# The
# Set-Up-to-Fail
# Syndrome

# The Set-Up-to-Fail Syndrome

*How Good Managers Cause*
*Great People to Fail*

Jean-François Manzoni
Jean-Louis Barsoux

HARVARD BUSINESS SCHOOL PRESS
BOSTON, MASSACHUSETTS

Requests for permission to use or reproduce material from this book should be directed to permissions@hbsp.harvard.edu, or mailed to Permissions, Harvard Business School Publishing, 60 Harvard Way, Boston, Massachusetts 02163.

**Library of Congress Cataloging-in-Publication Data**

Manzoni, J. F. (Jean-François)
    The Set-Up-to-Fail Syndrome : how good managers cause great people to fail / Jean-François Manzoni, Jean-Louis Barsoux.
        p. cm.
"In March-April 1998 we published an article in The Harvard Business Review entitled 'The Set-Up-to-Fail Syndrome : how bosses create their own poor performers.'"
    Includes index.
    ISBN 0-87584-949-0 (alk. paper)
    1. Supervision of employees.  2. Problem employees.  I. Barsoux, Jean-Louis.  II. Harvard business review. March–April 1998 (Supplement) III. Title.
    HF5549.12 .M354 2002
    658.3'15—dc21

                                                2002002904

The paper used in this publication meets the requirements of the American National Standard for Permanence of Paper for Publications and Documents in Libraries and Archives Z39.48-1992.

*To Anne and Astrid, and*
*To Suzy Wetlaufer,*
*Who were the first to believe . . .*

# Contents

*Preface*                                                      ix
*Acknowledgments*                                             xiii

1   The Set-Up-to-Fail Syndrome                                 1

2   When Common Sense Fails Us                                 17

3   Set-Up-to-Fail: A Vicious Cycle                            45

4   Labels, Biases, and Misperceptions                         67

5   Colluding to Collide                                       87

6   The Cost Iceberg                                          113

7   Blinders of Our Own Making                                135

8   Cracking the Syndrome                                     161

9   Preventing the Set-Up-to-Fail Syndrome:
    Lessons from the "Syndrome Busters"                        197

10  Getting There                                             221

    *Notes*                                                   251
    *Index*                                                   271
    *About the Authors*                                       279

# Preface

IN MARCH–APRIL 1998 we published an article in the *Harvard Business Review* entitled "The Set-Up-to-Fail Syndrome: How Bosses Create Their Own Poor Performers." The article seemed to hit a nerve and received enormous press coverage in the United States, in Europe, and in Asia. Every journalist seemed to report a personal story that illustrated the point we were making in the article. Many managers wrote to us, from everywhere—we remember vividly a letter from two medical doctors in Australia—to say, "I've seen what you describe, that's exactly right!" Some had been on the receiving end of the syndrome; others were bosses who were suddenly understanding better their responsibility in their subordinates' underperformance.

That response was of course very gratifying. It suggested that we had captured the phenomenon in ways that people could relate to.

Unexpectedly, an HBS Press editor asked us whether we would consider writing a book on this subject. We thought about it carefully, because we were not sure we had enough to add to the original article. After all, we had been working on the subject for years, and we had already researched it carefully.

First had come Jean-François's intensive cross-sectional study of fifty superior-subordinate dyads working in four manufacturing operations of Fortune 100 companies. The fifty subordinates and their bosses were interviewed at least twice and completed a questionnaire between the two interviews, in which the bosses evaluated the performance of their subordinates and the subordinates described their bosses' behavior toward them. Jean-François had also interviewed many individuals working close to these dyads and observed several meetings and interactions. In total, the study involved close to four hundred hours of interviews and observations, 75 percent of which were taped and later transcribed, providing a very rich base of information.

We had also been doing coaching and consulting work with many executives and their teams of first reports, often including discussions of each individual's 360-degree feedback results. The set-up-to-fail syndrome often manifests itself in 360-degree feedback through bimodal results, so these assignments provided ample opportunities to pursue our research on the subject.

Last but not least, by the time the article was published, we had discussed this subject with over a thousand participants in executive development programs, testing with them our ideas and interpretations, and asking them to volunteer and discuss their experiences. These executives had come from all over the world and from every level in their respective organizations, from junior to senior, from a single company to mixed-company groups. In almost every group we had worked with, a few participants had run up to us at the end of class to ask for individual meetings to continue the discussion, explaining, "I just realized that's what I've been doing to some of my employees," or "You just helped me understand what's been happening between me and my second child," or "That's exactly what my boss has been putting me through." We did not keep track of the number of such meetings we had over the years, but there were many.

How much more was there to learn, and what more could we say? With the benefit of almost four years of additional work on the subject, the answer to both questions has turned out to be a lot!

We have learned much from continued coaching and consulting work with executives and executive teams. We have also discussed this subject with an additional two thousand international executives taking part in development programs. We have used these contacts to share our findings, of course, but also to keep looking for new experiences, alternative explanations, and disconfirming evidence. We have also read a lot to try to understand better the psychological and social mechanisms underlying our Syndrome.

The basic story has remained the same: We still believe that many bosses unwittingly set up some of their subordinates to fail and, more generally, mismanage many of the subordinates they regard as acceptable but lower-than-average performers. But we now understand much better how and why managers do so. We also understand better how subordinates contribute to a process that we initially attributed largely to the bosses. We have learned much about what leaders can do to interrupt, and better yet to prevent, the development of the syndrome. We have also devoted more time to understanding the personal evolution some leaders went through to become more effective with their perceived weaker performers.

This book is the result of over fifteen years of combined research on a subject that we have cared deeply about because we have seen the human and performance toll it takes on so many bosses and subordinates, not only in their professional lives but also often in their personal lives as parents, spouses, and children. We have also seen the set-up-to-fail syndrome in motion in other settings. Indeed, and as a few of the examples in this book will show, the underlying mechanisms that we describe can and do play equally powerful roles in other types of relationships, at work (with peers, clients, suppliers, etc.) and beyond.

Completing a book is always a time of ambivalent feelings for authors. Competing with the sense of relief and accomplishment is a desire to hang onto the book for a few more days, "maybe just a week or two," to reexamine this or that tricky part. But there comes a point where you have to let the child wander into the world and make it on its own, and now is the time for this book.

We wrote this book to help people in positions of authority, particularly bosses, become more effective in the management of their subordinates, particularly their perceived weaker performers. We have had the good fortune to study a few bosses who got great contributions from such employees and, at the same time, avoided the human toll we have seen elsewhere so often. We have tried to understand what they did differently from the majority of their peers, and we have tried to explain it in ways that are actionable for managers—in other words, in ways concrete enough for managers to be able to visualize what their behavior looks like in practice.

It is now time for us to stop writing, and—we hope—for you to start reading. Completing this book does not signal the end of our interest in improving organizational performance and quality of life at work. We will continue our work in this area, and we hope some of you will share your reactions and experiences with us after you read this book and, maybe, act on its content.

# Acknowledgments

THERE ARE SOME DEBTS one can never repay. We have such a debt to the countless executives we have worked with over the years. They have given us time and energy, they have talked to us with candor, and they have helped us better understand boss-subordinate relationships. We won't attempt to list them here—the names would not mean much to you—but we will make sure at least a few of them know we had them in mind when writing this.

We do want to acknowledge a few people by name. Some of them trained us and have had an enormous impact on us as researchers and scholars: At Harvard Business School, Chris Argyris, Jack Gabarro, Bob Kaplan, and Ken Merchant (now at USC); at Loughborough University, Peter Lawrence; and at Oxford University, Rosemary Stewart. They are by no means responsible for our remaining limitations as scholars, but much of what we do well we learned from them.

Several friends and colleagues have helped us and believed in us over the years. They keep providing us with a wonderful blend of intellectual stimulation and emotional support. At INSEAD, we want to thank, among others, Henri-Claude de Bettignies, Linda Brimm, Mike Brimm, Yves Doz, Paul Evans, Manfred Kets de Vries, Chan Kim, Renée Mauborgne, Claude Michaud, Deigan Morris, Heinz Thanheiser, Jean-Claude Thoenig, and Vikas Tibrewala. Outside INSEAD, we have benefited from the help and support of Didier

Cossin (HEC Lausanne), Marc Epstein (Rice University), Susan Schneider (HEC Genève), and Larry Weiss (MIT).

There would have been no book without the initial *Harvard Business Review* article, and there would have been no article without Suzy Wetlaufer, then senior editor at *HBR*. Not only did Suzy select the article among the zillion submissions she receives every month, she also helped us immeasurably to write it up. There would also be no book without an editor. Marjorie Williams got the ball rolling by insisting that we still had much to say after the *HBR* article, and Suzanne Rotondo skillfully and enthusiastically took the relay when Marjorie left the Press. Suzanne's enthusiasm for the book's subject helped sustain our own energy, her questions and suggestions helped sharpen our thinking, and her remarkable clarity regarding deadlines helped us stay focused! Along the way, Jeff Kehoe also provided helpful comments and suggestions, and Astrid Sandoval expertly supported and coordinated the work of authors, editors, and reviewers. Penny Stratton made invaluable editorial suggestions and asked insightful questions that helped us tighten some of the arguments. Jill Connor then took care of the countless things that needed to be done to turn the manuscript into this book.

Last but proverbially not least, we want to thank our families without whom none of this would have been possible. Our parents, siblings, and children have inspired us and continue to do so. Most of all we thank our spouses, Anne and Astrid, who in addition to inspiring us and remaining outwardly confident that we would, one day, really press the "send" button, gracefully carried our share of the family responsibilities on top of theirs to give us the space and energy to see this project through.

# The
# Set-Up-to-Fail
# Syndrome

# 1

## The Set-Up-to-Fail Syndrome

The greatest blunders, like the thickest ropes, are often compounded of a multitude of strands. Take the rope apart, separate it into the small threads that compose it, and you can break them one by one. You think, "That is all there was!" But twist them all together and you have something tremendous.

—Victor Hugo

### Problem, What Problem?

When an employee fails—or even just performs poorly—managers typically place the blame outside themselves. The employee doesn't understand the work, a manager might contend; or the employee isn't driven to succeed, can't prioritize assignments, or won't take direction. Whatever the reason, the boss often assumes that the problem is the employee's fault—and therefore, the employee's responsibility.

But is it? The answer, of course, is sometimes yes. Some employees are not up to their assigned tasks, and never will be, owing to lack of knowledge, skill, or simple desire. But sometimes—and we would go so far as to say *often*—an employee's poor performance can be blamed largely on his or her boss.

Perhaps *blamed* is too strong a word, but it is directionally correct. In fact, our research strongly suggests that bosses—albeit

1

accidentally and usually with the best intentions—are often complicit in an employee's lack of success. How? By creating and reinforcing a dynamic that essentially sets up perceived weaker performers to fail. We call this the *Set-Up-to-Fail Syndrome*. It describes a dynamic in which capable employees who are mistaken for mediocre or weak performers live down to low expectations, and often end up out of the organization—of their own volition or not.

In our experience, most bosses have contributed to such a dynamic at one time or another. Our aim, therefore, is to unravel the multiple biases, blinders, and misperceptions—on both sides of the relationship—that fuel this degenerative process. By illuminating the mechanisms involved, we will provide the necessary platform to *interrupt* these downward spirals and, ultimately, to *prevent* them from taking hold.

This book is about leadership, not the grand, intellectual side of leadership as exercised by those at the apex of organizations. We don't deal with fancy concepts such as industry dynamics, corporate transformation, or the creation of sustainable competitive advantage through strategic positioning. Instead we dissect the everyday, interactive, human side of leadership. This is a leadership book for the masses, for all those with one or more employees reporting to them. It is about leadership in the sense of *mobilizing the people on one's team*.

Mobilizing subordinates is certainly not the only dimension of a leader's job, but it is the defining feature and it does absorb the lion's share of a leader's time and energy. It is a challenge that has the same resonance for chief executive officers as it does for the heads of business units, project groups, or task forces. The way bosses interact with their immediate team has a huge impact on how their leadership influence cascades. It is therefore a key driver of results. But it is also a major generator of stress and frustration.

Before exploring boss-subordinate relationships in more detail, let's agree on some terminology. Many of our colleagues make a clear and fundamental distinction between "managers" and "leaders." Managers, they claim, perform optimally within an existing frame, whereas leaders create a new frame. John Kotter, for example, tells us that "management is about coping with complexity. . . .

Leadership is about coping with change."[1] Warren Bennis likes to say that "a good manager does things right. A leader does the right things."[2] We recognize those differences, but in light of the aspect of leadership we focus on in this book—the interpersonal and execution part of the job that is common to both roles—this distinction is not as critical. Managers *and* leaders have direct subordinates whom they need to mobilize. We will therefore refer to them interchangeably as bosses, managers, and leaders.

We also had to choose a term to refer to the people working for these bosses. We could call them "subordinates," "employees," or "associates." Employees risks leading readers to think in terms of blue- and white-collar workers rather than managers, the type of subordinates we mainly studied. Associates describes employees in some companies but "peers" in others, and fails to highlight the position of power that bosses—even in the most empowering organizations—have over the people who report to them. As a result and although the term is a bit old-fashioned, we chose to mainly use the word "subordinate" to refer to the people who report to, and whose performance is evaluated by, their boss.

Last but not least, a clarification on the use of genders: When speaking about real managers we obviously refer to them using their actual gender. When speaking about bosses and subordinates in general, we used the plural form or alternated the use of "he" and "she." We may not have succeeded perfectly, but we did try!

## Walking a Tightrope:
## Concern with Results versus Concern with People

Meeting the numbers has always been a priority for managers, but in recent years managers have been increasingly held to their commitments. With ever more powerful and impatient capital markets quickly sanctioning underperforming companies, managers are themselves under intense pressure to hit short-term targets.

The pressure on managers to deliver results is compounded by the changing nature of their jobs. Advances in technology, allied to global competition, have made executives' work increasingly complex and fast-paced. For example, technology has allowed companies to set up committees or project teams that span geographical boundaries and time zones, coming together at intervals while keeping in touch electronically. As a result, we have seen a rising number of task forces and transitory, ad hoc types of structures in many companies. This trend has multiplied the activities that bosses have to manage concurrently, thus fragmenting their work and generating more setup costs. Managing projects also necessitates that bosses deal with people over whom they don't have full authority, which adds extra layers of complexity. And since those projects and assignments have short time frames, the pressure to show results intensifies.

Meeting tough performance targets under these frenzied conditions requires managers to motivate and provide clear direction for their people. To make sure that their subordinates execute tasks effectively, managers need to exercise strong discipline, control, and monitoring—which would seem enough of a challenge. But companies want *even more* from their managers—after all, there's a talent war going on out there! Therefore, companies *also* expect their managers to display positive values and to develop people. Companies know that good people have become highly mobile, and that a timely call from a headhunter, if they happen to feel frustrated or unappreciated, can prompt them to leave at any moment. Executives are therefore expected to coach, empower, encourage initiative and risk taking, foster loyalty and commitment, and show recognition. It's not just getting results that counts, but *how* executives get those results. Many companies have introduced evaluation systems that measure executives against results and according to the values and/or behaviors they display. Indications that a boss does not "walk the talk"—such as poor 360-degree feedback or excessive turnover—can spell serious trouble for that person.[3] Some companies also tie executive bonuses to the results of their 360-degree evaluations.

Thus bosses are increasingly held responsible for creating a work environment that is healthy and fulfilling for employees. At the same time, they risk getting canned for failing to meet the numbers. In effect, they have to negotiate a kind of tightrope. They are torn between wanting to empower employees and making sure that those employees can deliver on commitments; they want to show consideration toward subordinates without encouraging complacency; and they want to push for performance without alienating their subordinates.

You might expect that bosses would be either good or bad at walking this tightrope, but that is not what we observed in our research. Rather, we found that most bosses actually achieve the balancing act with some of their subordinates but fail with others. When we talked to employees rated as "higher performers," their comments suggested that their boss was striking that balance: Sure, targets were tough, but the boss's encouragement and support made them seem achievable, even stimulating. Of course discipline and measurement were necessary; how else could they learn and "own" their areas?

Employees rated as "weaker performers" presented an altogether different picture. According to them, their boss's drive for results was *not* tempered by the same levels of consideration, recognition, or autonomy. They often regarded their boss's help as interference, his or her suggestions inhibiting, monitoring unfair, use of metrics punitive, assignments unfulfilling, and so on. Instead of feeling challenged, they felt burdened and abused. Some of these subordinates' testimonies were poignant. Many really cared about being successful and helping their companies to be successful, but could not perform to the best of their capabilities *because of* the way their boss managed them. It was the difficulty bosses have in achieving that balance with perceived weaker performers that first drew our attention to this area—and that slowly led us to discover the intricacies of how these dysfunctional relationships develop and self-perpetuate.

An important point: We use the term *weaker performers* rather than *underperformers* because the research we discuss in this book does not relate to the small percentage of employees who underperform severely and fall short of the firm's minimum performance threshold. Our findings, and hence this discussion, pertain to employees whose overall performance is lower than some of their colleagues' but still exceeds the firm's minimum-performance threshold. They are not employees the firm wants to let go; rather, they contribute to the firm's performance, but not as much as some of their better-performing colleagues.

## Distress Signals

We don't want to give away the whole story in a few words at this stage, as it deserves to be unfolded carefully and systematically to make sure we highlight all the relevant mechanisms. Still, we can outline the basic problem as follows.

The set-up-to-fail syndrome begins innocuously enough. The triggering event could be specific—perhaps an employee misses a target or a deadline, loses a client, or gives a poor report or presentation. The trigger could also be quite vague—maybe the employee arrived from another unit with a lukewarm recommendation or reacted oddly to early advice from the boss. In any case, something sows a doubt in the boss's mind, and the boss begins to worry that the employee's performance may not be up to par. The syndrome is set in motion.

The boss then does what seems obvious in view of the subordinate's suspected shortcomings: He or she gives more time and attention to the subordinate. The boss starts providing more "guidance" when assigning tasks, tries to be more involved in the subordinate's decision-making process, and monitors corrective actions and progress more frequently and intensely (to make sure things are on track). The boss typically means well. He is only trying to boost performance and prevent the subordinate from making errors.

Unfortunately, subordinates often interpret that heightened supervision as a lack of trust and confidence. Their initial attempts to fight back seem to have little impact on the boss's opinion of them—and pretty soon instead of putting in more effort, they put in less. Deprived of elbowroom, they start to doubt their own thinking and ability, and they lose the motivation to make autonomous decisions. Feeling second-guessed much of the time, they figure, "Why should I take risks when the boss won't appreciate it anyway?" Or else they hunker down and get on with the job but try to steer clear of the boss.

Thinking—mistakenly—that the subordinate's withdrawal confirms that he is indeed a weaker performer, the boss begins to intensify her involvement in the subordinate's affairs. For example, the boss makes sure to define tasks very clearly, establishes precise and frequent milestones, and then closely monitors performance (to make sure the subordinate doesn't "get in trouble"). She sets challenging targets and objectives, to make sure the subordinate maintains the appropriate degree of drive and energy. Meanwhile, she increasingly steers important and risky assignments away from this subordinate and toward colleagues she deems more reliable. Frustrated, the subordinate may start to retaliate by ignoring instructions, failing to stand up for the boss in front of other employees, or even arguing with her. He begins to do only what is necessary to get along, devotes increasing energy to self-protection, and gives up any dream of making a meaningful contribution.

Of course, not all relationships degenerate to quite that extent. Sometimes, boss and subordinate just settle into a routine that is not really satisfactory but, aside from periodic clashes, otherwise bearable. In more extreme cases, the pair plunges into an adversarial relationship that really brings out the worst in each other. The subordinate sees the boss as intransigent, interfering, and hypercritical; the boss sees the subordinate as inept, uncooperative, and indecisive. They are well and truly caught up in the set-up-to-fail syndrome.

The sad reality is that once people are miscast as weaker performers, they tend to live down to that image regardless of their capabilities. Our research suggests that the set-up-to-fail dynamic can take hold in a remarkably short time—and that once it does take hold, it proves very hard to reverse. Our research also suggests that false perceptions play a significant role in the initial performance "categorization." That is why we call it a "set-up."

Why do we call it a "syndrome?" Because it is based on an array of observable behaviors. In medicine, a syndrome is a set of symptoms that, taken together, point to a particular pathology and suggest a specific cure. The symptoms here include a certain perceived lack of drive and motivation; an apparent lack of ability or willingness to act autonomously and to "own" issues and tasks; a tendency to resist innovation and new ideas and to hoard information; a propensity to focus on problems rather than solutions; and often a diminished ability to lead any subordinates to excellence.

The syndrome begins when the boss responds, seemingly reasonably, to the first instance of perceived poor performance. The boss thinks, "I've got to push and prod these subordinates to perform"; "I've got to give them more guidance to make sure they're approaching tasks appropriately"; and "I've got to monitor their work to make sure they don't let problems get out of hand." The response is reasonable, for sure. Its effectiveness is less obvious, as we will discuss later.

Note that we talk liberally about "bosses" in general, as if every boss reacts to perceived weaker performers the same way. This is a generalization designed to communicate our point quickly, but it is not that much of an exaggeration. As we will discuss in chapter 2, the research that we and others have conducted suggests that most managers across hierarchical levels, types of companies, and national cultures seem to ascribe to a "common-sense" theory of how to deal with weaker performing subordinates.

Note also that managers are not the only people in positions of authority to confront this problem. So do teachers, who encounter the "underperforming pupil syndrome" every day: A child doesn't listen properly, has a short attention span, is unresponsive, regularly displays inexcusable gaps on topics that were discussed minutes ago, and shows a propensity for unruly, sometimes delinquent behavior. Sports coaches, who face the "underperforming player syndrome" also grapple with this issue: A player displays inexcusable lapses of concentration, refuses to follow the coach's basic instructions, tries to do everything alone, or tries plays that she or he is not capable of performing while refusing to stick to basics.

Like most bosses, teachers and coaches respond in a clear-cut way: they discipline the student or athlete and exert more control, choosing to give a detention or bench the athlete until he or she understands better who's the boss! In any kind of leadership setting—business, school, sports—these responses are reasonable if you interpret the symptoms in a certain way. In many cases, however, not only will these responses *fail* to solve the problem, they will actually compound it. We wrote this book to help explain why, and to show how leaders can approach perceived weaker performers more effectively.

Do we mean all perceived weaker performers are potential solid performers? Of course not. There are such things as hiring mistakes, just as there are "pathological cases"—people who simply refuse to face reality and make no attempt to improve. And clearly, companies have to remove those people. But we would argue that the overwhelming majority of perceived weaker performers could improve significantly if they were better managed, better coached, or assigned to a position better suited to their capabilities. In fact, in our research we have seen several firsthand examples of bosses who achieve outstanding results with "regular" folks. The familiar notion of potential turns out to be dangerous, for who can really say how much "potential" someone has? What we do know is that when bosses get it into their heads that certain people have "limited potential," those bosses tend to behave accordingly—and will often end up causing the subordinates to deliver in a limited way.

We are not trying to lay the whole blame on bosses. This is clearly a two-way street—and we show in chapter 5 that one reason why the process proves so powerful is that the subordinate joins in, so that two people are setting each other up to fail. But because the traditional approach to subordinate underperformance is to look for explanations on the subordinate's side, we are saying to bosses: start by looking on your side.

## Why Should Bosses Care?

For bosses, it's important to know about this syndrome because of its cost to them and to their units. Working as researchers and consultants, we see how hard bosses try to make things work, the tremendous effort they devote to raising the productivity of certain subordinates. They work damned hard. They also create enormous amounts of pain. When we talk to the "weaker performers," they talk about not being heard, not being understood, not being fairly treated, being put under unnecessary pressure, and not being given a chance to contribute. That pain and frustration translate into forfeited performance. Perceived weaker performers may put in the same effort as their peers, but their creative and critical faculties are blocked, unappreciated, and ultimately unplugged.

The relationship also takes a significant human toll on bosses. Managers often tell us about the pain of working with weaker performers. They tell us that even when they engage in performance-improvement processes, the proportion of positive outcomes is disappointingly low—which represents a high opportunity cost. Those subordinates divert time and attention that bosses could be spending on more value-adding activities. They also consume inordinate amounts of energy, leaving bosses feeling depleted rather than revitalized.

Moreover, the stress spreads beyond the boss and subordinate. Weaker performers share their pain and misery with the members of their teams, corroding the team spirit or sense of joint aspiration. And, of course, they themselves may be bosses to other people, and the syndrome can cause their own subordinates to suffer in turn. Indeed, a recent McKinsey & Co. survey showed that people who work for weaker performing managers agree strongly that the experience "prevented me from learning," "hurt my career development," "prevented me from making a larger contribution to the bottom line," and ultimately, "made me want to leave the company."[4]

Beyond the current impact on performance, the ability to manage weaker performers also impacts a boss's career development. For over two decades, researchers at the Center for Creative Leadership (CCL), which specializes in leadership research and education, have been investigating career-success variables. They have found that the number-one success factor in the top three jobs of large organizations is "relationships with subordinates."[5] The Center has also conducted numerous studies of executive derailment—meaning resignation, removal, or demotion. Those studies have systematically shown that problems with interpersonal relationships and the inability to build a team are the dominant reasons executives fail.[6] The latest evidence, based on interviews with over eight hundred human resource executives, shows that failure to build good relationships with peers and subordinates is a major career-stopper, accounting for 82 percent of derailment cases.[7]

This phenomenon does not apply only to "Young Turks" who suddenly find themselves out of their depth. It applies to senior people, too. The fact that a boss "got away with it so far" is no guarantee that she or he will continue to do so, for three reasons. First, assets such as assertiveness and initiative, on which many outstanding track records have been built, can become liabilities as the leader moves up to senior levels where a more collegial approach is expected. Second, compelling evidence—from a study that tracked individual managers over a twenty-year period—indicates that interpersonal skills tend to decline over time (or else as one moves up the hierarchy).[8] Third, managers face increasing performance pressure, and pressure has a tendency to accentuate existing flaws.

From our discussions with executives, we know that under benign conditions, it is relatively easy to be supportive and to develop high-quality relationships with all subordinates. But when the pressure piles on, when bosses are overstretched and fewer resources are available, it is a different matter. Stress tends to make bosses more rigid, intolerant, and impatient—at least with subordinates who don't "get it" quickly or who seem less driven. Typically, bosses react by placing additional burdens on the top performers, those who can be relied on to deliver.

The net result is that bosses are overstretched, top performers are overworked, and "lower performers" are frustrated. Performance *may* improve, but mostly at the price of human pain: increased levels of stress, turnover, burnout, depression, and the like. It is not a sustainable approach.

## The Cost to Productivity

With executives at all levels under severe performance pressure, the chances of triggering set-up-to-fail syndromes multiply. Bosses involved with too many projects or task forces—such as those in flattened organizations with numerous direct reports, some of them in remote locations—may not notice that particular relationships are going sour, or may notice but simply not have the time or energy to invest in fixing them. The idea that many executives can be very good bosses to some of their subordinates, but downright bad ones to others, lies at the heart of this book.

Why should companies care that the set-up-to-fail syndrome exists? Because our research shows that this syndrome is common enough that it can seriously affect companies' productivity. For example, when discussing the incidence of the syndrome in their companies, human resources (HR) personnel have complained to us about how much time they spend on issues relating to dysfunctional boss-subordinate relationships. When bosses run out of patience and want people removed, when subordinates run out of patience and request a transfer or decide to quit, it's the HR specialists who have to clean up the mess. And when HR folks have to spend their time handling today's emergency issues, they are not attending to tomorrow's value-adding activities.

Another way to gauge the impact of dysfunctional boss-subordinate relationships on companies is to consider the reports of psychological abuse at work, which have exploded since the mid-1990s. In English-speaking countries, such abuse is often labeled "workplace bullying." It rarely involves physical intimidation or threats. More typically, it consists of unfair and excessive criticism, public insults, isolation, repeatedly changing or setting unrealistic work targets, undervaluing of work efforts, shouting, and verbal abuse.

According to Cary Cooper, a leading expert on occupational stress, workplace bullying is no longer the preserve of psychopaths and autocrats but now afflicts regular managers who are simply overworked and overstressed. "There has always been a small number of psychopathic bullies," Cooper says. "These people were bullies in the playground and went on to become bullies at work, but what is new is the growing number of overworked bullies, who suffer from stress, can't cope, and so take their anger and frustration out on the people they work with."[9] Not their dominant management style, bullying surfaces sometimes with particular subordinates—which can easily lead observers to dismiss it as unrepresentative or to put it down to "bad chemistry."

How common is this workplace bullying? A U.S. survey of workplace stress revealed that 42 percent of office workers work in environments where yelling and verbal abuse happen frequently.[10] Another U.S. survey found that 27 percent of the U.S. workforce is mistreated or bullied.[11] Similarly, a British survey of over five thousand employees found that almost half of the respondents had experienced or seen bullying, that one in ten had been bullied in the past six months, and that one in four had been bullied in the last five years.[12]

This phenomenon is not limited to English-speaking countries. In France, a book about workplace mistreatment, *Stop Psychological Violence,* was outselling the top fiction bestsellers within weeks of publication in 1998, and it sold four-hundred thousand copies within its first three years.[13] The book provoked important changes in French employment legislation, making psychological harassment punishable by a jail sentence of up to one year and a fine of $13,000, and it has been translated into twenty-four languages, including Japanese and Estonian. In Japan, a help line for employees who felt ill treated or intimidated received 1,700 calls in two months.[14] And in Sweden, workplace bullying is considered a factor in 10 to 15 percent of suicides.[15]

Some studies have also examined the substantial costs of these practices. For example, one U.S. survey showed that, in response to hostile treatment, 24 percent of employees decreased the quality and quantity of their work, 28 percent lost work time avoiding the bully, and 52 percent lost time worrying about the unresolved situation. The survey also showed that bullied employees took 50 percent more days off and developed 26 percent more chronic illnesses than their colleagues.[16] This adds up to a lot of lost productivity. It also has a toxic effect on morale. People who feel mistreated rarely keep quiet about it. They complain vociferously to colleagues, thus multiplying the time wasted, and they reinforce their views by finding others who feel similarly alienated.

The organization may also feel the cost indirectly in terms of increased resistance to change or higher turnover. As one authority in the field observed, "I've studied countless exit interviews and countless post-exit interviews. . . . Reason number one for leaving is usually some variation on the theme 'My boss was a jerk. [He or she] didn't support me, didn't communicate with me.'"[17] Of course, some readers may be thinking "good riddance," but a workplace where people are mismanaged, mistreated, and/or forced out is unlikely to elicit a lot of loyalty from *anyone*. People realize they are expendable, and the company is likely to have trouble retaining existing talent or attracting the best people in the industry.

On the basis of all these costs and consequences, improving boss-subordinate relationships would seem to offer enormous potential not only for bosses and subordinates but also for corporations as a whole.

## Addressing the Problem

When we outline the set-up-to-fail syndrome to executives, they quickly begin nodding their heads. They have witnessed it around them. They have seen how damaging it is for team spirit and productivity. Some have even been victims. But then comes the tough part: recognizing that they themselves have probably been perpetrators, without even realizing it. To address the problems this syndrome engenders, executives and other professionals must understand how bosses can trigger and remain blind to a dynamic that is hurting them, their people, and their companies, and that previous efforts to "fix the subordinate" have floundered because of a lack of awareness of the blinders and misperceptions afflicting both boss and subordinate.

By providing a framework that illuminates causes and effects, we hope that this book will give a better understanding of the traps and biases that influence perceptions of other people. Our objective, and our hope, is that more effective handling of these subordinates will contribute to improving individual and corporate performance, but also to decreasing the human toll these difficult relationships exact on the parties involved, as well as on other parties around them.

In the first six chapters, we describe specifics of the set-up-to-fail syndrome and its effects. Chapters 2 through 4 take a look at why bosses' responses typically fail to produce the desired results, often triggering instead an escalating spiral of malaise and underperformance, and why bosses remain blind to the ineffectiveness of their usual responses. Chapter 5 shows how subordinates contribute to fueling this spiral of malaise and underperformance, and chapter 6 examines the costs of this dynamic that bosses and subordinates have jointly created.

Beginning with chapter 7, we look at specific ways to address the set-up-to-fail syndrome. We discuss the mental adjustments bosses must make before trying to interrupt this dynamic, and then in chapter 8 we propose a framework to help bosses productively intervene with their perceived weaker performers. Chapter 9 examines how bosses can *prevent* the syndrome, and chapter 10 discusses the personal evolution leaders must undergo in order to take preventive action more often and more easily.

This book integrates years of research we and others have conducted. It addresses a real problem that each and every boss faces, has faced, or will face: "How do I get better performance from my subordinates, particularly those in whom I have limited confidence and whose abilities I do not trust as much?" We are going to argue, and try to show, that most bosses approach this issue in a way that is fundamentally flawed. This is not an easy sell. Let's get to it.

# 2

## When Common Sense
## Fails Us

Common sense is the collection of prejudices acquired by age
eighteen.

—Albert Einstein

HOW DO BOSSES get the best performance from their people? For
decades, scholars have attempted to answer this question by trying
to find a single "best" leadership style or a set of traits in a leader's
personality that would produce the best results. The findings of their
research were inconsistent, however. Some factors seemed to hold
some of the time, but they didn't hold systematically. So a new challenge emerged: to identify which approach was most effective *under
which conditions*. Results of this "contingency theory" research have
also been mixed.[1]

Most of these studies implicitly (and falsely!) assumed that individual bosses display a consistent style toward all their subordinates.
The style of each boss was measured by taking the average of the
responses provided by his or her subordinates. This process essentially dismissed differences among the answers of a given boss's employees as errors of perception or errors of measurement.

Today, companies invest considerable amounts of money, time,
and energy on 360-degree feedback programs, which involve collecting information on a manager's behavior from a variety of respondents, such as that manager's boss, peers, and subordinates. For

each category of respondents, the feedback delivered to the manager typically focuses a great deal more on the mean score (the individual's behavior "on average") than on the variance (the spread of differences between responses). Why? Because the process is aimed at capturing the individual boss's "management style." What matters is the central tendency. The variance between peers' or subordinates' answers might not be treated as an error, but all the same it tends to receive only limited attention. In addition, managers are often allowed to select to whom they give feedback questionnaires. This practice again implies that the individual's "leadership style" is reasonably uniform and that allowing the managers themselves to select, say, four out of ten direct reports for an assessment will produce a "representative" answer.

But what if we asked *all* of a boss's subordinates to describe his or her leadership style? What would they say? Picture for a moment the people who report to you. Imagine their faces. Would they all see you behaving the same way? Probably not. In fact, on reflection, definitely not. But who would say what? Can you make any predictions? This is the seed from which the idea for our book sprouted— just as it was the starting point for our research.

## A Puzzle Unfurls: Dr. Jekyll and Mr. Hyde

About a decade ago, while conducting research into leadership behavior, one of us stumbled across a fascinating case. Imagine the scene. The field research is at its halfway stage. You've interviewed numerous bosses and subordinates. Those subordinates have filled out questionnaires describing their boss's behavior toward them, and the bosses have sent you performance ratings for all their subordinates. It is now time to embark on a second round of interviews with a particular boss, Jack, and the four business managers (BMs) reporting to him. To prepare for these interviews, you decide to run through their earlier testimonies. Reading all the transcripts consecutively, you make a startling discovery: The descriptions of Jack by his direct reports evoke two extreme leadership styles. He comes across as some kind of Jekyll and Hyde character.

Two of Jack's subordinates (let's call them BM1 and BM2) describe him as a "people-oriented" manager who emphasizes frequent and informal conversations and treats them as his equals. He is demanding but supportive, available but empowering—in short, they say Jack is the "model boss." In sharp contrast, the other two subordinates (BM3 and BM4) describe a more formal manager, with whom interactions are often uncomfortable: a mean, meddling micromanager who never gives them an even break—in short, they say Jack is closer to being the proverbial "boss from hell."

These impressions were clearly reflected in the data collected from the BMs' questionnaires describing Jack's behavior. Answers from BM1 and BM2 were systematically close to one another, as were answers from BM3 and BM4, and each dimension of boss behavior—such as level of coaching, participation, or consideration—showed a clear gap between the two pairs. This gap was mirrored in the four subordinates' performance ratings completed by Jack: BM1 and BM2 received similar high ratings, and BM3 and BM4 received similar lower-than-average ratings.

The contrast was baffling. This was the stuff of schizophrenic disorders, yet Jack was a well-adjusted manager! In fact, Jack's bosses perceived him as an outstanding manager. He held an M.B.A. and in business school had specifically focused on people issues. He came across as reflective and thoughtful. So how could some of his reports brand him as "wonderful" and others as "impossible"? Were these differences in behavior perceptual or real? We decided to go straight to the source and ask Jack to clarify the situation. Initially, he gave us a textbook answer:

> Individuals have different levels of maturity. Those with high maturity need less attention, whereas those with low maturity need more direction. Also, you need to understand the personality traits of people: Some are thick-skinned so you can be more blunt with them, whereas others are thin-skinned so you have to be more careful.

When challenged about the clear split among the four people reporting to him, Jack became more hesitant. After some time he eventually conceded:

> Yes, I do behave differently with these people. With the better performers I need to reinforce where they are heading and let them know that I don't take their efforts for granted. So I show my recognition, my appreciation, and I keep the reinforcement going. With

the others, my behavior is more into counseling, how it can get better. So maybe overall, I act more like a teacher to the weaker ones and more like a facilitator with the better ones. Plus, when the weaker ones call, I'm only human, I sometimes feel a bit exasperated, like "Now what?"

This testimony was puzzling. Here was a boss who was convinced of the benefits of delegation, coaching, and recognition, but he was intentionally behaving differently with some of his subordinates.

Although Jack's case was extreme, a similar pattern emerged in the rest of the study. When asked to describe their behavior, managers' self-descriptions matched closely with the reports made by their "better performers." When asked whether they behaved in an identical manner with all their subordinates, however, most managers acknowledged that they did not: "With the weaker folks it's different," they reported. "Unless you're on their back, nothing happens." In their eyes, this counted as "remedial action" and somehow did not reflect their "true leadership style." So they were empowering and encouraging, but only with the people who "deserved it." To assess the extent of this effect, we started surveying groups of executives with whom we were discussing these initial findings.

## The Plot Thickens: How Managers Spot and Treat Weaker Performers

We started by asking executives whether they could distinguish between higher and lower performers to make statements such as "In general, better performers tend to _____, and tend to be _____, while weaker performers tend to _____, and tend to be _____." We emphasized that the so-called lower performers were not "people about to be fired"; they were employees whose performance was above the minimum acceptable performance threshold but who overall were "less good" than their "better-performing" counterparts. This is an important distinction. Once a manager has decided to get rid of a subordinate, the manager's main objective ceases to be "getting the best from this employee" and becomes instead "encouraging the employee to leave and building a case for dismissal." This was *not* the case for the subordinates we studied.

Executives told us that they did make such a distinction and had little trouble articulating the main differences. Specifically, executives explained that compared to "stronger performers," "weaker performers" tended to be:

- less motivated, less energetic, unlikely to go "beyond the call of duty"

- less autonomous, not "taking charge" of problems or projects—"you have to do their thinking for them"

- poorer communicators; often defensive, insecure, looking for excuses—"you have to drag it out of them"

- less proactive, not anticipating problems very well and sometimes hiding them, inclined to let themselves get swamped

- less innovative, less open to change, less likely to bring up new ideas

- more parochial, inclined to get lost in detail, often lacking in vision and "big-picture" perspective

- weaker leaders to their own subordinates, failing to develop or show confidence in them, prone to hoard information and authority

- more likely to bring problems, less likely to come up with solutions

To date, we have surveyed over three thousand international executives. To our surprise, these "distinguishing features" of weaker performers have proved remarkably consistent across varied groups of executives, regardless of hierarchical level, corporate affiliation, or national culture. In light of the perceived differences between high and low performers, we then asked executives about their behavior toward subordinates. Do they do the same things in the same way with all their subordinates? Or do they do different things with some? Or do they do the same things, but differently, or to different degrees, with some? Again, managers are happy to volunteer that they behave "differently" and proceed to spell out how their behavior varies between "higher" and "lower" performers. Often, they start off with abstractions like "more trust," "more delegation," or "less supervision," so we ask them to be more concrete and to stick to directly observable behaviors. Table 2-1 shows a list of responses representative of those we have received from executives.

The picture that emerges is that stronger performers typically benefit from less defined and more challenging tasks, where the boss is more available but less present, with richer "freewheeling" exchanges and a "sparring partner" type of relationship. With the perceived weaker performers, on the other hand, bosses talk a lot more about "what, how, and by when." Discussions are more structured and tasks more mundane. Because bosses don't perceive these subordinates' ideas as good, they tend to push their own recommendations a bit more. They then have to monitor actions and results more closely to make sure that things stay on track and to provide help before the subordinate starts to flounder. Again, these sharp distinctions in managerial behavior have largely held true across all the national and organizational cultures we have worked with.

Overall, the three thousand managers we surveyed were *conscious* of behaving in a more controlling way with their perceived weaker performers. Some of them preferred to characterize their approach as "supportive and helpful" ("these subordinates can't really perform on their own, so I try to help them, to coach them, to support them"), but this "help" and "support" looked very much like the behaviors outlined in table 2-1. This awareness is significant because it signals that such controlling behavior exhibited by the boss is not an implementation error, as in "I try to give them more autonomy but I fail." When these bosses go to work in the morning, they have a clear intention of engaging in specific behaviors with their perceived weaker performers.

Some bosses also acknowledge that, although they try not to, they tend to become more easily and more quickly impatient with perceived weaker performers. As one boss told us, he typically set out with the aim of developing weaker subordinates but sometimes resorted to "spoon-feeding the person just a little bit if [he or she is] not coming up with the idea."

It's the time factor. That's no excuse, but it is a reality of life. If I had spent another five or another fifteen minutes asking questions

**TABLE 2 - 1**

## How Bosses See Their Behavior toward Their Subordinates

| With "Weaker Performers" Bosses Tend To . . . | With "Stronger Performers" Bosses Tend To . . . |
|---|---|
| Be more directive when discussing tasks and goals. Focus on *what* needs to be done, as well as *how* it should get done. | Discuss project objectives with limited focus on project implementation. Focus on *what* and *why,* with limited focus on *how.* |
| Set more targets, more deadlines. Establish clear action plans and checkpoints. Give limited decision-making autonomy overall. | Give subordinates more freedom to choose own course of action. Set checkpoints farther apart and invite them to "get in touch" if need be. |
| Follow up regularly to ensure things are on track. Pay close attention to unfavorable variances and get more systematically involved when subordinates run into difficulties. | Perform less obtrusive follow-up; make themselves available, as in "let me know if I can help." Treat unfavorable variances, mistakes, or incorrect judgments as learning opportunities. |
| Focus discussions on operational issues; ask precise questions. | Engage in more casual and freewheeling conversations. |
| Limit open-ended contact and focus on tasks at hand. Tell more than ask. | Use subordinates as "sparring partners." Solicit their views on strategy, execution, policy, and procedures. Follow up on their suggestions. |
| Impose their own views in case of disagreements. Make "strong suggestions" that more closely resemble recommendations. | Often defer to their opinions. Emphasize that suggestions are only that, meant to encourage them to try things their way. |
| Give them more routine assignments and projects. | Offer more interesting or challenging stretch assignments. |
| Be more distant physically and emotionally. | Be more comfortable with subordinates, resulting in warmer relationships. |

rather than telling the person what I wanted them to do, would the person have got it? I hope so, but I don't know for sure, and there are usually other problems I need to attend to.

Our findings that managers behave differently toward different subordinates are not isolated. They fit in with a large body of research known as leader-member exchange theory, which has established that 80 to 90 percent of managers have sharply differentiated relationships with their subordinates.[2]

In the first major investigation of this issue in the mid-1970s, researchers tested groups of subordinates reporting to new bosses.[3] Just one month into the relationship, it was already clear that the vast majority of bosses were making a broad distinction between two clusters of more and less trusted subordinates. Compared to their colleagues, the more trusted subordinates, labeled the "in-group," reported receiving significantly higher amounts of leadership attention and support. As they saw it, they had more influence on decisions affecting them, and they received more complete information and feedback and more help with their problems. They also noted more expressions of confidence, more signs of concern for their needs and feelings, and more public backing from the boss. Were they just imagining it?

Checking with bosses, the researchers found that subordinates' impressions were accurate. Relationships with certain subordinates were based on high reciprocal influence and consideration, while others were based more on rules, policies, and formal authority. Bosses were conscious of these differences, reporting that they indeed showed their trusted "in-group" subordinates more signs of concern and confidence. Tracking these evolving relationships at three-month intervals for a year, the researchers found that the initial differences of treatment did not regress; to the contrary, they tended to grow more pronounced. Predictably, staff turnover in the year following the study was over 50 percent higher within the "out-group" than within the "in-group."

Numerous studies have supported these early findings.[4] The evidence that bosses behave differently toward different subordinates seems fairly conclusive. But this statement now begs two questions, which we often hear when we discuss these issues: First, "Isn't this simple common sense? Isn't this why so many managers behave this way, because it's common sense?" And second, "So what? So what if a boss monitors subordinates differently, helps and advises them differently, or relates to them differently? So far, you have not established that this is in any way dysfunctional!"

The first question is easy to address: Yes, managers' behavior seems to make sense. Perceived weaker performers are seen as less capable of functioning effectively when left to their own devices, so it is "only natural" for the boss to want to provide more help, coaching, direction, and monitoring. But as helpful as common sense can be, it is not infallible. For example, common sense suggests that the earth is flat and that the sun revolves around the earth. These "observations" made so much common sense that they were held as true for centuries, and many years after contrary evidence started to be reported.

The second question—"So what?"—is more complex to address. A first answer could be that in the studies we have conducted, the perceived weaker performers reported more negative attitudes than their colleagues toward their job, toward their boss, and toward the company in general. They exhibited less trust, less comfort, a stronger feeling of being controlled, and, overall, less commitment. But you may object, as do many managers in our seminars: "Of course they are less happy; they are *meant* to be less happy! We are trying to motivate them to become better performers so that they get out of the out-group. You wouldn't want us to make the out-group feel comfortable, would you?"

In part, this reaction is slightly shortsighted. Much research shows that intangibles such as employee trust, and confidence in the boss and the organization tend to be associated with many favorable outcomes within the company. In the absence of trust, for example, employees are less likely to share knowledge and engage in "corporate citizenship" behaviors such as helping peers with their work, orienting new hires, and volunteering for extra projects.[5] Ultimately, the company does suffer from the absence of these positive behaviors. In addition, low morale and high turnover can quickly have an impact on customer service levels, supplier relationships, the company or business unit's ability to attract fresh talent, and ultimately the bottom line.

But executives do have a point that today's corporate life is harsh. Executives are under severe pressure and many would endorse the opinion of one seminar participant whose line was worthy of Gordon Gekko, the heartless corporate raider in the film *Wall Street:* "If you need affection, get yourself a dog. . . . Oh, and leave it at home!" Executives may also have a point that making the out-group somewhat uncomfortable might indeed motivate people to knuckle down and work their way out of it. The question is, what impact does it actually have?

## Withdrawal Symptoms

Returning to the list of boss behaviors in table 2-1, we ask executives what they think it feels like to a member of their out-group. In fact, we often do not even have to ask. One executive, looking at the list, will often volunteer something like this: "Gee, seeing this now, I realize this is absolutely what I do, but I really wouldn't want to be in that [weaker] group." Why not? "Well, because it can't be fun to work under these conditions, plus this type of behavior is more likely to make me perform worse rather than better!"

This last reaction is quite reminiscent of what we have observed in our studies. How do "weaker performers" react? From our observation and interviews, many perceived weaker performers—but not all, and we will come back to this—tend to withdraw in two ways: They disconnect from the boss, and they disconnect from the job.

### *Reducing Contact with the Boss*

Disconnecting from the boss is typically the first response. Subordinates retreat into themselves, largely because exchanges with the boss tend to be negative—focusing mostly on operational matters, on problems, on deadlines—on the whole, not very pleasant. One subordinate explained, "I used to initiate much more contact with my boss until the only thing I received was negative feedback, then I started shying away."

Besides avoiding unpleasant exchanges with the boss, perceived weaker performers want to avoid any further tainting of their image. They know that their boss does not think highly of them, so they tend to nod their heads rather than ask for clarification when they have not fully understood advice or instructions. Believing "better to keep quiet and look a fool, than open your mouth and prove it," they avoid asking for help for fear of further exposing their limitations.

They also cover up problems and tend to volunteer less unsolicited information. A simple "heads-up" given by a perceived weaker performer can cause the boss to overreact, jumping into action when none is required. As one subordinate recalled, "I just wanted to let my boss know about a small matter, only slightly out of the routine, but as soon as I mentioned it, he was all over my case. I should have kept my mouth shut; I do now."

In some cases, the subordinate in question remains firmly committed to the organization or the job but adopts a kind of siege mentality: "Just leave me alone and let me do my thing." Feeling hemmed in by the boss's close supervision and tight boundaries, the subordinate tries to reestablish a margin of maneuver. By pulling back, the subordinate hopes to reinstate some space, some sense of freedom and choice. As one perceived weaker performer explained, "I kept doing my job to the best of my abilities, without that constant interaction, feeling that if there's no trouble, why wave the flag?"

## Disconnecting from the Job

By disconnecting from the job, the subordinate withdraws intellectually from the task at hand. Many subordinates who are treated as weaker performers experience a loss of drive, enthusiasm, or initiative. Tired of being rebuffed or ignored, they lose the will to fight for their ideas. As one subordinate put it, "My boss tells me how to execute every detail. Rather than arguing with him, you end up wanting to say, *'Come on, just tell me what you want me to do and I'll go do it.'* You become a robot." Another perceived weaker performer explained, "When my boss tells me to do something, I just do it mechanically." If the boss never defers to their ideas, or comes up with fifteen ideas per day on their behalf, why should subordinates take the trouble to generate any?

Taken to extremes, employees can begin to feel second-guessed all the time and start to think, "Why bother trying if I am going to be overruled anyway?" They begin to channel their creativity and surplus energy into outside activities—and they no longer link their sense of self-worth to their work. Ultimately, subordinates can lose the motivation to make autonomous decisions—or even to take any action at all.

## The Erosion of Self-Confidence

These disconnections also affect the subordinates' relationship with colleagues, employees, and customers, and they have repercussions on the corporate culture as a whole, as we discuss in chapter 6. Overall, our research shows that while most bosses' behavior toward "lower performers" seems like common sense and is meant to improve subordinate performance, it actually undermines many a subordinate's sense of self-determination. The subordinate's efforts become contractual (contingent on definite and immediate rewards), and intrinsic motivation is crowded out by a strong focus on gaining the approval, or avoiding the wrath, of the boss. If this sounds bad, it only gets worse.

The boss's behavior also communicates a lack of trust and low confidence in the subordinate's ability—which has a further impact on performance. Bosses intuitively know that self-confidence drives performance. When people firmly believe they can execute the behaviors needed to achieve something, chances are that they'll succeed—because they try harder and don't give up so easily. The problem with bosses' behavior toward weaker performers is precisely that it erodes subordinates' self-confidence.

When we explain this dynamic to executives, some agree with the reasoning behind it, but explain that they do not fall prey to this trap. These bosses say they are aware that they risk hurting their subordinates' self-confidence, and so they work hard to hide their reservations. They say things like "I do exert more control over my weaker folks, but I make sure I sound encouraging and supportive."

We believe what these executives tell us. That is, we believe that they *do* try hard to disguise their intentions. When we talk to their subordinates, however, we find that these efforts are mostly futile. In fact, our research shows that few employees have difficulty telling what their boss thinks of them. In particular, they know full well whether they fit into the boss's in-group or out-group. Bosses who think they can mask their real opinions should think again. They are not getting away with it.

## Reading the Boss's Hidden Thoughts

From our interviews with and direct observation of groups of subordinates reporting to the same boss, we know that subordinates are highly sensitive to the comparative signals sent out by their bosses. Setting aside the dead giveaways, such as who gets the best assignments or who sits in for the boss at meetings—subordinates listen, observe, and compare. They watch their boss interact, they listen to what the boss says or doesn't say, they see the body language, they take note of the choices offered and the controls imposed. Bosses reveal their true beliefs in many ways. Consider these six indicators.

**Unsolicited Advice.** Bosses giving advice to "lower performers" tend to overdo it—they offer too many suggestions too quickly. These subordinates complain that when they approach their boss with a problem, they barely get a chance to expose the problem before the boss fires off a list of more or less appropriate suggestions—without first inquiring what the subordinate had in mind. Conversely, when the subordinates' star colleagues come forward with problems, the boss takes care to consult them on what they have already done or intend to do and feels less obliged to offer such unsolicited advice.

Here is a test: When a subordinate comes forward with a problem, does the boss (a) assume that the person has already taken the key measures, or (b) does he or she start with the blindingly obvious? For example, one perceived weaker performer remembered feeling very insulted and demeaned when after announcing to his boss that three production lines went down, the boss asked: "Have you called maintenance?" The boss wouldn't have asked such an obvious question of a perceived stronger performer.

**Disguised Directions.** Not only do bosses offer suggestions to weaker performers too quickly, they also tend to offer them too forcefully. As one subordinate commented:

> When I tell him that I have a problem and what I've done with that problem, there is never any feedback like *"That was a good thing to do"* or *"Not bad—I think I would add this other aspect."* The communication in that type of situation is always one-sided: *"Here are the things you have to do,"* period, with no comment on what I've done. I can feel his lack of confidence.

Weaker performers have told us that their boss tends to impose solutions in the case of disagreements and conflicts. To "impose" solutions does not require heavy-handed dictatorship; bosses have more subtle ways of using their influence or expertise to ensure that their own approach prevails. For instance, rather than telling a subordinate to "do it this way," the boss may simply argue until the subordinate capitulates. The boss's tenacity in pushing this "advice" makes it clear to the subordinate that this is not an offer to be refused. The boss *says*, "This is only a suggestion. . . . " The boss *means*, "I would *really* like you to do this. . . . " The subordinate *understands*, "Just do it!"

Alternatively, the boss may let weaker subordinates implement their own solution but then offer faint praise, however successful the outcome. The unspoken reproach is that "things would surely have worked even better if you had done it my way." Perceived lower performers quickly recognize that they'll get more credit when they use the boss's ideas than when they rely on their own.

**Disregarded Ideas.** Subordinates are highly sensitive to the boss's reaction to their ideas. Members of the in-group tend to get supportive feedback on their ideas and often get clearance to "try it their own way," even when the boss does not fully share their views. On the other hand, the boss often ignores or squashes out-group members' ideas, with little consideration for the idea or person. In one particular team, the "higher performers" believed their boss gave equal weight to her and their points of view and interests. "She is very attentive to our input," one of them said. In contrast, one of the team's "lower performers" complained, "She just never refers back to my proposal. We only talk about hers." The implication was clear: *She does not find mine very good!*

A more subtle variation is the boss who gives an illusion of listening to the recommendations of weaker performers but fails to act on their input or tries to reshape it. As one "weaker-performing" manager recalled, "After a while, it became obvious that my advice had no weight." Another frustrated manager commented, "He sometimes lets me have my say, but then he tries to change it to something that is closer to his own ideas. So you stop raising ideas because you know you're going to fight him for three months and, in the end, it won't resemble your idea anymore."

**Response to Failure.** Perceived weaker performers remark that their bosses are quicker to seize on their failures, sometimes unfairly. For example, after a tour of the shop floor, one manufacturing manager circulated an e-mail contrasting two of the areas he visited. In particular, he highlighted a number of performance measures posted by one area but not the other. The head of the lower-performing area was incensed:

> It was on the screen for everyone to see. He never came and asked me why these things were missing, or why we weren't doing it, or how he could help us to do it. I was very angry when I saw the message. It was a put-down, without discussing it, without working the issue.

Even when discussions with weaker performers do not revolve around shortfalls or failures, bosses often have difficulty resisting a parting salvo. As one subordinate noted, "Whenever he gives me feedback, there's always a *but*. . . . " Another made a similar observation:

> At the end of the conversation, if we have not talked about, say, customer satisfaction, he will throw out the zinger: *"Customer satisfaction needs to be improved!"* And that's the way the conversation ends, on a low note rather than a high note. So one way or the other it will always get around to something negative.

This comment was in stark contrast with the testimony of this subordinate's better-performing colleagues, who reckoned that their conversations with the same boss tended to end on an upbeat note, something along the lines of "You're on the right track, keep up the good work!"

**Response to Success.** Weaker performers often complain of feedback asymmetry when compared to their better-performing colleagues. As one weaker performer observed:

> There are very few times, I can count them on one or two fingers, where he has come across with a positive reinforcing comment. I do take negative feedback as an incentive to improve, but it's wearing after a while. Every so often you need a little positive reinforcement, and it's never forthcoming.

Even when they *do* acknowledge the successes of weaker performers, bosses may find it difficult to reconcile the achievement with their image of the subordinate. One "poor performer" recalled her boss's response to a spectacular result: *"You got zero returns from customers this month? You really did? I don't believe that!"* The incredulity expressed the boss's low expectations of the subordinate; it also signaled that he would probably dismiss the result as a "one-off" occurrence and therefore would not change his opinion of this subordinate. When managers hold strong opinions about their subordinates, even praise can come out all wrong!

At the other extreme, some bosses go overboard and congratulate weaker performers on every little achievement. Indiscriminate praise comes across as patronizing and betrays the boss's real opinion of the subordinate just as clearly as the "blindingly obvious suggestion."

**Harsher Style.**  Underpinning the boss's skewed attention to success and failure is a more subtle difference of style toward "lower performers," which can be characterized as "a presumption of guilt." As one lower performer observed, "When we talk about service levels, in particular, he has very strong words to say. His demeanor changes, the harshness of his words changes. He is very direct."

Another poorly regarded manager discussed the way his boss decided to review the client bids his area put together. The subordinate explained that he was disturbed *not* by his boss's involvement, but rather by the way the boss approached the issue:

> What bothered me was the negative approach he used. *"I don't believe you, I don't believe your subordinate. I want to go through this in detail. Why didn't you do it this way? Why did you overlook this? Why didn't you do it that way?"* It was those kinds of questions rather than, *"Gee, I don't understand your business and I need some help in understanding how you go about quoting these jobs. Can you show me some examples?"*

Another weaker performer observed, "I've noticed that with me, she tends to ask very specific, detailed questions, like *'How are things going with this?'* or *'What's happening with a, with b, with c? Are you satisfied that enough is being done?'* The details." Such exchanges have the feel of an interrogation rather than an inquiry, much less an exercise in joint learning. Weaker performers often get a sense that the boss is trying to put pressure on them, catch them making a mistake, or show them up. That sentiment gets reinforced by the cross-checking and "trick" questions that bosses sometimes use to test these subordinates.

Subordinates see their boss's behavior for what it is: a reflection of the boss's lack of trust in them. In other words, the boss's behavior is saying that unless he or she presses the subordinates on specific issues, they will not invest enough energy into solving those issues, nor will they volunteer information that might make them look bad or signal impending problems.

Without denying that they make occasional distinctions in their treatment of subordinates, some bosses believe that these distinctions are minor and hardly noticeable. But when all these "little differences" are put together, how large is the overall impact? How accurate is the subordinate's impression? Imagine we asked your subordinates, whom we've never met, to describe your behavior as their boss. They get a short questionnaire asking them for some simple one-to-five ratings on various dimensions of your managerial behavior. At the same time, you complete a questionnaire on each of them, again using a one-to-five scale to rate them on five different performance dimensions. If we looked at each subordinate's questionnaire, could we accurately predict whether you rate that person's performance above or below average?

The answer is yes. To our amazement, our regression analyses showed that we could predict correctly almost 90 percent of the time. Given the huge scope for measurement error in social sciences and the differences in how people apply rating scales, the fact that we misjudge only one subordinate in ten says a lot. It underlines that bosses' behavior is quite unmistakable. Tell us how your subordinates see you behave, and we will tell you what you think of them!

Subordinates can read bosses' minds; they can *feel* the under-confidence. The differences in boss behavior are very significant. Yet, as important as they are, these elements do not explain why boss behavior has such a detrimental effect on many subordinates' motivation and performance.

## Killing the Drive in Others: Three Perspectives

Executives often ask us, "Are you sure you didn't study particularly weak subordinates? Shouldn't managers be more resistant? If these people are really capable of improvement, shouldn't they simply demonstrate their drive and fight to change their bosses' poor opinion of them?" Some subordinates clearly have more drive than others and hence do a better job fighting off the tendency to "give up," but our observations suggest that loss of motivation or confidence has a strong impact on performance. People's willingness to fight back has its limits and is often short-lived.

So far, we have dealt with our own empirical evidence, based on our observations of boss behavior and subordinate responses. Let's now briefly look at three lines of research dealing with the power of expectations and the levers of motivation, which help explain why this is the case.

### "I Can Do It!": Self-Efficacy Theory

Research into "self-efficacy" shows that self-confidence drives performance. In other words, when self-confidence is undermined, performance is undermined. People's level of self-efficacy has been found to predict important health behaviors such as the likelihood they will lose weight, lower their cholesterol, or exercise regularly (see "Believing You Can").[6] In the workplace context, it has been shown to influence blood pressure and whether people cope positively or negatively with job stressors.[7]

The impact of self-efficacy on business performance was also demonstrated in a study involving a simulated organization.[8] Participants were asked to match people to jobs and had to master some complex decision rules about how to guide and motivate those people. Half the participants were told that decision-making skills are innate; the other half were told that they could be acquired through practice. At the outset, both halves of the group expressed moderately high expectations of success. As the simulation became more demanding, however, those in the "innate" condition showed a marked decline in perceived self-efficacy, while for those in the "acquired" condition, it remained stable. Those in the "innate"

---

**BELIEVING YOU CAN**

How much difference does your belief in your ability make? Smokers wishing to quit were *randomly* assigned to one of three groups, supposedly (but not really) based on previous questionnaire responses. In the first group, they were told that they had been selected because of their strong willpower and high potential to quit. They were put through a fourteen-week program that taught them how to quit, for example, by starting out with easy nonsmoking situations and gradually working up to the toughest situations. Participants in the second group went through the same program but were told they had been selected at random. Participants in the third group were told they would be contacted later, but received no special instructions and did not go through the program. At the end of the fourteen weeks, 67 percent of the first group had quit, compared to 28 percent of the second group and only 6 percent of the third group.[9]

---

condition also became harsher toward their employees, considering them impossible to motivate and deserving of termination.

The impact of self-efficacy on performance is further supported by research into "mindlessness" and "learned helplessness," two conditions in which a sense of self-efficacy is undermined, either through lack of practice or through repeated setbacks.

For example, our finding that perceived weaker performers sometimes adopt a "mechanical" approach to their work is understandable from research into "mindlessness."[10] Mindlessness is a mental state in which people are not especially alert, thoughtful, or creative. When instructions are regular, specific, predictable, and leave little room for objection, people end up "going on automatic pilot." They stop wasting time evaluating the merits of a request and focus instead on its execution. Over time, they are liable to develop a range of requests with which they will comply unthinkingly. That may be good for efficiency, but it also dulls their sensitivity to things that are out of the ordinary. They become less adaptive to new signals or situations. They are not "switched on."

If people's ideas and initiative are stifled for long enough, they may become more passive still, as suggested by research on learned

---

## NOTHING I DO MAKES A DIFFERENCE

Researchers place a dog in a kind of sling from which it cannot escape and give it small electric shocks. Twenty-four hours later, they place the same dog in a two-compartment box and expose it to shocks again. This time, though, the dog can escape simply by jumping over the barrier between the two compartments. Two-thirds of the dogs in the study failed to learn the simple escape response—whereas *all* dogs *not* previously exposed to shocks readily learned to escape from the shocks. Dogs that failed to escape had simply learned that nothing they did made any difference—and this expectation persisted even when the situation changed.[11] The experiment shows that lack of control over outcomes leads to withdrawal of effort and helplessness.

The same sort of "learned helplessness" has been demonstrated in a variety of settings with mice, cats, and even humans. People are first given insoluble problems to crack and are later asked to work on some straightforward anagram puzzles. Their performance on the anagram task is poorer than the performance of people who were initially given soluble problems.[12]

---

helplessness.[13] When they perceive their actions as having no impact on outcomes—in other words, when they have a total lack of self-efficacy—they begin to feel helpless. Exposed to repeated setbacks or uncontrollable events, they see themselves at the mercy of external forces, and they see no link between their efforts and their rewards. Feeling they can't win, they often give up trying. They figure, "I can't do anything about it. They wouldn't listen to me anyway, so what's the point?" And that passivity can persist even when the negative environment is altered (see "Nothing I Do Makes a Difference").

### "I Want *to Do It!": Self-Determination Theory*

This research stream looks at conditions that sustain or undermine people's development, performance, and well-being.[14] Self-determination theory posits that we show more interest, excitement, and confidence—and hence perform best—when our behavior is self-driven. Conversely, the greater our sense of being controlled, the more we lose interest in what we are doing and the lower our

---

### PROMOTING SELF-DRIVE

Participants enrolled in a six-month, very-low-calorie weight-loss program were asked why they were participating. Some gave reasons that suggested external control, such as "because my partner insisted" or "because I would feel guilty if I didn't." Others gave more autonomous reasons, such as "because it's important for my health." During the program, the participants also evaluated the autonomy support of the health-care providers—that is, the extent to which staff were seen to give choices and options.

Participants who felt more autonomous—either because of their initial motivation *or* because of their treatment by the staff—attended more weekly meetings and lost significantly more weight over the six-month program. Better still, a follow-up measurement, a year and a half later, showed that they had maintained their weight loss to a greater extent.[15]

---

satisfaction.[16] Clearly, the behavior of the perceived weaker performers in our studies was a lot more controlled than it was self-determined.

The performance consequences of controlling people's actions have been repeatedly shown in various contexts (notably in education and health care—see "Promoting Self-Drive"). With students, for example, the more they felt externally regulated, the less effort they expended. They also showed more signs of anxiety and coped more poorly with failures, tending to disown responsibility for negative outcomes and blaming others, such as the teacher.[17] More autonomous contexts, on the other hand, have been shown to promote more engagement, greater resistance to setbacks, more persistence (lower dropout rates), and enhanced creativity, as well as more effective learning outcomes with enhanced curiosity and better retention of knowledge.

Self-determination theory also helps explain perceived weaker performers' loss of drive and motivation. The theory, supported by studies in a wide variety of settings, tells us that people perform better when they feel (a) autonomous, (b) competent, and (c) valued as individuals. Bosses' more controlling approach toward "lower performers" systematically thwarts all three of these core needs.

With respect to autonomy, for example, weaker performers have fewer opportunities to exercise their judgment and initiative, to make choices, or to solve problems relevant to them. With respect to competence, the routine assignments weaker performers tend to be given rarely allow them to develop new skills. Furthermore, the boss's focus on negative variances gives feedback a punitive, competence-decreasing edge rather than a learning orientation. And with respect to individual worth, discussions with the boss rarely extend beyond immediate operational concerns, nurturing little sense of group membership—indeed suggesting that the individuals are valued exclusively for what they do, not for who they are.

### *"You* Can *Do It!": The Pygmalion Effect*

Research into the Pygmalion effect considers the impact of the expectations of "powerful others" on people's performance. This research stream is particularly important to our discussion because its very powerful findings establish a direct link between bosses' expectations and subordinates' performance.[18]

The research started out in classrooms.[19] A researcher told teachers that their pupils had been tested, and that one group showed high potential for development, whereas another group had normal potential. This statement was *completely false.* The students had indeed been tested but then sorted into two equivalent groups. In another IQ test conducted three months later, however, the supposedly "gifted" group actually *did* score a significantly higher average than the supposedly "normal" group. Remember, the two groups produced similar test results at the beginning of the study. But the teacher was led to expect more from one of the groups, and that group's average performance rose up to the teacher's expectations.

Numerous studies have replicated this staggering result, showing that the Pygmalion effect is alive and well in schools.[20] It is also powerful and long lasting. One study followed the mathematics performance of a group of children over seven years, to assess how long teachers' expectations would be related to student performance. How many years would you predict teachers' expectations would matter? Until the following year, when kids typically would get a new teacher? Or maybe two years? The surprising, and frightening, answer is *six* years. Controlling for other important variables such as actual student performance and student self-efficacy, teachers' expectations were still significant predictors of student performance *six* years later.[21]

Of course, children's egos are not yet fully developed, which may make them more impressionable and more easily encouraged or discouraged than adults. But subsequent research focused on adults, notably in military and organizational settings, has produced similar results. The studies conducted within the Israeli army by Dov Eden and his colleagues are particularly compelling.[22] The first study basically reproduced the classroom experiment.[23] An army psychologist told platoon leaders in charge of officer training that half their incoming trainees had high potential, whereas the other half had "regular" potential. Again, that statement was a total bluff. At the end of the training course, those who were supposed to be "better" scored 15 percent higher on tests than their colleagues did. Different population, same result.

The second study investigated whether this effect could be generated for a whole group. In other words, do the "bright" trainees need to *see* the instructor treating them better than peers in order to feel inspired? This time, the psychologist told some platoon leaders that their *whole platoon* had high potential. Other platoon leaders got the same pep talk except that nothing was said about the platoon's potential. Again, at the end of the training course, the supposedly high-potential platoons scored significantly better in tests, suggesting that the Pygmalion effect can work for a whole team.

Now, before some of you decide to capitalize on this finding and go running to tell your subordinates "you folks are all great," keep in mind that the training officers in these studies were genuinely convinced that the tests had value and hence truly expected their recruits to be exceptional performers. You have already made up your mind about your subordinates, which will make it very difficult for you to set aside your existing beliefs and behave toward all your subordinates as if you really believed all were high performers!

The third study was set up to compare the impact of raising *leader* expectations versus raising the *trainees'* self-expectations.[24] The trainees were divided into four categories. Imagine you're one of the platoon leaders. You hear that half your platoon has been properly tested and, as in the typical Pygmalion manipulation, half have outstanding potential and the other half are average. You learn that the tests for the other half of the platoon were inconclusive, so they have "unknown" potential as far as you're concerned. At the end of seven weeks, the power of expectations has once again worked its magic. The supposedly superior trainees significantly outperform their "control" peers, with the difference in average performance amounting to 12 percent.

Taken together, these studies strongly suggest that subordinates' (in this case, officer trainees') performance tends to adjust up to bosses' (in this case, trainers') expectations. The next question is, Does this work in the other direction? Do *low* expectations *restrict* achievement? Testing that proposition poses serious problems because of the ethical issues associated with inducing low expectations, but researchers found a clever solution. Instead of inducing low expectations, they decided to try to wipe out naturally occurring low expectations.

Platoon leaders were in the habit of receiving the physical fitness scores of incoming trainees.[25] The research targeted the "weaklings." Half the platoon leaders were told that the standard fitness test was proving unreliable at its low end—suggesting that a low score was no sign of fitness potential. The other platoon leaders were not told anything about the reliability of the test. The "weaklings" were retested at the end of the course. In squads where leaders had been led to dismiss their low expectations, the trainees had improved faster than in the other squads. On average they could do around 10 percent more pull-ups and sit-ups, and they completed faster times when running 2 kilometers. But even more significant, they were three times more likely than the "weaklings" in the control group to ultimately feature among the top third of performers! This reverse Pygmalion effect has been dubbed the "Golem effect."[26]

Such studies provide powerful evidence that performance tends to adjust *down* as well as up to the expectations of authority figures. So wherever bosses have access to test scores or performance ratings that differentiate among their subordinates, the likelihood is that something similar is happening. Taken together with the streams of research just described, they help explain why, when bosses hurt subordinate confidence or motivation, they can expect subordinate performance to decrease correspondingly.

What about the second half of the third study? For the half of the platoon for whom bosses were told that "tests were not completed," the psychologist worked directly on *trainee expectations*, telling half they had been found to have high potential and telling the other half that they had "regular" potential. We might expect this manipulation to work "even better" than the manipulation of trainers' expectations, since in this case we are working directly on subordinates' self-confidence. Indeed, results were consistent with this intuition: The average performance of the supposedly gifted trainees exceeded the control group's average performance by 15 percent.

Note that working indirectly through trainers' expectations produced a difference of 12 percent, which is very close to the 15 percent obtained when working *directly* on trainees' expectations. The lesson, of course, is that working indirectly on subordinates' self-confidence through bosses' expectations and actions is a *pretty efficient process*. We do not lose much effect. In other words, bosses' actions have a very strong impact on subordinates' expectations and self-confidence.

## Perverse Effects

We have covered a lot of ground in this chapter, so let's summarize some of the main ideas. Based on widely shared tacit theories of how to pull up weaker performers, bosses tend to behave in a more controlling and less supportive way with subordinates they perceive to be "lower performers." In doing so, they drive down subordinate performance because their approach reduces self-determination, reflects low expectations, and saps subordinate confidence—and we have presented various bodies of research to support that claim.

The odd thing is that holding these beliefs about weaker performers does not prevent bosses from getting high performance from their perceived better-performing subordinates. It seems that the same bosses can be both very good leaders and rather mediocre ones depending on their opinions of the subordinate facing them. In effect, bosses tend to lavish a disproportionate amount of their leadership resources on their perceived better performers. We have

FIGURE 2-1

## Living into Expectations

SUBORDINATES LIVING UP/DOWN TO EXPECTATIONS

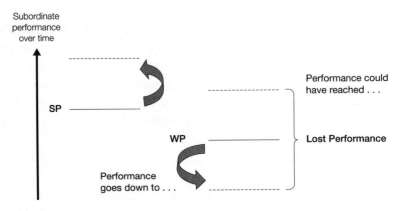

Note: SP = stronger performer; WP = weaker performer

also shown how bosses unintentionally betray their real thoughts about the capabilities of subordinates and how clearly subordinates read those thoughts.

The net result is that performance among subordinates tends to polarize, with some individuals progressing, while others have a tendency to disengage—both from the boss and from the job itself. We do not have to claim that all these "lambs" could be turned into "lions," in other words, that they all could be better, or at least just as good as the stars. Even modest improvements from the weaker performers would be a big bonus compared to what is happening at the moment, with performance steadily deteriorating and the boss investing more and more effort into slowing down that deterioration. The performance that weaker performers could deliver *if they were better managed* leaves tremendous room for improvement. Figure 2-1 illustrates the performance forfeited by bosses when perceived weaker performers live down to lower expectations.

Here is the punch line: When there is a performance issue, bosses think that the performance problem persists *in spite* of their best efforts. We are saying that in many cases the problem persists *because* of their best efforts. Bosses are producing their own misery, and often creating their own poor performers!

These are alarming findings. They suggest that you have a theory in your head, a theory that is supposed to help you but in fact is hurting you. The way you are trying to help perceived weaker performers has a very high probability of actually making things worse—which may explain why past attempts to redress the performance of weaker performers have often proved unsuccessful. How can thousands of bosses have a theory that is dysfunctional but somehow fail to see and correct it? That is the subject of chapter 3.

# 3

---

# Set-Up-to-Fail

*A Vicious Cycle*

That is what learning is. You suddenly understand something you've understood all your life, but in a new way.

—Doris Lessing

A READER exposed for the first time to our assertion that bosses often create their own poor performers might reasonably react with some surprise: "Come on. You mean to tell us that there are countless managers out there clinging to a theory that is dysfunctional, but somehow none of them have realized this? And you two are the only people in the world who happened to have noticed?"

Well, our answer is yes, and no. Yes, we mean that countless managers are relying on a theory of how to deal with perceived weaker performers that is meant to improve the situation, but instead often makes it worse. But no, we don't think we are the only ones who have noticed. In fact, we would argue that people *have* noticed at least parts of what we are discussing. For example, bosses have noticed how difficult it is to redress subordinate performance and to pull a weaker performer out of a rut. They have noticed how frustrating it is to help weaker performers, how much time and effort it drains. They have noticed that their efforts typically produce diminishing returns and that, over time, weaker performers often become worse.

This view—that weaker performers absorb disproportionate attention and resources—is widely accepted as a given. In some companies, HR policies encourage managers to focus their efforts and coaching on the better performers, where the return on investment is assumed to be higher. Indeed, a few companies, notably those with an up-or-out philosophy, actively encourage weaker performers to leave—that way no one has to try to manage them.

A large high-tech company we work with recently introduced a new performance appraisal system designed to, among other things, identify the bottom 10 percent of the employee performance distribution. The company communicated clearly to its employees that the purpose of the exercise was not to single out the "lowest performers" for dismissal. Rather, these employees would be enrolled in a well-defined, individual performance improvement process. Privately, however, a senior manager of the company acknowledged that he expected as much as 75 percent of these processes to fail and hence lead to employee dismissal. Essentially, he was saying, "We don't know how to work with underperformers."

So individuals and companies have clearly noticed that managing weaker performers, and particularly improving their performance, is a difficult and often unsuccessful process. What they have not noticed as much is that this difficulty may arise not in spite of, but *because of*, bosses' behavior, which triggers and nurtures a dynamic that almost condemns these subordinates to fail. Understanding this aspect of the problem is crucial: If the boss is part of the problem, the diagnosis clearly must be different—and so must the cure.

In this chapter we discuss three reasons why managers and companies have not really caught on to the boss's role in the process.

1. They tend to underestimate the demotivational power of bosses' behavior toward perceived weaker performers.

2. They also tend to underappreciate how, and how much, bosses' behavior constrains that of "weaker performers."

3. Bosses and subordinates are caught in a *self-fulfilling process:* Bosses get the behavior and performance outcomes they expect from perceived weaker performers. This match between expectations and outcomes validates bosses'

assessment of the subordinates and gives them no reason to reexamine the process and their role in it.

These three factors, which we will consider in turn, combine to create a vicious cycle of degenerating performance. Though it is a very powerful dynamic, people's capacity to resist it clearly varies. As a result, some underrated subordinates will fight back harder than others. We go on to examine why their efforts are often short-lived and why, in some cases, they backfire.

## The Powerful Undertow of Expectations

We mentioned in the last chapter how bosses drive their subordinates' behavior through their impact on expectations and on subordinate confidence. Once perceived weaker performers start to pick up signals that their boss views them less favorably than their peers, they are liable to start "living down to expectations." Those signals can be very subtle. For example, research has shown that when interviewers send negative nonverbal signals to an interviewee— such as sitting farther away, reducing eye contact, and refraining from nodding or smiling—the interviewees actually perform more poorly. Watching the interviews on video, independent judges rated these interviewees as far more nervous and far less effective than those in a control group.[1]

In working relationships, low expectations sap the morale of subordinates and their drive to succeed. Bosses often have trouble understanding why subordinates react like this. Why don't they fight the label? Clearly, some do—and we will discuss their chances of success toward the end of this chapter—but most employees shut down in some way.

Bosses typically underestimate how demotivating it is for subordinates to feel they are in the "out-group." Yet when we ask them whether *they* have ever been in *their* boss's out-group, many acknowledge having "spent some time in the doghouse." They describe their feelings with words such as unfair, lonely, devastating, frustrating, infuriating, wearing, unpleasant, and even soul-destroying—thus revealing powerful underlying emotions such as anger, fear, and anxiety.

Now, the fact that bosses behave differently with different people is not in itself the issue. At any point in time, some subordinates will be more experienced, more competent, or more motivated than others. Managers are accountable for results and thus have incentives to entrust critical tasks to people who are more likely to perform them successfully and to monitor more closely the performance of subordinates in whom they have less confidence. Thus the problem is not that bosses treat their poorer performers differently but that they do so in a way that projects underappreciation and low confidence.

As we've mentioned already, self-confidence is a volatile substance; it takes surprisingly few signs of disapproval or indifference to erode an individual's confidence. We know from research, for example, that if study participants are led to believe (based on false information) that they are weak problem solvers, they become more easily discouraged when trying to solve troublesome problems. We also know that when athletes are fooled into believing that they have been outperformed by an opponent in a competitive sports trial, their competitive endurance in subsequent physical tests diminishes significantly. This effect is so strong that when male athletes are discouraged while female athletes are encouraged (through false feedback), the impact of objective gender differences in physical strength is nullified.[2]

One might of course argue that managers, particularly senior managers, would not have reached their position without a stronger than average belief in their capabilities. Decades of research suggest that self-confidence is indeed associated with leadership effectiveness and career advancement.[3] That does not make managers—even senior managers—immune to self-doubt. As leadership scholar John Hunt put it, "It is frightening for a researcher like me interested in patterns of motivation, to find how easily high achievers, when rejected continuously, can become underachievers."[4] This phenomenon is particularly noticeable among expatriates when they return home from job assignments overseas. The self-confidence they acquired from the autonomy and challenges they experienced abroad is quickly eroded when they do not have a specific job to return to, which is allegedly the case for over half of them.[5]

When their self-confidence is shaken, perceived weaker performers start to doubt that they have anything worthwhile to contribute. They begin to question their own thinking and to feel that they are out of step with the organization. This uncertainty translates into increased self-censorship or lack of conviction in follow-through. They do not bring up potentially interesting ideas for fear of being shot down, and they tend to implement key initiatives in a half-hearted way that precludes success.

Their enthusiasm and sense of excitement also evaporate. Consigned to the out-group, they take a more cautious approach to avoid further interference or censure from the boss. They stop taking risks, figuring that the boss is not going to appreciate their efforts anyhow. Denied the chance to shine, they can quickly become less entrepreneurial, less committed, less communicative, and more reactive.

Over time, these subordinates' view of their work changes. Work is what they do, but it no longer reflects who they are—their job does not provide the sense of purpose or connection with others that it once did. They still work well enough to get along, but they don't find satisfaction in their work, nor do they look for ways to excel at it. They become "satisfactory underperformers." While this situation may sound fairly relaxed, it is actually distressing and uncomfortable—especially for people whose careers to date have been relatively successful.

This is a pattern that we have observed many times. Most executives we have worked with have seen it too, including Jack Welch—better known for his intense performance drive than for his patience with underperformers. Yet, in his recent book, Welch emphasizes how bosses' behavior can trigger a downward performance spiral even in the most seasoned managers:

> Piling on during a weak moment can force people into what I call the "GE Vortex." It can happen anywhere. You see the "Vortex" when leaders lose their confidence, begin to panic, and spiral downward into a hole of self-doubt. I've seen it happen to strong, bright, and self-confident general managers of billion-dollar businesses. . . . They became willing to agree to anything just to get out of the room and make it through another day. It's terrible to see.[6]

The full measure of the power of the Pygmalion/Golem effect is best illustrated by the *speed* at which it operates. How long do you think it takes for the boss's misgivings to get through and start wearing down the subordinate's defenses? Most subordinates have a track record of success that should sustain their self-confidence for a while, so we might assume that it would take several months, even in the worst cases. After all, the chain of events is complex. It starts with a doubt in the boss's mind. The boss validates that impression. Very subtly, the boss starts to behave differently. The subordinate notices. The subordinate makes efforts to correct the boss's impression and "fights back." Then, slowly but surely, the subordinate realizes that the extra effort has not changed things. The subordinate perhaps tries again, to no avail. The subordinate begins to lose confidence and performance starts to drop, slightly at first, then more and more noticeably.

We know from the Pygmalion research studies described in chapter 2 that by the end of seven weeks, the process has run its course and the boss's low expectations have had a significant impact on test scores. But how quickly did this process take hold? After how many weeks did performance of the two groups start diverging? Five weeks? Three weeks? Surprisingly, the answer is *within days*. In a Pygmalion study, researchers tracked performance scores weekly.[7] Trainees who were (falsely) expected to do well had opened up a significant performance gap with their peers *at the end of the very first week*. That gap never closed. Consistent with the performance data, trainees' expectations of success started equal but continued to drift apart throughout the course.

Other research has shown that low expectations could produce observable behavioral differences within *minutes*.[8] Researchers showed interviewers photos of people who allegedly represented the people they were going to interview. The interviewers thus developed initial impressions of each interviewee based on his or her facial attractiveness. (Attractiveness is, of course, a matter of personal appreciation, but the researchers had pre-tested a series of photos and selected the photos that rated as the most and the least attractive of the series.) Each interviewer then conducted a ten-minute "getting acquainted" phone conversation. When independent assessors who, of course, did not see the photos, listened to a tape recording of the interviewees' half of the conversation, they rated the supposedly unattractive interviewees as less confident, less animated, and less sociable. In other words, it only took minutes (and a restricted communication toolkit, i.e., voice) for the interviewers to nurture in the interviewees the type of behavior they had expected.

Overall, then, we have a very powerful, and surprisingly fast, process. It is easy to underestimate it, to argue that managers "surely are" more resilient than this. Our own studies of managers did not capture how quickly the process works in real-life managerial settings, but like John Hunt, we have certainly been impressed over the years by the impact bosses' behavior and evaluation of their subordinates can have, even on successful subordinates. As posited by self-determination theory researchers, most of us have strong needs for competence, autonomy, and relatedness, and bosses can restrict weaker performers' ability to fulfill these needs in a way that quickly becomes personally and professionally inhibiting.

In addition to its morale-sapping and self-confidence-destroying consequences, the behavior of bosses also has negative consequences on subordinate performance through some simple, almost mechanical processes. Here's how.

## Encouraging Underperformance

Let's go back to the lists compiled from our work with executives, discussed in chapter 2 (see also table 2-1). The first list showed the bosses' perceptions of stronger versus weaker performers' *attitudes and behavior;* the second list showed the *bosses' behavior* toward the two groups of subordinates. These two lists helped explain why, based on their perceptions of subordinates' attitudes and actions, bosses behave the way they do. For example, a boss is more likely to be directive with a subordinate who shows limited initiative.

Let's now reshuffle these lists to focus exclusively on the perceived weaker performers (see table 3-1). By reversing the presumed order of causality, we can see that the subordinate behaviors observed by bosses (right column) actually become quite predictable in light of the bosses' behavior toward the subordinates (left column). Working with the raw material generated by the executives themselves, a number of disturbing connections can be made between the two columns.

TABLE 3 - 1

## How Bosses' Behavior toward Their Subordinates Reinforces Their Perceptions

| With "Weaker Performers" Bosses Tend To . . . | ➡ | Bosses' Perception of "Weaker Performers" (WPs) |
|---|---|---|
| Be directive when discussing tasks and goals. Focus on *what* needs to be done, as well as *how* it should get done. | ➡ | WPs are less autonomous; they don't take charge of problems or projects. |
| Set more targets, more deadlines. Establish clear action plans and checkpoints. | ➡ | WPs don't take the initiative; "you have to do their thinking for them." |
| Give limited decision-making autonomy. | ➡ | WPs are less likely to delegate autonomy to their own subordinates. |
| Give them more routine assignments and projects. | ➡ | WPs are less motivated, less energetic, unlikely to go "beyond the call of duty." |
| Follow up regularly to ensure things are on track. Pay close attention to unfavorable variances and get more systematically involved when they run into difficulties. | ➡ | WPs don't ask for help. They don't bring problems to their boss's attention quickly enough and let themselves get swamped. |
| Be more distant physically and emotionally. | ➡ | WPs are often defensive, insecure, looking for excuses. |
| Focus discussions on operational issues and ask precise questions. | ➡ | WPs are more parochial, often lacking in vision and "big-picture" perspective. |
| Limit open-ended contact, focusing on tasks at hand. Tell more than ask. | ➡ | WPs are less effective "sparring partners." |
| Impose own views in case of disagreements. Make strong "suggestions," close to recommendations. | ➡ | WPs are less innovative, not as open to change, and less likely to come up with solutions. |

When juxtaposed, the two columns make startling reading. Without claiming a perfect match between two sides, we can certainly argue that the bosses' behavior is not exactly helping subordinates overcome their perceived weaknesses. But let us examine some of those contradictions in more detail to highlight the systemic aspect of the subordinates' predicament.

For example, weaker performers are said to exhibit poor judgment. According to bosses, this lack of judgment manifests itself in various ways: They "let themselves get swamped by issues," "get lost in detail," "don't anticipate problems," "hoard information," and "fail to see the whole process." Yet these weaknesses are not helped by the bosses' self-confessed tendency to focus on *what, how,* and *by when* but not to bother much with the *why.* Less privy to the thinking behind strategic decisions, the weaker performers inevitably acquire a more limited understanding of how their work fits into the big picture. This is exacerbated by more routine assignments, involving less exposure upward or outward, fewer opportunities to make contacts or to understand how things fit together. Weaker performers also know that the boss monitors their unfavorable variances more closely and has a tendency to take over when results seem to be lagging. Under these circumstances, subordinates may indeed feel the need to protect themselves and may think twice about volunteering information or signaling problems. Bosses may thus feel compelled to "drag it out of them."

Weaker performers are also considered to be poorer bosses for their own subordinates, less inclined to delegate information and authority and less effective at motivating them. But how surprising is that? Clearly, generating confidence in others is not easy when your own confidence is shaken. Second, and probably more constraining, perceived weaker performers work under tight targets, checkpoints, and deadlines, which leaves them limited room to maneuver and hence limited ability to empower and develop their own people. How can weaker performers approach their team and honestly ask, "How do you think we should go about this?" when they received very detailed instructions from their own boss? It is hard to delegate authority you don't have! The fact that weaker performers get more than their share of routine tasks is not helpful either in terms of subordinate development. Last but not least, the model of management that perceived weaker performers observe in their own bosses is a controlling one. It may also become the model they are most familiar with and hence most likely to replicate.

Bosses also often tell us that the "give-and-take" ratio is poorer with weaker performers and that they are less valuable as idea generators or sounding boards. But it is difficult to act as a sparring partner for the boss when one is not privy to high-level information and when one is rarely exposed to the latest thinking in the field (through training opportunities, international assignments, or deputizing for the boss at trade forums). In discussions with weaker performers, moreover, bosses systematically focus on operational issues, rarely solicit opinions, and generally impose their own solutions. If bosses never defer to their ideas or proposed solutions, why should subordinates bother to venture any suggestions? And if bosses are inclined to make strong "recommendations," how will perceived weaker performers develop the self-assurance to push back, develop an independent view, or advance their own ideas? Under these conditions, bosses may indeed "have to do subordinates' thinking for them."

Finally, bosses allege that weaker performers distinguish themselves by their poor attitude, such as their low enthusiasm and resistance to change. But their failure to go beyond the call of duty is understandable if they receive fewer choices, fewer informal rewards, and fewer challenging assignments. Also, if the boss tends not to share inside information with them or to probe their thoughts on impending changes, then they may struggle to anticipate or develop an openness to change. They always seem to be the last to know, always presented with the fait accompli.

The perceived weaker performer's situation is made worse by the way the boss monitors their performance. The boss observes the poor performer more closely, sets more intermediary targets and deadlines, and is more sensitive to weak signals. In fact, the boss is constantly on the lookout for these signals, scanning for them and cross-checking with people who are likely to disclose them—for example, by asking leading questions of the subordinate's internal or external customers. If the boss is on their case all the time—especially when things are not going well—then he or she is also bound to see more problems. With stronger performers, on the other hand, monitoring is looser and less frequent. If a strong performer encounters a problem and fixes it on her own, the boss may well never know.

We are not arguing that perceived weaker performers never actually display any of the behaviors that bosses observe. Some subordinates really do have faulty judgment and lack motivation and drive. But we wanted to highlight how, given subordinates' initial propensity to display these attitudes, bosses' typical behavior toward them is bound to make things worse.

Until now we have laid out a series of individual elements. The following two sections revisit these elements, but this time in a dynamic context. Highlighting the *interdependence* among these elements will help us show they are part of a process that is both *self-fulfilling* and *self-reinforcing*.

## Bosses' Expectations Are Fulfilled

When we add the *mechanical* effect of a boss's behavior to its *motivational* impact, the expectation of major performance improvements starts to look like wishful thinking. Sensing disregard or disrespect, perceived weaker-performing subordinates struggle to keep their drive and self-confidence intact. Granted fewer opportunities or resources than their higher-performing colleagues, deprived of discretion, influence, and valuable information, they are hard-pressed to disprove the boss's assessment of them. They quickly become locked into a situation from which they find it difficult to recover. Meanwhile, the boss's behavior, which is meant to improve the situation, is having the opposite effect: The alleged "help" actually discourages and disempowers subordinates.

Regardless of how these subordinates fell into the out-group, it is not clear how they can hoist themselves out. Seen from the subordinates' angle, the situation has the makings of a classic catch-22: To escape the out-group, they have to perform better. But to be seen to perform better, they have to be part of the in-group. In other words, they need to benefit from the support, attention, and challenges only on offer to the better performers. They cannot hope to match the standards of high performers given the way they are treated by their boss!

Seen from the boss's angle, on the other hand, *subordinates are exhibiting the very behaviors their bosses had anticipated.* Bosses see very little evidence of what have been called the "E factors"—energy, enthusiasm, excitement, effort, and excellence.[9] What they notice instead are individuals who lack commitment, intensity, urgency, and imagination; who are defensive, reactive, risk-averse, cynical, and not very dependable; and who delegate upward or double-check every little matter with the boss; precisely the kind of employee their bosses already suspected they were. And when overall performance starts declining, bosses get tangible evidence of trouble, confirming their suspicions.

This is known as a *self-fulfilling process*. Bosses expect a certain behavior from subordinates. They select their own behavior in order to avoid this problem, but in fact their behavior actually contributes to subordinates behaving as bosses feared. In the end, bosses actually observe the behavior they feared to observe.

The problem is not *just* that bosses create their own weaker performers. It's also that they do so in a way that is bound to blind them to their own responsibility and that spurs them to dispense more of the wrong remedy. In other words, this process is not only self-fulfilling, it is *self-reinforcing*.

Consider the case of "Richard" and "Michelle." Richard, the boss, has a theory of how lower performers are likely to behave: They will not ask for help when they are in trouble, and they don't drive to excellence on their own—they need to be pushed to it and often try to evade accountability. Richard regards his subordinate, Michelle, as a less-than-excellent performer. Accordingly, he monitors her work more closely, asks her more specific questions, and generally provides less positive reinforcement than he does to his better performers. Richard also pays closer and more regular attention to Michelle's results, so he immediately notices when Michelle hits something that looks like a problem.

Believing that Michelle will not ask for help even if she needs it and that she will not drive to excellence on her own, Richard is convinced that he must get involved and help Michelle to analyze and resolve the problem she faces. Like most managers, Richard is very busy, so he tries to coach but sometimes lacks patience with those he considers weaker performers. As a result, he often ends up giving Michelle very clear instructions, spelling out in detail how she should approach the task.

On the receiving end of such behavior, Michelle steadily gives up on her hopes of personal autonomy and gets used to being told what to do. She begins to execute Richard's directives in a mechanical and uninspired manner: "He never likes what I do, so I'll just do it his way and get it over with." Put off by the prospect of having to argue with him over the right course of action, Michelle prefers to keep her ideas to herself and to avoid unnecessary contact with Richard.

The problem is that these are exactly the behaviors that Richard feared, but also halfway expected, from Michelle. He's looking out

FIGURE 3-1

## No Harm Intended

DEGENERATIVE SPIRAL TRIGGERED BY THE BOSS

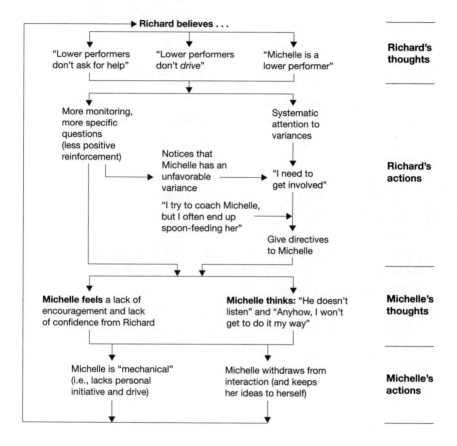

for them and observes them, which only confirms his initial feeling that Michelle is indeed a lower performer, rather than a self-starter capable of setting and striving for stretch targets. The facts are now unambiguous, Richard must *really* keep close tabs on Michelle, and he must *really* make sure she understands what needs to be done. He suspected that this was the case, it's now been confirmed. From now on he'll redouble his efforts.

This is a perfect example of how the self-fulfilling process has become self-reinforcing as well. Richard and Michelle are caught in a vicious cycle, which is mapped out in figure 3-1.

## Caught in a Web

The vicious cycle quickly develops momentum. We noted in chapter 2 that often the weaker performer's immediate reaction to micromanagement or unwanted help is to disconnect from the boss. Unfortunately, it also happens to be the first thing that the boss notices. This increased distance lessens the boss's sensitivity to the difficulties the subordinate faces or indeed the progress the subordinate makes. It also diminishes the boss's ability to contribute to the decision-making process and to obtain reassurance that the subordinate has things well in hand. This in turn fuels the boss's anxiety about being blindsided, the frustration with the subordinate, and the desire to exercise greater control. Interactions become progressively more painful for the subordinate. He or she becomes increasingly nervous or resentful of more contact and pushes back harder. In our experience, the boss-subordinate relationship often degenerates before the subordinate's job performance actually falls off.

Feeling cut off and anxious, bosses tend to overreact to minor performance anomalies. They jump into action at the first hint of trouble, sometimes reacting in directive and punitive ways. Understandably, weaker performers become more reluctant to report worries. This "discretion" can result in delayed problem recognition, so that when the problem finally surfaces, the boss must take drastic action. As one manager put it, "When the barn is on fire, you don't get into a debate, you just step in and put out the fire!" Yet a forceful intervention by the boss merely confirms the subordinate's view that it is best to try to solve problems alone (which may include hiding them from the boss), because when the boss gets involved, he or she takes the issue away. Alternatively, a forceful intervention by the boss may encourage the subordinate to veer the other way, clearing even routine decisions in advance for fear of being overruled later. This response also confirms the boss's view that the subordinate lacks initiative and judgment and needs close supervision.

Another aspect of the self-reinforcing dynamic is the subordinate's intensified search for excuses in response to the boss's intensified scrutiny. Not only does this preoccupation distract the subordinate from more productive activities, it also becomes self-defeating. The subordinate spends more time looking in the rearview

FIGURE 3-2

## How Subordinates' Efforts to Break Free Only Get Them More Tangled Up

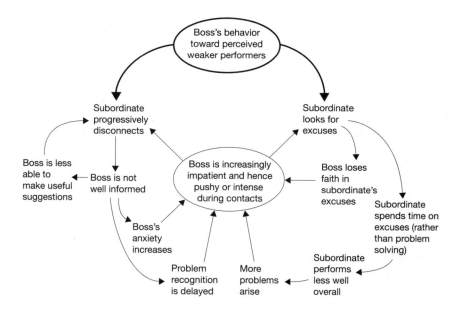

mirror for self-protection. But when not looking at the road ahead, he tends to hit more potholes. Moreover, the boss begins to sense that he always seems to have a good excuse ready. At that point, even valid justifications will stop carrying weight. The subordinate's efforts will have a diminishing impact on the boss's assignment of blame—and the subordinate will feel doubly persecuted compared to colleagues: "First, they give me dead-end assignments and inadequate support. Then, when things don't work out, they take no notice of the reasons." Figure 3-2 illustrates the systemic nature of the set-up-to-fail dynamic.

Moreover, the efforts devoted to trying to "fix" these relationships or improve the subordinate's performance with increased supervision prevent the boss from attending to other issues or activities. And this in turn may generate its own cycle: Feeling resentful or aggravated at being sidetracked from other matters, the boss is likely to be more impatient, making the subordinate feel nervous and less likely to initiate interaction or reveal discrediting information—which means that the boss is forced to squeeze and probe all the harder. When bosses set out to coach perceived weaker performers, they find it difficult to hide their real feelings. Sensing their bosses' impatience or discomfort, subordinates tense up and refrain from asking for clarification. They become anxious and distracted learners—only confirming their bosses' view that they could have spent their time more profitably.

## Breaking Out of the Cycle Is Hard to Do

Clearly, not all subordinates give up or disconnect at the same rate. Many persist. They work hard to maintain high standards, take on more responsibilities, beat deadlines, stimulate their staff, and show commitment and energy. Yet their chances of success remain slim. Even subordinates who are hell-bent on proving that they have been misjudged face considerable difficulties in pulling clear of the out-group, for three key reasons.

1. *It's hard to stay motivated.* Not only is it difficult for out-group subordinates to impress their boss when they're stuck on unchallenging assignments with very clear directions and limited resources, it's also difficult for them to feel any kind of motivation or drive when they aren't given any encouragement. Bosses themselves are reluctant to offer praise lest it lead weaker performers to decrease their effort and become complacent. Under highly monitored work conditions with little appreciation, even robust individuals may see their confidence start to melt. Persistence requires tremendous self-belief. And to persuade the boss to alter significantly a deeply anchored opinion of them, they must deliver exceptional results.

2. *It's easy to overstride.* In a bid to impress the boss, some subordinates tend to overstride. They typically don't do so consciously; they simply end up biting off more than they can chew because they lack big-picture information and experience at running their own show. Others, however, do consciously take on big challenges, convinced that they have to make a *huge* impact in order to change the boss's

mind, like the subordinate who pledged to prove his boss wrong: "His characterization of me was flat out wrong, and I would perform so well that he'd have to eat his words."[10]

To show their energy and competence, some weaker performers set excessively high goals for themselves—promising to hit a deadline three weeks early or to finish six projects at once, or else attempting to handle a large problem without help. Sadly, this strategy is more likely to lead to failure, thus reinforcing the boss's negative opinion of the subordinates' capabilities on one hand and judgment on the other. (Someone with "good judgment" would have known to set the bar at a more realistic level.)

3. *It's hard to live with conflict.* The third problem is that fighting back requires considerable resolve. It takes a significant amount of drive, determination, and self-confidence to say, "I'll show that boss." In addition, this resolve is likely to come across as aggressive or deliberately provocative. Fighting back generally means sticking to one's guns, discreetly ignoring advice or instructions, and possibly even defying the boss in public. The boss is unlikely to appreciate such behaviors—and what starts off as legitimate opposition can easily degenerate into a personal quarrel or grudge. So the period during which a perceived weaker performer tries to fight his way out of the boss's out-group can be very uncomfortable from an interpersonal point of view.

Some bosses don't understand why subordinates would consciously set unattainable goals, take on too many projects, or confront them head-on. "Get real," they tell us. "That would be totally irrational." But that really depends on how you define irrationality. An important line of research on a process called "self-handicapping" shows that people often deliberately create obstacles to their success in order to give themselves plausible excuses on which to fall back if they do fail. Of course, if they succeed, they can also expect more credit for having beaten the odds. (See "Looking Bad in Order to Look Good.")

Notwithstanding these pitfalls, we have met perceived weaker performers who battled on regardless, including some who even

## LOOKING BAD IN ORDER TO LOOK GOOD

We can all recall situations when fellow students claimed not to have prepared for a big test or else to have spent the whole night partying. These claims illustrate a form of self-handicapping that could be called "getting your excuses in early."

Research has identified two levels of self-handicapping behavior. The first is to *claim* that certain factors may inhibit your performance. At work, these factors might include stress, overwork, illness, or lack of resources or support from colleagues in other units. The more extreme version of self-handicapping involves actually *creating obstacles* that genuinely impede the likelihood of success. For example, an employee might deliberately neglect one area of his or her job, withhold effort or prepare poorly, while at the same time presenting these tactics more positively as "winging it" or doing "back-of-the-envelope planning."

Why do people sometimes engage in behaviors that might contribute to the failure they so fear? Quite simply, to protect their ego. Failure in itself is certainly no fun—but failing due to lack of commitment, inattention, insufficient time, or a personality clash with the boss tends to be easier to accept than failure due to lack of ability. By making it easy to attribute failure to external and unstable causes, rather than to a stable and internal factor such as personal ability, self-handicappers try to preserve their self-esteem and sense of competence.

There are two schools of thought on the impact of self-handicapping on performance. One view is that self-handicapping impairs performance as self-handicappers come to believe the excuses they have offered and reduce their effort. The other view is that self-handicapping may actually liberate the individual by reducing the anxiety of evaluation.[11] The fact that most people self-handicap to some extent, in some settings, suggests that this strategy has some benefits. Certainly by offering both protection against failure and enhanced personal credit for success, self-handicapping is one possible strategy to attain very rational objectives.

managed to break out of this vicious cycle. Yet the rare examples we have come across seldom involved a straightforward switch from the boss's out-group to the in-group. Take the case of a banking executive we'll call "Paula." In total disagreement with the operational direction her boss proposed and her colleagues pursued, but in agreement with a consultant's recommendations, Paula discreetly swerved down another path. After a few months, top management realized that Paula had been right all along, so that Paula's boss and several of her colleagues were forced to leave. Essentially, Paula "over-performed" them out of the organization. The removal of the boss and his clique was a spectacular vindication of Paula's tenacity, but this strategy was clearly very risky. Pulling off such a coup requires impeccable judgment and assurance of your re-employability.

"Don" is someone else who decided to go it alone. While his boss and colleagues took one route to implementing a just-in-time production system, Don adopted a less flamboyant approach that he regarded as more sustainable. His colleagues in other units had rapid success while Don's unit made disappointing progress. On the crest of the wave, two of Don's top-performing colleagues moved on to bigger jobs outside the organization. Meanwhile, Don's results started to improve exponentially and subsequently overtook sister units, where progress had flattened out altogether. Ultimately, Don carried the day and his boss came around to his approach. Reflecting on the transition period, however, Don recalls many adversarial feelings. Daily meetings with his boss, for example, had been very painful for weeks on end, tempting Don to throw in the towel.

In our experience, this kind of breaking out is more likely among employees who perhaps disconnect from the boss but whose performance remains strong. They manage to fight it out emotionally, stay committed, and avoid overreaching. Subordinates whose performance has slipped, or whose relationship with the boss has become acrimonious, stand little chance. Those we might call "re-sisters" essentially manage to limit the damage, circling just below the surface rather than being sucked down into a full-blown self-defeating spiral. They bide their time and keep their noses clean, often in the hope that a new boss will arrive to give them a fresh chance before the current relationship becomes unbearable.

Escape *is* therefore possible. But given how tough, painful, and risky it is to escape, fighting back is not the most obvious response. There are nontrivial chances that the subordinate's efforts may in fact worsen the situation. Weighing the fight-versus-flight options, flight makes more sense. For some, as we saw in chapter 2, flight means disconnecting from the boss or the work. For others, it means changing jobs and switching to a unit or an organization that appreciates their talents better. So why don't all weaker performers leave if they are as capable as we maintain? A key reason is that over time, their view of what is tolerable treatment from the boss shifts to accommodate the new "reality."

Imagine the boss's behavior as a kind of normal distribution, ranging from pleasant on the left to unpleasant on the right. Occasionally the boss will behave in a way that falls just within the subordinate's "zone of indifference"—but is really borderline acceptable. As the boss repeats this behavior, the subordinate gets used to the new situation, and her zone of indifference shifts to the right. Previously borderline acceptable, the boss's behavior becomes the center of the subordinate's new zone of indifference. As the boss becomes ever more controlling, the subordinate stays because the boss's new behavior remains within the revised zone of indifference. This zone will keep shifting to the right as the subordinate adjusts to the boss's increasingly coercive behavior. Eventually, she greets behavior that would initially have fallen well outside the bounds of acceptable treatment with indifference. Had the full change in the boss's behavior come from one day to the next, she certainly would not have accepted it. But fighting a gradual change is harder because resisting keeps the subordinate in a state of unease. The path of least resistance is to learn to live with the boss's new behavior.

## When It's as Bad as You Feared

This chapter asked why so many smart executives do not notice that they are heavily contributing to creating their own poor performers, and hence fail to adjust their behavior accordingly. The main reason is that in spite of their best efforts, bosses get the behavior they expect, or fear, from their perceived weaker performers. This match between expectations and outcomes reinforces bosses in their belief that they understand the situation well and certainly does not lead them to examine their own responsibility in the process.

In addition, bosses tend to underestimate how powerful an impact their expectations and behavior have on subordinates' motivation and drive. They also underestimate how much their behavior toward perceived weaker performers constrains these subordinates' responses. Among other constraints, perceived weaker performers cannot pass on to their own employees a sense of autonomy and empowerment they themselves do not have.

The process we've described in this chapter is not indefinitely self-reinforcing, else these weak relationships would always disintegrate—and people would systematically leave. The vicious cycles we describe do not all spiral downward at the same speed or to the same depth. Boss and subordinate often learn to live with a professional and personal relationship that is not very satisfying but is bearable, at least for some time. And as we have discussed, not all subordinates give up. Some resist. Setting aside the fact that this resistance sometimes backfires, we must stress again what these subordinates are up against. Once the boss develops low expectations, the subordinate's ability to deflect these and to fight back is severely limited. The inhibiting power of the boss's low expectations and associated behavior is both very fast to set in (from a week in Pygmalion studies to minutes in interviewing settings) and very powerful once in place.

We are obviously going to want to offer solutions that will interrupt the patterns we discussed in this chapter. Before turning to the cure, however, we need to make sure we have a complete diagnostic of the symptoms and causal mechanisms. Chapters 4 and 5 explore in more detail how bosses and subordinates unwittingly fuel the set-up-to-fail syndrome through their respective mental biases.

# 4

---

# Labels, Biases,
# and Misperceptions

We don't see things as they are, we see them as we are.

—Anaïs Nin

"HAVING FORMED AN OPINION," an English philosopher once said, "our minds draw on all possible evidence to support it. When confronted with evidence that contradicts our viewpoint, we overlook it or denigrate it, or find some other way of writing it off. That way we can cling to our original opinion as though it were a universal truth."[1]

These sentences could have been uttered yesterday. They have bite and self-awareness, and they echo recent findings of modern social psychology. And yet they are the words of Francis Bacon, written close to four hundred years ago! So the idea that we first make judgments and then set out to confirm them is not exactly new. But if we have known about it for so long, why do human beings remain so vulnerable to these mental biases? That question is at the heart of this chapter.

The very nature of the set-up-to-fail syndrome does not encourage bosses to examine their own contribution to it. The odd thing is that we have so little difficulty identifying such processes in others. For example, when we see a friend overparenting a child or a colleague overmonitoring a subordinate, we seem to notice it immediately. This suggests that it is more than just a self-fulfilling process.

On discovering the disastrous and self-reinforcing consequences of being labeled a weaker performer, we initially assumed that these labels were at least triggered by concrete performance problems. The weaknesses were perhaps magnified by the boss's inappropriate response, but the blame for setting all this in motion essentially lay with subordinates. It was regrettable, but they had really brought this on themselves. We were in for a surprise!

Only by examining the development of individual relationships—and trying to trace the point at which the relationship had gone sour—did we discover the true extent of the "set-up." Sometimes the trigger was a real, but eminently curable, performance problem. However, it was often a case of the boss unilaterally, and often mistakenly, *deciding* that the subordinate had a problem—and thereby *creating* a problem. In these circumstances, subordinates really seem to be set up to fail, getting caught up in intricate webs from which they cannot extract themselves.

## Why Managers Label

A large part of the problem that we have described in the previous chapters clearly relates to the labeling process—specifically, the implicit sorting of subordinates into in- and out-groups. Managers clearly have a vested interest in getting the best out of their people, and labeling apparently does not help much. So why on earth do managers persist in labeling?

Fundamentally, they do so because they're human beings, and we all tend to categorize. We attach labels to our family, friends, acquaintances—even to "weirdos" we happen to pass in the street. Indeed, evolutionary psychologists claim that categorization was one of the "competencies" that enhanced our development and chances of survival back in the Stone Age. They suggest that our ancestors developed prodigious capabilities for classifying information—both about the natural environment and about their social environment—and that these abilities have become part of our nature, such that it now takes a conscious effort to overcome the sorting instinct.[2]

Whether or not one buys this evolutionary argument, labels can be a big help. They enable us to function more quickly and efficiently, providing rough and ready guides for interpreting events and interacting with others. The need to label is especially acute for managers. Working in an uncertain and information-rich environment, labeling is critical to reducing ambiguity. It helps managers decide *ex ante* or at least very quickly and without much effort who should get what tasks, what information they should act on, or where they need to direct their attention. It allows them to process information in real time and to move forward without turning every decision into a major research project. One reason they have succeeded in their careers so far is precisely because they have tended to be good at labeling and have developed a reliable gut instinct.

So managers label because labeling happens to be functional. It makes their lives easier, saving thinking capacity for more complex issues. These mental shortcuts are efficient and usually lead to acceptable decisions in a reasonable amount of time. So what's the problem? The problem is that the labels are less accurate than managers think they are—and when we say less accurate, we mean specifically that labels are unreliable indicators of performance and potential.

## Premature Classification

The first hint that managers' labels have dubious reliability relates to the speed with which they're applied. When we ask executives how long it takes them to make a good assessment of someone, their answers range from "a few months" to "a few minutes." They begin cautiously, telling us that it depends on the job and how far away the person is physically located—and that clearly it can take months if you *really* want to do a good job assessing someone's strengths and weaknesses. But then there's always someone who jumps in and says, "It takes me about ten minutes!" At that point, everybody laughs, and they start to joke about whether it takes ten minutes or two.

These executives are essentially saying that they quickly develop a first impression, which they then try to submit to some kind of testing process before they formalize serious performance expectations. The question remains, how fast are labels activated?

Research that tracked boss-subordinate relationships at monthly intervals showed evidence that in- and out-groups had been formed by the second month of the new working relationship. So one month seems to be "enough." But could it be less? A subsequent study, which tracked the evolving relationship at shorter intervals, showed that bosses' perceptions of their subordinates after just *five* days of working together predicted the quality of their relationship six weeks later.[3] If it takes only a week for bosses to start "typecasting" their subordinates, how likely is it that performance is the determining factor?

Actually, the fastest instance of labeling we have come across showed up in a laboratory study of eighty boss-subordinate pairings, which found that distinctions had developed within *ninety minutes* of starting work on a simulation problem.[4] Now we are not saying that bosses establish firm labels in under two hours. But they do develop an initial opinion and, as we know from research on decision processes, these first thoughts can have a disproportionate influence. For example, two groups of managers were both asked the following two questions:

1.  Do you believe that six months from now the prime interest rate will be above or below X percent?

2.  What is your best estimate of the prime rate six months from now?

For one group, the first question mentioned the figure of 8 percent, and for the other group it was 14 percent. (This was in 1983, when the real prime was around 11 percent.) Managers' answers to question 2 then showed an average gap of 70 basis points—with the first group estimating 10.5 percent and the second 11.2 percent.[5]

This simple test showed how managers' thoughts could be dragged one way or the other by bogus information, even though they knew better. It illustrates the mental phenomenon of *anchoring,* the tendency to give disproportionate weight to the first information received. Where subordinates are concerned, many sources of information can serve as anchors, even throwaway comments. For example, a meaningful "Good luck!" from a colleague who learns that a particular subordinate has been assigned to your task force may be enough to trigger the process.

## Attitude, Not Performance

To get a clearer picture of what role performance *does* play in initial labeling, we surveyed executives. What caused them to lose confidence in subordinates? What were the triggers? Performance was bound to play some role. Examples could include missed deadlines, weak reports or presentations, covering up a problem, losing key clients, undershooting targets, and poor knowledge of the product or operation. Here are the factors they mentioned:

- *Disloyalty:* bad-mouthing previous bosses or other managers, bypassing you
- *Complaining:* about his or her own employees or own lack of career success
- *Negative attitude:* "glass half empty"
- *Low engagement or energy:* failure to communicate desire and drive
- *Low self-confidence:* how they hold themselves, talk, and look at you
- *Insensitivity to signals:* poor listening, failure to read the new environment or grasp the prevailing norms
- *Know-it-all:* too much unsolicited advice or failure to admit ignorance (new hires aren't expected to know everything immediately)
- *Disrespect for boss's time:* how they use your time and what information they give
- *Blatantly political:* for example, how they send e-mails—especially if you are on blind copy
- *Extrinsic motivation:* excessive concern with compensation aspects versus job tasks and responsibilities
- *Trying too hard:* try too hard to impress, to be likable, to demonstrate their skills, or to be overly visible

To our surprise, executives' answers were conspicuously short on performance specifics. They mainly stressed attitudes. While subordinates' attitudes clearly have repercussions on certain aspects of performance, they are not necessarily related to their ability to do the job. The bosses, then, are focusing on the qualitative part of performance, not the quantitative part. Other research confirms that impression. For example, one study measured how many calls employees in a telephone company handled and how many service complaints they entered into the computer.[6] Their weekly performance was averaged over six months and compared with the subjective performance ratings their bosses gave. It turned out that in-group status was linked to the bosses' subjective ratings but *not* to objective performance measures.

In another study in retail stores, researchers looked at the interplay between sales performance and in-group status.[7] When salespeople received their sales targets for the second quarter, they were confidentially asked to rate their commitment to those goals. They were also asked to rate their perceived relationship with their boss, to indicate broadly who was in-group and who was out-group. At the end of the quarter, the researchers looked at the actual sales figures for each person. Predictably, those who performed best were in-group employees with high goal commitment. More surprisingly, those who performed worst were in-group employees with low goal commitment. The out-group salespeople performed close to average, regardless of their commitment (see figure 4-1). It seemed that in-group employees could afford to turn in a sales performance that probably would not be tolerated of an out-group employee—and that out-group employees with high goal commitment were not enabled to perform at higher levels.

So while "objective subordinate performance" certainly enters into the equation, it is not always clear how or to what extent. Indeed, when researchers look at factors other than performance to try to predict who is in the out-group, they often get stronger results. For example, factors that managers refer to as "personal chemistry," "empathy," and "fit" play a bigger role than many bosses would care to admit. Compatibility can be a product of actual similarity, of perceived similarity, or of liking. One study of bank managers showed a remarkably high correlation of 0.73 between liking and the subordinate's in-group status.[8] A manager is more likely to favor someone who "reminds me of me ten years ago," who "sees things in much the same way," or who "seems to be on the same wavelength."[9]

FIGURE 4 - 1

## Goal Commitment and Sales Performance

### HOW IN- AND OUT-GROUP EMPLOYEES COMPARE

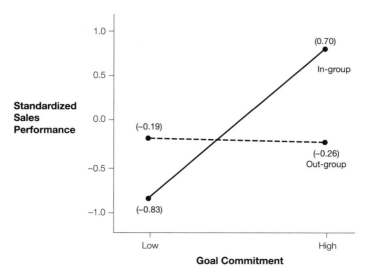

Source: H. J. Klein and J. S. Kim, "A Field Study of the Influence of Situational Constraints, Leader-Member Exchange, and Goal Commitment on Performance," Academy of Management Journal 41 (1998): 88–95.

Perhaps the best illustration of both the speed and subjectivity of labels was a study of new working relationships from day one.[10] The study looked at in-group composition versus out-group composition six weeks into the boss-subordinate relationship. It measured the boss's early expectations of the new hire, captured during the first week of the relationship ("Do you think that the new employee will be a high performer?"), and the boss's evaluation of the individual's actual performance after two weeks on the job ("How effectively has the subordinate been fulfilling his or her roles and responsibilities?"). Bosses' expectations at the end of week one proved to be a much better predictor of subordinates' future in-group status than their evaluation of subordinates' actual performance at the end of week two.

The notion of performance turns out to be so multifaceted that the distinction between good and satisfactory performance is very much in the eye of the beholder. Good people can quickly end up with bad labels. That needn't be a problem. The boss's inaccurate label *becomes* a problem because it is so hard to change.

### First Impressions Last

The durability of labels is confirmed by researchers who have tracked boss-subordinate relationships over time.[11] Interviewing new boss-subordinate pairings at three-month intervals, they detected hardly any movement between the in-group and the out-group. The subgroups identified at the start of the second month remained very stable throughout the course of the year. Research tells us that relatively few people actually manage to transfer from out-group to in-group. Why is this the case?

A key reason is that managers are overconfident about their judgment. They're smart, they have good intuition, and they have a lot experience identifying the prospective hotshots and the duds. And often they have been right—but not as often as they think. Numerous studies indeed show that people tend to put too much trust in their own opinions.

A classic demonstration of overconfidence in judgment involved a group of practicing clinical psychologists and psychology students, who were asked to form clinical judgments about a thirty-year-old man who had experienced "adolescent maladjustment."[12] The case study was divided into four parts, to be read at intervals: first, the man was introduced as a war veteran, along with details of his current job; part 2 described his childhood; part 3, his high school and college years; and part 4, his army service and later activities.

After reading each part, subjects had to answer the same set of questions and then estimate the likelihood that each answer was correct. After reading the first part of the case study, subjects answered 26 percent of the questions correctly, and had a mean confidence of 33 percent—so there was a fairly close match between estimated accuracy and true accuracy. As they read more material, they became increasingly confident, though their accuracy hardly improved at all. By the time they finished reading the fourth part of the case study, they were about twice as confident as they should be—showing 28 percent true accuracy versus 53 percent estimated accuracy.

Subsequent research has confirmed this overconfidence effect with experts in various fields—including computing, oils and chemicals, advertising, automobiles, and money management. Of particular interest here is that overconfidence has also been shown in people's predictions about their behavior and the behavior of others—and that overconfidence actually *increases* under conditions of stress.[13]

Although overconfidence seems a fairly universal phenomenon across cultures and occupational categories, managers may well be particularly prone to succumb to it. In fact, when we talk about overconfidence to executives, they argue that they couldn't do the job without it. Similarly, a respected business journalist has pointed out, "If you are not that way inclined, you are not going to make it up the ladder."[14] The problem is that excessive assurance about your assumptions and opinions means you won't notice, much less seek out, contradictory information.

Also, to be fair to managers, the business context does not make it easy for them to revisit their labels, for two reasons:

- Managers are under intense time pressure that precludes extensive reanalysis of causes and consequences or corrections of false impressions. As Debra Speight, CIO at Harvard Pilgrim Health Care, puts it, "We are all afflicted with what I call the 'MTV Syndrome': We process so much information so fast that it's easy to hear only what we want to hear."[15]

- The managerial process itself is messy. As a result, clear-cut evidence that might disconfirm a label is limited. Performance is frequently ambiguous, there are no right or wrong answers, and the uncertainty is often compounded by the geographical remoteness of subordinates. Under these conditions, objective measures of managerial effectiveness or potential remain elusive.

Clearly, we are not claiming that *right now* all your subordinates are actually performing on par and that your ratings are unfounded. What we *are* saying is that the performance differences you see now are largely driven by your actions at an earlier stage, when you first stuck labels on the poorer performers. Perhaps those weaker performers really were less competent than their colleagues, but that is not the issue. Our point has to do with the evolution of performance. Instead of putting them on a trajectory of continual improvement, your label has placed them on a downward spiral. That's why we call it the set-up-to-fail syndrome: first, because it is not necessarily triggered by the subordinates; and second, because once they fall prey to it, they have little hope of getting out of it!

## The Reign of Error

Some executives we talk to think we make too much of subordinates' hopeless situation. They argue that subordinates still have a good chance to succeed, even if their assignments are a bit on the boring side. After all, they still have deadlines and profit targets to meet, or even beat. And the boss is still there to give advice, even if subordinates feel somewhat cramped and the advice is at times painful. Sure, the subordinates in question may not exactly be helped, but they are not doomed either. Or so these executives think.

Well, just consider what perceived weaker performers have to do in order to have their labels revisited. First, the subordinate must fight hard to maintain self-confidence and not grow discouraged. Assume also that the subordinate resists the temptation, highlighted in chapter 3, to fight back in unproductive ways such as overreaching or confronting the boss head-on. Then assume that his intensified efforts actually produce visible performance improvements. How likely is it that the boss's opinion will change? "Very likely," bosses tell us, with genuine sincerity. But unfortunately their minds get in the way. Considerable evidence shows that what bosses notice and what conclusions they draw depend very much on who they are dealing with.

They fall prey to what psychologists call a *confirmatory bias,* elegantly illustrated by the following study. Take a group of people who believe in the death penalty and a group of people who don't. Give them two thorough reports of research on capital punishment—one concluding that it is effective, the other concluding that it is not. We might expect that exposure to such conflicting evidence might cause the subjects to doubt or at least to become more open to the other point of view. In fact, when retested, both groups were *even more convinced* of their positions than before.[16] Note how powerful this dynamic is: In real life, when we have made up our minds, we are unlikely to go out of our way to consider contradictory evidence as in this test.

Thus, for weaker performers to shake off their label, they would have to breach *three* successive filters in the boss's mind: what bosses notice, how they interpret their observations, and the way they remember these interpretations.

### Bosses' Observations Are Selectively Biased

The first obstacle is the boss's *selective observation*. Bosses often don't notice perceived weaker performers' achievements because that is not really what they are scanning for—they are mainly on the lookout for bad surprises. As one subordinate lamented:

> [My boss] didn't pay an awful lot of attention to the fact that we reduced customer complaints by 50 percent. He just doesn't give a lot of weight to the things [our unit] achieve[s]. With me, he focuses primarily on cost. I mean, that's the only thing he ever focuses on!

In other words, the labels we give to subordinates act as sieves, straining out information that is contradictory to or inconsistent with those labels. What we notice or ignore is guided by our expectations.

A classic demonstration of that bias involved a class of students and a guest lecturer. Researchers told students that the university was interested in how different classes reacted to different instructors. Students read brief biographical notes about the instructor before he arrived. In addition to information about his age, background, and experience, the biography included one sentence describing his personality: "People who know him consider him to be a _____ _____ person, industrious, critical, practical, and determined." For half the students, the missing words were "rather cold," while for the other half they were "very warm." When asked to assess the instructor afterward, those who expected him to be warm gave him significantly higher ratings than their colleagues. They found him more participative, open, and considerate.[17]

These are impressive findings! Changing two words in the document set students' expectations of their instructor and had a massive impact on their perception of reality during the subsequent twenty-minute class discussion. Contrary to what we might tell members of the other group if we had attended this class, *neither* group was blind to reality. They just picked up on *different aspects* of an ambiguous reality.

Another example of biased observation involved people observing a student trying to solve multiple-choice questions.[18] The observers saw one of two scenarios. In both, the student correctly answered fifteen of the thirty questions. In one scenario, the student got most of the first questions right but tailed off. In the other, the student began poorly but got most of the last items right. When asked to recall how many questions the student had got right, those who had seen the student start well overestimated his success (17.7 out of 30), whereas those who had seen the student start badly underestimated it (13.8 out of 30). This elegant experiment shows the speed and power of first impressions.

The chances of distorting what we see are even more pronounced in organizations where managers have to contend with a barrage of information in different forms—some of it observed directly (both verbal and nonverbal), some of it reported by others, and some of it inferred from data. Much more than the students in the experiment, managers operate under high-pressure and high-information conditions, which only increase the possibilities of selective observation.

## *Bosses Don't Give Credit Where It's Due*

Even if a boss notices a perceived weaker performer has obtained a positive result, it does not guarantee the subordinate will get credit for it. The boss first has to decide, in a process that may or may not be conscious, how much credit the subordinate really "deserves" for achieving the desired outcome. To determine why things happen and why people do what they do, we make attributions. In particular, we can attribute people's actions to the stable characteristics of the *person* (i.e., the individual's dispositions and capabilities) or to the specific conditions of the *situation*.

A considerable amount of research shows that human beings go about this attribution process in ways that feature a few systematic biases, known as *attribution biases*. The first such bias is so well documented that it is called the *fundamental attribution error*. Human beings—particularly in the Western world—simply have a strong propensity to overestimate the extent to which others' behavior is driven by their dispositions, and thus to underestimate the impact of situational factors. This result has been obtained even in situations where situational factors could fully account for the behaviors observed.

When explaining our own behavior, however, we are much more likely to emphasize situational or unstable factors.[19] We have observed this *actor-observer bias* many times in our classes when we discuss with executives why people resist change. (See "Resistance to Change.")

The same action can therefore trigger different attributions depending on whether we are observing the behavior or performing it. But the distortion is actually more subtle than that. When we are explaining outcomes rather than behaviors, we tend to make different attributions depending on whether we experience success or failure. We are inclined to take personal credit for successful outcomes but to blame the situation (or others) for our failures. This tendency is known as *self-serving bias*.

Some of us are more vulnerable to self-serving bias than others. It is a matter of self-awareness, humility, and probably of national culture as well. But human beings are basically all, to some extent, more prone to attribute their success to internal causes and their failures to external ones. This is not news.

The fascinating thing is the fact that *we tend to extend the self-serving bias to members of our in-group*. We can see this effect when we watch sports teams we support. If our team wins, we think it is because the players are talented, they try hard, and encourage each other. If the opposition wins, it is because they were lucky, they cheated, the referee was biased, or we fielded a depleted team. This process was confirmed by the following study.

Students from two rival schools were asked to watch their school teams play a football match. The two groups of students were asked to note, as objectively as possible, the number of infringements each

## RESISTANCE TO CHANGE:
## AN ILLUSTRATION OF ATTRIBUTION BIASES

When we ask experienced managers why people resist change, they typically come up with a list that includes such things as inertia, intolerance of uncertainty, anxiety about the unknown, fear of new working relationships, and loss of status or rewards. It is not a particularly flattering list for the resisters (See table 4-1.).

When we turn the question around and ask the managers if *they* ever resist change, they answer affirmatively. When we ask them why, they offer a very different set of explanations: because the change initiative was poorly conceived, because it addressed the wrong problem, because it did not fit with some other aspect of the organization, because of a lack of resources or training to implement it properly—essentially, "because we carefully considered the initiative and decided it was not appropriate under the existing conditions."

So when "other people" resist change, they do so for personal and emotional reasons: anxiety, stubbornness, complacency, self-interest, inertia. But when we resist, we do so for rational and contextual reasons—in short, because the change itself stinks.

This example highlights the asymmetry between the way people explain their *own* behavior compared to how they explain the behavior of *others*. We overintentionalize the behavior of others, meaning that we play down the role of outside forces or constraints and explain their actions by their attitudes or character traits. This phenomenon is known as the *actor-observer bias*.

team committed. The game turned out to be rough, with several injuries on both sides. When researchers examined the results, they found that both sets of students recorded significantly more fouls from the opposition team than their own team. Each group noticed different things and attributed different intentions to the actions. They tended to dismiss their own team's questionable acts as tough but fair, but they deemed the opposition's actions as unsportsmanlike and worthy of being called fouls.[20]

Not surprisingly, bias toward people we regard as part of our in-group can also be seen in the workplace. In one study, bosses were

TABLE 4 - 1

## The Unreasonableness of Others

| Why Others Resist Change | Why I Resist Change |
| --- | --- |
| Fear of uncertainty | Ill-conceived initiative |
| Risk-averse | Bad timing |
| Don't understand the vision | Wrong priority at this time |
| Cynicism (bad experiences in the past) | Not achievable (e.g., insufficient resources) |
| Not their idea (NIH syndrome) | Insufficient consultation |
| Won't benefit from change | Low trust of change agents |

asked to identify two subordinates: one on whom they could depend for help (to represent the in-group) and another to whom they would most likely *not* turn for help (to represent the out-group). Next, the bosses had to think of critical incidents when each subordinate's performance was effective and alternatively, of incidents when each subordinate's performance was ineffective. From these four scenarios, the bosses then had to judge what caused those outcomes. For effective outcomes, out-group subordinates were credited with significantly less effort and ability than in-group subordinates. But for ineffective outcomes, out-group subordinates' lack of success was more likely to be attributed to lack of effort and low ability.[21]

In other words, bosses tend to attribute better performers' success to their judgment, competency, and effort. When better performers fail, bosses tend to be more indulgent and less likely to penalize these subordinates: It's probably a case of bad luck, an unreasonable client, or lack of support from another part of the organization. With the perceived weaker performers, however, things work exactly the other way around. If there's a performance problem, the immediate reaction is "She messed up again" or, in a more positive vein, "I'm not really surprised." Bosses aren't as ready to make allowances. And when good things happen to weaker performers, the attributions are reversed. The explanation is probably situational: "It must have been a soft target," or "The client must have been desperate," or "She must have followed my advice," or "I wonder who helped him out?"

Imagine that you notice "Gloria," one of your subordinates, going out of her way to help others, including you. How might you interpret it, depending on whether you saw her as a high performer or a low performer? Would this count as "good citizen behavior"— that is, behavior that is neither required nor rewarded but that enhances the functioning of the organization? Or would you rather see it as ingratiation, in other words, as an attempt by the subordinate to influence the way you think of her? Earlier, for example, we mentioned that "trying too hard" sometimes raised managers' doubts about the subordinate's motives. Yet the distinction between "trying hard" (dedication) and "trying too hard" (in order to look good) is clearly subtle. Similarly, who is to say whether volunteering for additional work or helping your boss and colleagues is an act of altruism or of impression management?

Or again, consider feedback-seeking behavior by the subordinate. You can interpret it as evidence of a learning orientation: a drive to improve by seeking diagnostic information, or an attempt to assess the correctness and adequacy of her behavior and enhance her future performance. But you could also view the same behavior as a sign of personal weakness and insecurity—or worse still, as a highly calculated attempt to prompt your memory before a performance evaluation.

The problem is that motivation cannot be observed; only behaviors can. Bosses have to *infer* motivation from their perceptions of the authenticity of the behavior. They have to decide whether it is "typical" behavior or whether it is "put on." In reality, motives are often mixed. A subordinate may be quite conscious that joining a certain task force will be good for visibility but will also require efforts that "go beyond the call of duty." Similarly, even "model employees" may tailor the *type* of citizenship behaviors they display to an authority figure's known preferences. Quite conceivably, then, a similar set of behaviors will lead one person to be labeled a model employee and another to be labeled a "political animal" (see table 4-2).

The ease with which we sometimes make these attributions is emphasized by a tendency known as *spontaneous trait inference:* Without even intending to do so or being aware of it, we tend to infer personality traits from someone's behavior or appearance.[22]

**TABLE 4 - 2**

## Same Behavior, Different Takes

|  | *"Model Employee"* | *"Underperformer"* |
|---|---|---|
| **Inferred Motive** | To improve the welfare of others, to promote the effective functioning of the organization | To make himself or herself look good, to secure unfair share of rewards or resources |

| | Interpretation | |
|---|---|---|
| **Observed Behavior** | *"Model Employee"* | *"Underperformer"* |
| Seeking feedback | Sign of learning orientation (desire to improve) | Sign of weakness, insecurity, or trying to prime boss's memory |
| Complimenting the boss | Useful upward feedback | Flattery, brownnosing |
| Helping a colleague/ listening to problems | Altruism | Manipulation, coalition building |
| Not complaining | Sense of self-sacrifice, under-standing of the greater good | Conformity tactic |
| Working long hours | Dedication, owning the issue, taking responsibility | Value of input over output, inability to prioritize, slow employee, slow mind, trying to make others look bad |
| Volunteering for a difficult assignment | Sense of responsibility, sense of obligation | Seeking visibility, unaware of own limitations |
| Running errands for the boss | Respect for boss's time | Sycophancy, bootlicking |
| Publicly thanking colleagues | Selflessness, team spirit | False humility, hypocrisy |
| Agreeing with the boss | Good judgment, respect, effective followership | Weak, useless, ineffectual |

Thus if we hear that a subordinate has been working long hours, we infer that the employee is either "dedicated" or "slow-minded." We do this because trait cues are easier to store than concrete behavior information—which brings us to the issue of recall.

### Bosses' Recollections Are Selectively Biased

We have seen that mental biases influence what people observe and how they interpret these observations. Related biases also influence how they store and retrieve information. Of course, part of what makes incidents or behaviors easy to recall is how we interpret them. You remember something if you think it's relevant. If you do not think the event is relevant, you are more likely to dismiss it.

For example, you may hear a perceived weaker performer make an intelligent suggestion, and you may even compliment him. Yet somehow it doesn't stick in your mind for long because you regard it as uncharacteristic or irrelevant. It requires much less effort to accommodate confirmatory evidence than contradictory evidence. We can process consistent evidence automatically, without awareness: "Bjorn didn't win the contract. Yep, it figures." We can't store away inconsistent evidence with the same ease.

Therefore, handling good news from weaker performers is more problematic. "How do I reconcile this outcome or behavior with the label?" The easiest way is simply to dismiss it: "Helena was bound to land a contract some time. Law of averages." This is the exception that proves the rule. Another way is to hold the incongruous information "in abeyance" to see if it happens again—but for it to register, it had better happen again quickly. Modifying the label to accommodate the information requires the most effort. It demands mental energy and presence of mind that busy executives do not always have. When we receive a lot of information, we tend to store away what is easiest to remember. (See "Impressionistic Recall.")

Even assuming that we store the information, our recall may be less than reliable because our memories don't function like computer files. Information that we store away does not simply stay there unaltered. It perishes; it gets mixed up with other memories. It even gets corrupted by information we receive after the event has occurred—a process known as *memory reconstruction*.[23] For example,

---

### IMPRESSIONISTIC RECALL

Two lists of well-known men and women were read to different groups of people. Each list included an equal number of men and women, but on some lists the men were better-known figures and on others the women were better known. Afterward, respondents had to assess the proportion of men and women on each list. Those who heard the list with more memorable women thought there were more women on the list, and those who heard the list with more memorable men thought there were more men.[24] Imagine how this parallels your ability to recall the successes of perceived higher and lower performers.

---

people in one study saw a film of a woman engaged in various activities. Some of the subjects were told she was a librarian. When asked to recall what she had been drinking in the film, they answered wine, because this seemed consistent with her occupation. Actually, she had been drinking beer. The other subjects, who were told the woman was a waitress, got the beverage right.[25]

## Fighting a Stacked Deck

We are not claiming that bosses set out to treat people in a biased manner. Most bosses do try to be evenhanded. The problem is that their mental biases get in the way. Bosses have a strong tendency to process information in ways that confirm their initial labels. They start by noticing different things for "high" versus "low" performers. And even when they do notice the same behaviors or consequences, they attribute different causes to them depending on who is involved.

Given what subordinates are up against, it is not surprising that many eventually give up. Even if the subordinate achieves superior results, it may take some time for these to register because of the boss's selective observation and recall. One outstanding result can be dismissed as a fluke. Worse still, it may be chalked up to the boss's clear directions and guidance rather than to the subordinate's ability or effort. The subordinate will therefore need to produce a string of hits in order for the boss to even contemplate revising the initial label. Inevitably, this increases the chances that subordinates will either overreach or vote with their feet.

So far we have focused on how the boss's labeling and mental biases trigger and fuel the dynamic. The subordinate has been portrayed as playing a submissive role—pulling back in order to accommodate the stress, frustration, or anguish induced—and inadvertently fulfilling the boss's expectations. While we maintain that the initial responsibility mainly lies with bosses, subordinates actively contribute to the process, too. They have their own expectations, blind spots, false assumptions, and warped responses. In turn, they set up their bosses to fail.

# 5

## Colluding to Collide

No one can make you feel inferior without your consent.

—Eleanor Roosevelt

AS IF THE SET-UP-TO-FAIL SYNDROME weren't convoluted enough, we're now going to add one more level of complexity. So far, we have highlighted the boss's responsibility in activating the process, but part of the reason why the dynamic quickly becomes entrenched is that the subordinate joins in. In this chapter we consider how *subordinates* unwittingly, but actively, contribute to the set-up-to-fail syndrome, through their cognitive processes and through their actions. That is, by interpreting their boss's actions so as to confirm an initial negative impression, and by behaving toward the boss in ways that actually make her react negatively. We'll explore how this happens, and how the boss's biases interlock with the subordinate's biases to produce a self-perpetuating dynamic.

Let's start by looking at the way the subordinate's own cognitive biases contribute to this dynamic.

### Subordinates Label Too

In chapter 4, we discussed bosses' premature labeling of subordinates. Based on their impressions of subordinates' attitudes and their interpretations of performance signals, bosses tend to decide that particular subordinates are struggling, have limited potential, or show poor judgment. Those labels tend to stick whether they are accurate or not.

But this is not just a one-way process. Subordinates, too, form expectations about bosses. Just as bosses appraise subordinates, so subordinates also assess bosses. A number of researchers have examined this angle. In one study, subordinates were asked to rate their first impressions of the boss, based on questions such as whether they shared the same outlook, perspective, and values, or whether they expected the boss to do well in the organization. The findings mirrored bosses' expectations, as discussed in chapter 4. Subordinates' expectations of the boss, measured in the *first five days* of their relationship, predicted how the subordinates would assess the working relationship six months later.[1]

Often, based on flimsy evidence such as rumors that accompany the boss's arrival, early disagreements, or misinterpretations of unexplained decisions, individual subordinates can quickly develop an unflattering view of the boss. In particular, those who sense that they may not be part of the in-crowd may start to suspect that the boss is somewhat aloof, insensitive, insecure, difficult to please, egotistical, or even mean.

As we've mentioned, one major problem is that we often assume intentionality where there is none. This tendency to overintentionalize means that when we don't know why someone is acting in a particular way, we tend to assume the cause is rooted in the person, rather than the situation.[2] It also means that when the action is directed at us, we are more liable to take it personally. For example, when we receive bad service in a bank or restaurant, we tend to take personal offense rather than dismissing it as a function of the situation. Similarly, when the boss has no time to consult or inform the subordinate about an issue, the subordinate can easily interpret this as a sign of disrespect. Simple oversights by the boss can quickly lead the subordinate to give the boss a negative label.

In truth, what a subordinate perceives as deliberate mistreatment from the boss may have the following varying degrees of intentionality:

1. *No choice:* The boss's hands were tied and circumstances "forced" her to cause harm. Only one course of action was possible, and those on the receiving end are unfortunate victims of the consequences.

2. *Quick choice:* The boss adopted this course of action because it made good sense, it came to him reasonably quickly, and there did not seem to be counterindications. He did not necessarily think through all the consequences. He consciously chose which action to take, but his focus was not to cause harm—and certainly not to cause distress to anyone in particular. If he foresaw some harm, he probably rationalized it by thinking something like "You can't make an omelet without breaking some eggs."

3. *Considered choice:* The boss chose a course of action after careful deliberation and reflection, in the full knowledge that it would have a negative impact on some subordinates. Or she may have specifically designed her action to send a strong message to the subordinates.

These three possibilities are helpful in showing how misinterpretations could occur. Most managerial decisions would fall into the gray second category. Indeed, Herbert Simon earned a Nobel Prize in 1978 for his theory of bounded rationality, which suggests that managers tend to *satisfice*—meaning that they often settle for the first "good enough solution" rather than looking for the very best alternative.[3] That first acceptable solution is seen to address the main features of the problem in hand. An everyday example of *satisficing* is finding a radio station to listen to in the car. You cannot optimize this process because it is impossible to listen to all the stations simultaneously. Your search therefore stops when you find the first station that's playing a song you don't mind hearing and where the reception is reasonable. Satisficing makes a lot of sense given time and attention constraints on managers, the cost of acquiring more ample information, and the unpredictable consequences of even the "best possible course of action." As one manager memorably told us, "You're as likely to do the right thing for the wrong reasons as the wrong thing for the right reasons." Given that perspective, why would a boss overinvest in sifting through all the possible alternatives and their consequences? Better to try it and see.

So we know that bosses often make decisions without determining all the alternatives or thinking through all the consequences. The problem is that those on the receiving end tend to *overestimate* the breadth and thoroughness of the decision-making process.

The model of decision making we tend to carry in our heads is much closer to the rational view, which assumes that a decision maker carefully evaluates competing alternatives, weighs the pros and cons, and selects the best option—having pretty much worked out all the consequences. It follows that he or she must have known in advance about any negative impact—and either chose to ignore it or else willfully decided to pursue the negative impact. In short, the boss must have known the decision would cause distress, offense, or embarrassment, and did it anyhow (signifying that the subordinate is not especially important to the boss); or worse, the boss made the decision with the aim of upsetting the subordinate.

One of the factors that probably reinforces subordinates' tendency to overintentionalize is that they attribute substantial power to their bosses. They know that they themselves have limited budgets and discretion, but they tend to look at their bosses and think, "I can't, but *she* can." They thus underestimate the fact that their boss is also a subordinate and, as such, also has to work within constraints—even if she happens to be the CEO.

This discrepancy between the boss's view and the subordinate's view is well illustrated by an incident that occurred in a medium-sized company we know well. The newly appointed CEO realized that his span of control was excessive—so he decided to reduce it by half. He asked eight people to report to him via the head of operations. The reactions of those eight—who essentially were pushed down a rung—varied considerably. Some had been sounded out by the CEO and reluctantly acknowledged the pressures he was acting on. Others were utterly disgruntled, feeling that the reshuffle had been sprung on them. One senior manager, who had experienced a few rows with the head of operations he would now be reporting to, was livid. Within an hour of the announcement, his letter of resignation was on the CEO's desk.

Clearly, the incoming CEO had not thought through the full ramifications of this reorganization—he failed to identify or pay sufficient attention to existing rivalries. In the abstract, the overstretched CEO made a satisficing decision—but in reality, those on the receiving end read his decision very differently. The CEO saw this reorganization as a way of making his workload tolerable. The manager who quit saw it as a deliberate affront, possibly an attempt to force him out—or at best, as a sign that the new CEO would not value his opinion or input.

The strength and speed of the manager's reaction shows how closely subordinates analyze their bosses' behavior. As we've mentioned in previous chapters, subordinates are very sensitive to their relative treatment, and they tend to read errors of omission as errors of commission. Of course, it is rare for a boss's action to provoke such a tough-minded response as in this case. Usually, when subordinates feel let down, betrayed, or singled out for mistreatment, they give the boss an unfavorable label and reduce their effort on the job. But these two things are enough to set the vicious cycle in motion.

### Validating the Label

To quickly summarize: Like bosses, subordinates develop rapid assessments that lead them to label their bosses, often by overintentionalizing. Once they form those labels, subordinates fall prey to very much the same *confirmation biases* as their bosses. For example, subordinates who think their boss is stubborn will notice and remember the times when the boss was inflexible, but they'll conveniently overlook times when she was open to important new ideas. In other words, they observe and recall selectively, and they show overconfidence in their judgments, just as bosses do.

In fact, subordinates' normal propensity to observe and recall selectively is probably magnified by two factors. First, subordinates are going to be especially vigilant about signals coming down from the boss. Second, they are likely to compare and reinforce labels and impressions of the boss through social corroboration with their peers.

**Vigilance: Scrutinizing.** We saw in chapter 2 how sensitive subordinates are to the differential verbal and nonverbal signals they get from their bosses. This is understandable. Their relationship with the boss is asymmetric, in the sense that subordinates cannot do to their boss what he or she can do to them, including fire or hire, promote or give a raise, assign work or delegate. As a result of this power imbalance, subordinates are more dependent on their boss's perceptions than vice versa. Subordinates therefore are constantly scanning boss behavior for indications of their relative standing within the group and of their overall job performance.[4]

That type of vigilance is a good thing, most of the time. Being alert to social signals is a healthy adaptive mechanism that allows individuals to respond effectively to threats and opportunities. But this sensitivity can also encourage subordinates to overreact to casual comments from the boss or to impute more weight to suggestions than the boss intended. As one of our former bosses once put it (when reminded of a previous declaration), "Why do you pay so much attention to the specific words I use? I certainly don't." This is especially the case with negative comments and cues.

When subordinates feel in some way threatened or anxious—especially when they are part of the out-group—they begin to scan conversations more carefully for negative signals. If their initial impressions are confirmed—that they are being targeted for unfair treatment—they are liable to become particularly alert, or *hypervigilant*.[5] They scrutinize every exchange for sinister purpose or hidden meaning; the slightest affront becomes a pretext for reinforcing the view that their boss is mismanaging the team. They mentally replay discussions for further evidence of the boss's unfairness, which they may have "overlooked" at the time. Even nonverbal cues, such as a meaningless averted glance or the failure to return a greeting, can be viewed as loaded with meaning.

**Social Corroboration: Discussing.** Social processes are another key driver of this confirmation process. Research has shown that out-group members spend more time discussing and analyzing the leader's differential treatment of subordinates than do in-group members.[6] That preoccupation is understandable, but it also fuels the dynamic by reinforcing subordinates' negative perceptions.

For example, one of the first things that people do when they feel unfairly treated is to try a "reality check" with someone—but when someone presents the information from a particular vantage point, the unbiased observer can often do little but sympathize (which conveniently passes for corroboration). At best, the observer will suggest alternative interpretations of the boss's behavior that will lead the subordinate to suspend judgment for a while. Often, however, managers who seek support pick an observer who is not unbiased, such as another member of the out-group—someone who may not only confirm their interpretation but actually provide further evidence to reinforce it or take it even farther.[7] Just as a boss who monitors a subordinate more closely is bound to be exposed to more problems, subordinates who invest more time in "boss watching" are more likely to see things they don't like. Not only do weaker performers become more sensitive to signals of injustice or mistreatment, they also become *hyperinformed* about them. By engaging in "bitch sessions" or "water cooler discussions," disenchanted subordinates develop an even more unbalanced view of the boss, reinforcing their sense of injustice and distrust. If the boss makes any kind of misstep, they'll hear about it. Any colleagues with a gripe know they will get a sympathetic hearing and commiseration from them. So they become repositories for sob stories. A colleague who tries to defend the boss may be told, "Look, I talk to a lot of people— and they all see what I see."

People fool themselves about feedback, not just by what they buy or discard, but also by their choice of informants. Where we look for feedback determines the kind of feedback we get.

### The Label as a Distorting Lens

Once armed with a strong label, whether positive or negative, subordinates will use that lens to interpret subsequent boss behaviors, especially ambiguous actions. In particular, out-group subordinates are more likely to see the boss's decisions as unfair, which they may indeed be. After all, a key aspect of *satisficing* is that the decision maker takes into account only a limited number of problem criteria. A boss may consider the impact of the decision on the career or motivation of a star performer, but he may be less likely to examine its impact on members of the out-group. He doesn't make a conscious choice to inflict harm on the weaker performers—their well-being simply doesn't weigh heavily on his mind. It's like the famous exchange in the film *Casablanca*, when Peter Lorre says to Humphrey Bogart, "You don't think much of me, do you?" and Bogart answers, "I guess if I thought about you at all, I wouldn't."

Members of the in-group may be more inclined to give the boss the benefit of the doubt on some issues, even if the outcome goes against them, *if* they think that the boss has demonstrated trustworthiness in the past. Out-group subordinates, on the other hand, will judge any "harsh" decision in isolation—they will not cut the boss any slack. They will overintentionalize, pinning the blame on the boss's personality and not considering the context. In other words, subordinates are likely to see a bad decision as evidence of malice, selfishness, or insensitivity rather than as evidence of the boss's workload, organizational constraints, or time pressures.[8]

One subordinate's view of a boss's actions can be quite different from another's, depending on each person's labeling of the boss, as table 5-1 shows. The label serves as a mechanism for channeling and amplifying blame. If you compare this table to table 4-1, you'll see that this process is the mirror image of the process that bosses follow when interpreting subordinates' actions.

### Beyond Total Recall

So far we have discussed how out-group subordinates confirm their labels by their unbalanced attention to negative evidence, their feedback-seeking biases, and their tendency to categorize ambiguous actions in unfavorable ways. They also have ways of filling the gaps in their evidence and seeing patterns where none exist!

We've seen that the tendency to overintentionalize leads subordinates to make negative inferences about boss behavior. Research suggests that subordinates may store away those inferences as *likely* causes and later remember them as *actual* causes. In other words, over time suppositions become facts. An interesting study illustrates this process of "phantom" recollections.

Researchers showed the study participants forty slides of an everyday activity, in a logical sequence—for some it was going

**TABLE 5 - 1**

## Taking Sides

TWO VIEWS OF THE SAME BOSS'S BEHAVIOR

| | Interpretation | |
|---|---|---|
| **Observed Behavior** | *"Great Boss"* | *"Impossible Boss"* |
| Giving critical feedback | Development-oriented | Negative, mean-spirited |
| Making a unilateral decision | Intuitive, decisive | Autocratic |
| Instructing work to be redone | Has high expectations and aspirations | Stickler for details, intolerant, impossible to please |
| Imposing discipline | Driven | Intimidating, treats people as resources |
| Setting stretch targets | Demanding, has high aspirations | Unrealistic |
| Sticking with a doubtful course of action | Single-minded, focused | Stubborn, impossible to influence |
| Sending mixed signals | Politically astute | Manipulative |
| Giving unsolicited advice | Helpful, caring | Meddlesome, untrusting |
| Asking specific questions | Encouraging, coaching, informed, close to the pulse | Control freak, micro-manager, evaluative |
| Delaying response to proposal/request | Thoughtful, busy | Uncommunicative, aloof, unsupportive |
| Not condemning a big mistake | Allows self-discovery | Weak, prone to favoritism, has low performance standards |
| Losing temper in public | Passionate, incisive, mercurial, (at worst) impulsive | Impatient, tempera-mental, unpredictable |
| Resisting a proposed change | Realistic, better judge, aware of interdependencies, victim of a poorly sold change | Ignorant bureaucrat, clueless, defensive |
| Giving a routine assignment | Considerate, letting me recover | Stifling my development |

grocery shopping, for others, eating at a restaurant. Included in the sequence were "effect slides": for example, the person visiting the supermarket sees that the floor of the fruit section is littered with oranges; and in the restaurant sequence, a person is cleaning up wine from a restaurant table.

Participants later took a recognition test to determine which slides they remembered. Interspersed with the slides they saw were some "dummy slides," including "cause slides," that is, slides showing the most likely causes for the accidents: for example, one showed a person taking an orange from the bottom of the stack, and another showed a person knocking over a glass of wine. The participants showed a significant tendency to "remember" seeing the cause slides. They thought they had observed something that they had only inferred.[9]

This study confirms that memory is a reconstruction of the past, not simply a reproduction of it. One of the tricks our minds play on us is to make us see patterns where none exist.[10] As a result, what outsiders would regard as minor or unrelated incidents come to be perceived as a coherent whole—and so a series of satisficing decisions can be interpreted as a sophisticated conspiracy. Put simply, subordinates' cognitive processes are just as imperfect as their bosses' are. If they *want* to see the boss making unfair differences between them, they *will* see him or her doing it, and the ones who can't see it will make it up.

Of course, subordinates who have an unfavorable image of the boss are going to find it difficult to conceal their opinion when they interact with the boss. So having dealt with the cognitive aspects, let's now consider how subordinates actually fuel the dynamic through their actions, by setting up the boss to fail. This is the *behavioral* side of the subordinate's contribution.

## How Subordinate Actions Fuel the Process

In chapter 2, we documented how subordinates unwittingly contributed to the set-up-to-fail syndrome by producing the very behavior that bosses feared. In particular, perceived weaker performers tend to withdraw from interracting with the boss. They stop seeking the boss's advice as much and perhaps are not very forthcoming with information or prompt in returning the boss's phone calls—which only confirms the boss's suspicions. Of course, subordinates simply can't avoid some exchanges with the boss, such as mandated meetings and reviews, or interactions initiated by the boss. Let's look at the behavior of subordinates during these unavoidable exchanges.

We've found that subordinates tend to engage in any one or all of five different behaviors, consciously or not. And these behaviors tend to put an extra spin on the vicious cycle of the set-up-to-fail dynamic. Though many appear provocative, occasionally to the point of self-destruction, they are behaviors that often have constructive intentions and invariably make sense to subordinates who feel that they are unfairly treated by their boss.

### Discounting Feedback

When bosses notice an underperforming subordinate, their well-intentioned reaction is often to try to coach him. As discussed previously, these "coaching" efforts are often characterized by the boss issuing series of unsolicited directions or the boss firing off a set of indiscriminate questions without first checking on what the subordinate has already done or plans to do.

Out-group subordinates are unlikely to act on such advice, for two reasons. First, because they regard the advice as unhelpful, maybe even unworkable. As we saw in chapter 3, weaker performers are less likely than their in-group counterparts to volunteer information and keep their boss in the loop. They also have fewer informal contacts with the boss and are less involved in informal give-and-take. Thus even though the boss tries to monitor weaker performers more intensely, he or she may have more difficulty making intelligent suggestions to them because the subordinates have "shut down." At a minimum, the boss may not have as a good a grasp of some details, which makes it easier for out-group members to discount the advice (e.g., "He didn't even know about such-and-such. How can he comment intelligently on the overall problem?").

The second reason the subordinate would not listen to the boss or implement her advice is that he perceives her as unfair. Subordinates who feel "the boss is picking on me" may well decide to attribute the negative feedback to the boss's disposition rather than to their own performance flaws. Again, the boss's very approach to coaching may reinforce this perception, because it has a punitive feel. Recent research supports this idea, showing that subordinates consider the following when they judge whether negative feedback is fair or not:[11]

- *The procedure:* Subordinates tend to consider the feedback unfair when the boss fails to collect all relevant data, does not allow or consider clarifications the subordinate offers, and does not apply consistent standards.

- *The interaction:* Subordinates tend to deem the feedback unjust when the boss fails to respect their dignity, or when the boss is insincere or impolite.

Keeping in mind that both dimensions are in the eye of the beholder, the evidence presented in previous chapters clearly suggests that perceived weaker performers *are* going to attribute very low degrees of fairness on both dimensions. And largely, they would be right. Bosses *do* have selective observation and recall; bosses *are* sometimes curt and impatient with them; bosses *don't* always give them a fair hearing. None of this means that the boss's advice is invalid—but it does lower the subordinate's *willingness* to accept the feedback. And of course, if the subordinate doesn't accept feedback, then the chances he or she will act upon it are even lower. This study on the acceptability of negative feedback is all the more compelling in that the same patterns hold true in two different national cultures, the United States and China.

In-group subordinates, on the other hand, take the criticism more constructively because they feel the boss listened to them and showed them respect and support despite the disagreement. This situation coincides with bosses' comments that better performers tend to be more receptive to their feedback. The net result is that better performers will focus more on the *content* of the feedback and may even request from the boss further suggestions or clarifications, rather than simply nodding or paying lip service to the advice—so that the criticism is more likely to bring about improvement efforts.

In this context, it is not surprising that bosses' feedback to weaker performers tends to fall on deaf ears—which then just confirms their belief that those subordinates are not very gifted, or not interested in learning, or both.

## Bringing Up the Past

Right or wrong, perceived weaker performers often feel that in the past they have been victims of a number of injustices. Over time, they may get over these injustices or learn to live with them. We all do. We may not always forgive and forget, but the burn of the perceived injustice becomes less salient and the wound starts to heal. But this process takes time—all the more if the perceived injustice was serious.

Therefore, at any given moment, weaker performers are likely to have a few perceived past injustices still fairly present in their minds. They may feel disrespected, taken advantage of, or strung along with false promises. A rich body of evidence tells us that people will, over time, try to restore equity in their lives according to their own perceptions.[12]

Attempts to restore equity can take many forms, both direct and indirect—for example, subordinates will periodically bring up issues that have stuck in their throats. At the most benign level, the subordinate's objective may simply be to air the issue in the hope of getting some form of redress—such as the lowest paid member of the team who "keeps going on about" his salary. The subordinate may also be trying to "warn" the boss in order to prevent further abuse.

Another possibility is that the subordinate brings up the issue in order to vent. Even though this venting may not help the relationship with the boss, it can be personally satisfying, certainly in the short term. Indeed, research on the subject suggests that people who feel bad try to repair their moods—and that aggression is partly motivated by the assumption that letting off steam will make them feel better.[13]

In all these cases, the fact of bringing up the past may appease the subordinate, and possibly even achieve a measure of repair— "the squeaky wheel gets the grease"—but it will nevertheless annoy the boss. The typical reaction of bosses tends to be, "Look, it's water under bridge. Can we look forward instead of backward?"

In more extreme cases, undigested injustices can lead subordinates to try to restore equity in more damaging ways—from covert actions like "bad-mouthing" the boss or phoning in sick to self-destructive behaviors like whistle-blowing, humiliating the boss in public, or even becoming violent. The urge to get even can be so powerful that it defies rational explanation.

From the boss's point of view, all these behaviors indicate a tendency to rehash the past and a failure to face reality, which will do nothing to improve the subordinate's standing in the boss's eyes.

## Standing Up to the Boss

Disfavored subordinates also commonly "stand up" to the boss: Publicly or privately, they challenge the boss's positions, explicitly reject his or her suggestions, or turn down assignments, for example. Subordinates may act this way for different reasons. As we saw in chapter 3, some weaker performers are going to *persist* in trying to improve performance and to change their boss's low opinion of them albeit at the price of numerous run-ins.

Even among those with more limited hopes of seeing their boss change his or her mind, some subordinates will occasionally take a stand. For example, one out-group manager we interviewed recalled deliberately starting a meeting on time even though his boss had not yet arrived. The boss arrived ten minutes later and joined the meeting underway. At the end of the meeting, as they were left alone in the meeting room, the boss gave the subordinate "a schoolboy lecture about 'Don't start a meeting without me here [banging on the table], and don't ever interrupt me again!' [banging]."

In another example, a manager was losing a subordinate and knew his boss would want to try to avoid replacing that person. Such was indeed the boss's position—and yet for an hour and a half, the manager fought tooth and nail to change his boss's mind. At the end of their discussion, he told the boss, "I knew you would say that." Talking to us afterward, the boss commented, "If you know I'll eventually get my way, why on earth would you do this? Why do you argue with your boss for an hour and a half, and annoy him in the process, if you know he'll have his way in the end? What kind of judgment is that?"

In both cases, the poorly perceived subordinates knew full well that their actions would annoy their bosses, yet they carried on regardless. Why? A line of research in psychology called *reactance theory* provides one explanation.[14] According to this theory, when people are told they *can't* do something, their motivation to do it is increased as a way of reasserting their personal freedom. So for an out-group subordinate, the reasoning might be "I know my opinion carries no weight. In fact, I know you don't even want to hear my opinion. But I'm going to voice it anyhow!"

Because being powerless is so debilitating, opposition seems to be a way to reestablish a measure of self-determination. The French writer and philosopher Albert Camus noted a similar reaction when people were told they *must* do something: When deprived of choice, they had only one freedom left: the freedom to say no. For out-group subordinates, contradicting the boss is a way to create a voice for themselves. And since they have no goodwill to manage with the boss, they have no need to "pick their battles," as in-group subordinates would do.

Indeed, in some cases this opposition stance may even become systematic and become part of the subordinate's workplace identity. It is not uncommon to come across very bright or capable subordinates whose successive run-ins with the boss have led them to position themselves as the "resident rebel" or "thorn in the side." Deprived of any way into the in-group, the subordinate bolsters a shaky self-image by constructing a favorable out-group status as "the only one around here prepared to stand up to the boss." This self-appointed role may even prevent the subordinate from responding to the boss's conciliatory efforts—since accepting the boss's extended hand would be socially perceived as having "sold out." On the far side of frustration, systematic opposition may be a way for individuals to assert that they still "make a difference."

From the boss's point of view, subordinates' attempts to affirm their existence and bolster their self-esteem come across, at best, as annoying and reflective of bad judgment. At worst, they come across as a deliberate obstruction of the boss's intentions.

## Provoking the Boss

The idea of provoking the boss is to some extent an extension of the previous section: Many of the behaviors are identical, but the intention is different. The aim here, whether conscious or not, is to make the boss react negatively in order to validate their view of the boss as an unreasonable person. Subordinates have various ways of triggering "blatantly" unfair reactions.

For example, an easy way to guarantee a poor response to almost any suggestion is to make that suggestion at the wrong time, such as when the boss clearly has no bandwidth to process it. Nick Baker captured such a case in a cartoon that features an enterprising employee hovering outside his boss's high-rise office window thanks to a handheld flying machine. He is knocking on the window to attract the boss's attention, but the boss is rushing to put his jacket on and tells him: "Not now, not now! I have to go to an entrepreneurial meeting!" The cartoonist clearly expects our sympathies to lie with the enterprising subordinate whose boss is incapable of recognizing innovation when it's staring him in the face. But the opposite case could also be made.

An even surer way to see one's point dismissed is to raise an important issue during a meeting that the boss clearly intends to be a short informational meeting. In that same vein, some bosses particularly dislike being challenged in public. In-group subordinates know this and tend to offer challenges in a private setting where the boss feels comfortable. Out-group members—in part because they do not always have such privileged access to the boss, but also to "yank the boss's chain"—sometimes take advantage of meetings to express their disagreement. A related tactic is to rekindle an issue that has been discussed numerous times in the recent past and one that the boss considers settled.

At the extreme, subordinates can needle the boss into losing control once a discussion is under way, especially if they feel threatened. One familiar tactic is *button pushing*: raising an issue that the subordinate knows will trigger the boss's anger, such as comparing the boss with a predecessor or hinting that the boss is unprincipled, unfair, or incompetent.

Overall, it is relatively easy to *make* just about any boss react like a "jerk" by catching him or her off guard or under pressure. Subordinates can make sure that the boss does not listen or even reacts forcefully by raising the wrong issue, in the wrong way, in the wrong setting, at the wrong moment. Comforted in their expectations, they can then return to colleagues and relate the latest "horror story" of what the boss has said or done: "You'll never believe how she responded when I proposed. . . . "

Clearly such provocations will not endear the subordinate to the boss, but they do allow the subordinate to transfer the blame. If the boss can be made to react impulsively or unreasonably, it is reassuring. It exonerates the subordinate's own contribution to the dynamic and confirms the subordinate's self-image as a "reasonable person" and a "competent employee" who simply works for an "impossible boss." This may have been one of the objectives of the subordinate, mentioned in the last section, who argued with his boss over an issue for an hour and a half, an argument that he knew he could not win.

## Looking for Senior Allies

Perceived weaker performers typically find themselves short on resources, short on autonomy, and unable to push their ideas through with their boss. So, in an attempt to create a bit more space for themselves or support for their ideas, they may appeal to people higher up in the organization. For example, when they run into the boss's boss or other senior people, they may expose their ideas, mentioning in passing that the idea does not appeal to their immediate boss—hoping that the senior executive can somehow exercise some influence or even hoping to establish a fallback position if relations deteriorate further and the subordinate must seek alternative employment within the firm. We can easily understand why a subordinate who feels cornered may try to activate other alliances and other networks within the organization.

This strategy is often called *covert lobbying*. An increasing number of companies are creating formal mechanisms that allow employees to communicate beyond their immediate hierarchy, such as breakfast, lunch, or coffee sessions with the CEO, skip-level meetings, or even GE Work-Out-style practices.[15] Once relationships exist throughout the hierarchy, covert lobbying is facilitated and,

TABLE 5 - 2

## How the Subordinate Fuels the Boss's Bias

| Subordinate's Action | Purpose/Intention | What the Boss Sees | What the Boss Infers about the Subordinate |
|---|---|---|---|
| Discounting Feedback | To avoid implementing wrongheaded or biased feedback—own solutions more effective and appropriate | Unresponsive to feedback: "My help/advice is ignored" | Anti-learning, unreliable, lacking potential and respect |
| Bringing Up the Past | To get redress, to avoid repetition, or simply to "get it off my chest" | Rehashing and backward-looking | Lacking judgment and emotional maturity |
| Standing Up to the Boss | To be heard and to create space | Indiscriminately challenging, foolish resistance | Lacking judgment, self-control, and discipline |
| Provoking the Boss | To validate beliefs, to reassert control, to force resolution | Insulting or confrontational behavior | Lacking judgment and respect |
| Looking for Senior Allies | To build support for self or ideas, to establish fallback positions | Personal betrayal | Lacking loyalty and integrity |

in principle at least, should be better tolerated by bosses. Still, most subordinates we talked to believe that if they did this informally in their organizations and were discovered, some form of retaliation from their boss would ensue.

For example, one boss who merely suspected his subordinate of circumventing him "vowed to cut off her access to other decision makers"—eventually forcing her out of the organization. Another manager who complained about his boss to his boss's boss later realized that the conversation had been reported "line-for-line" to the circumvented boss. "Until he decided to leave," recalled the subordinate, "he made my life miserable."[16]

Such reactions from the boss are understandable insofar as the subordinate's action shows a lack of trust in the boss's judgment or fairness, is evidence of disloyalty to the boss, and can inflict significant damage to the boss's reputation. The boss's view of the subordinate as untrustworthy and lacking in judgment is thus confirmed or enriched.

As before, given the high risk of upsetting the boss, why might subordinates act this way? Quite simply, because they have given up on trying to influence the boss. They are stuck, and in order to persist or break out, they need to get support elsewhere.

To recap then, why do these subordinate behaviors all fuel the dynamic? Because in every case the boss looks at the subordinate's reaction and thinks, "This is exactly what I dreaded!" Table 5-2 summarizes the five different behaviors that help fuel the boss's bias against weaker performers. It highlights the purpose associated with each type of behavior and thus makes it easier to see why in-group subordinates are less likely to feel obliged to resort to such behaviors. These subordinates typically trust their boss's intentions toward them and hence have fewer reasons to reject his or her feedback. They are less likely to feel wronged and have things that they feel the need to rehash, and they don't have to fight with or otherwise circumvent their boss to gain autonomy, as they are more likely to be given the opportunity to try their idea.

And even if perceived better performers exhibited some of the behaviors listed in table 5-2, these actions would probably be interpreted much more positively by the boss. After all, better performers don't "discount feedback," they "try it their own way"; they don't "defy the boss," they "push back and challenge"; they don't "bypass and betray the boss," they "leverage their network to gather support for an initiative."

## Mixed Motives

For the purposes of illustration the preceding section carefully separated the five types of behavior perceived weaker performers tend to produce. In reality, these actions often come together as a package. Take the example of Paula, the banking executive who successfully stuck to her guns on a project against her boss's wishes—but in accordance with a consultant's recommendations—which ultimately led to her boss's removal.

When Paula resisted her boss, she actually engaged in several different behaviors:

- Seeing her boss as unfair and as an obstructionist, Paula ignored her boss's feedback that this was not a good idea.

- Determined to prove the boss wrong, she refused to let go of the idea, persisting regardless of the career risk.

- Feeling boxed in and exposed, she did some covert lobbying to establish alliances with other senior people in the organization—those who had appointed the consultants.

- She cut her boss out of the loop and worked covertly. This could easily have triggered a backlash from the boss if he had found out and would merely have confirmed her attributions that he *really* was an "obstructionist" and a hindrance to progress.

- Paula's opposition to her boss did not last long enough for her to develop deep-seated grudges she would feel the need to rehash. She was not actively looking for revenge either, but her boss's removal did restore some equity by "punishing" him for his errors.

Paula was smart, persistent, and lucky. Others are not so lucky—and wind up in a destructive chain of events partly of their own making. The box "How Subordinates Also Set-Themselves-Up-to-Fail" summarizes a number of traps that combine both the behavioral and cognitive faults of certain out-group subordinates.

## HOW SUBORDINATES ALSO SET-THEMSELVES-UP-TO-FAIL

The following five habits are essentially traps of the subordinate's own making:

**Never giving the boss an even break:** The subordinate interprets the boss's decisions or behaviors from the position that the boss is incompetent, unfair, or uncaring. Should the boss hold out his hand, ignore it or bite it ("I can't be bought!"). If the boss offers advice, just nod.

**Seeing folly everywhere:** Past mistreatment creates an overdeveloped sense of injustice and distrust. The subordinate reads negative meaning into everything and picks up condemning evidence from all quarters.

**Selling problems:** The subordinate never brings good news and only proposes difficult ("half-baked") solutions. If the subordinate requests a meeting, the boss can guarantee that it spells trouble.

**Swinging at every pitch:** The subordinate feels obliged to point out what's going wrong even in areas that don't concern her. She gets drawn into fighting other people's fights for them, wasting ammunition (residual goodwill or credibility) on battles that can't be won. She refuses to back down.

**Sounding like a broken record:** Complaining becomes a way of life. To outsiders, the complainer seems to wallow in it. People stop taking much notice of his comments: "There goes Eli again." He grows embittered. He also knows that standing up and complaining about it will just make things worse. He feels trapped.

## Subordinates Who Retaliate First

Until now, we have really highlighted the impact of the boss's behavior or decisions on subordinates. We have shown some of the unproductive ways in which subordinates respond to a process generally set in motion by the boss. But we also need to keep in mind that when bosses inherit subordinates, the subordinate is coming to the relationship with a particular history. The way subordinates approach a relationship with a new boss is influenced by the way they have been (mis)managed in the past. In some cases, subordinates may have difficulty erasing the legacies of their negative interactions with past bosses. When this happens, subordinates may go farther than merely fueling the set-up-to-fail syndrome; they may actually *trigger* a fresh dynamic with the new boss.

As far as these disabused subordinates are concerned, a new boss does not walk in with a clean slate. Right from the outset, he is tagged ("the new bozo from head office," "an outsider who knows nothing about our business," "another young hotshot who'll use us as a springboard for his career"). With such a negative predisposition, these subordinates are on the lookout for the same kind of mistreatment they received from the previous boss. Essentially, they pick up with the new boss where they left off with the last one. They do so because they have grown cynical, they have internalized antagonistic patterns of behavior towards authority, or they may be protecting themselves against being disappointed yet again by another boss. In some cases, the role of "dissident" has become part of their self-image or positioning within the group.

It is easy for the new boss to get dragged into this process. First, an incoming boss is bound to make a number of decisions, some of which have ambiguous motives or consequences. Interpreting some of these decisions in a negative light may be enough to validate the label that the boss "doesn't listen," "lacks courage," or "has no clue." Going one step farther, the embittered subordinate can engage in some of the retaliatory tactics—say, standing up to or provoking the boss—in an anticipatory way. For example, we noted that bosses are often riled when subordinates bring up past injustices. Clearly, that is doubly frustrating for the boss when the alleged injustices were committed by a predecessor. Even if this does not provoke and intensely irritate the boss, why should she be held responsible for or feel obliged to repair the misdeeds of others? The incoming boss sees these as crimes committed under a previous regime. Yet the disgruntled subordinate is still living with the consequences—in terms of diminished status, career damage, low pay, and so on. Even if the boss sympathizes with the subordinate, it may be difficult to put matters right. Therefore, the new boss gets blamed not for what she has done, but for what she refuses to do.

The boss ("Cynthia") feels she cannot put a foot right with the subordinate in question ("Alberto"), whom she starts to view as argumentative, unmanageable, or a "lost cause." Alberto feels he has recognized a pattern of behavior and neglect from Cynthia that suggests he can't trust her any more than he could trust her predecessor. As a result, he quickly reconstructs with this new boss the adversarial context that had characterized the relationship with his previous boss.

## Whose Fault Is It? The Blame Game

When analyzing a particular instance of the set-up-to-fail syndrome, it's hard to figure out who started it. On the one hand, we could blame the boss whose first impressions of a subordinate led him to perceive that person as someone with limited potential or poor judgment. On the other hand, we could blame the subordinate for overintentionalizing and reading mischief or disregard into innocent or constrained actions.

Part of the problem is that *no one sees the full causal chain*. If we ask a boss and a subordinate what triggered their bad relationship, they will give very different answers. In the series of exchanges between them, each would point to different elements as critical and dismiss others as irrelevant.[17]

The fact that each party sees the causal chain differently has two vital consequences in terms of keeping the dynamic going. First, each is convinced that the other party initiated the problem. By holding each other responsible, they each feel perfectly justified in attempting to restore the balance or defend themselves, thus keeping the dynamic going. Second, the fact that they construct reality differently means that each party "keeps score" differently. Different harms are difficult to quantify. For example, one manager reasoned, "He didn't stand up for me in the promotion meeting. So I decided, Why stand up for him when he needed me [when the boss was under attack in meetings]?"[18] This sounds very much like an eye for an eye, but the two actions do not carry the same weight. Who feels more betrayed? That makes it pretty much impossible to even the score and therefore "call it quits."

Such dynamics cannot resolve themselves. Even if the boss proposes a truce, the subordinate will tend to resist because "too much has happened." For example, one employee who was publicly ridiculed by her boss recalled, "I felt so angry and betrayed. There was nothing she could say or do to make me feel better after what she did. Nothing."[19]

If boss and subordinate sit down to try to discuss the situation, they must consider that they are probably starting from very different versions of the "facts." The situation they now find themselves in is a joint creation, fueled by biases on both sides.

## It Takes Two to Tango

Whether or not subordinates initially deserve to be classified as lower performers, that is what they become. What is even more worrying, as became clear in chapter 4, is that many lower performers really don't deserve that label in the first place. They were set up to fail.

There may be an initial spurt of employee resistance, an effort to "turn round" the boss's label, but once the set-up-to-fail syndrome takes hold, both parties keep it going. The full-blown syndrome is really a reciprocal set-up. The escalating dynamic is underpinned by well-researched mental biases that protect us from the inadequacies of our own actions. Premature labels that boss and subordinate have thrown at one another are quickly confirmed through selective observation and recall, and hasty attributions. Both parties think they see "reality," but perception turns out to be a highly imperfect process. As Will Rogers once put it, "It's not what we don't know that gives us trouble. It's what we think we know that ain't so."

This adds up to a complex phenomenon for many reasons. We are dealing with normal human behavior, including tendencies such as labeling. We are dealing with past misdemeanors on both sides and accumulated mistrust. We are dealing with contradictory views of who started it and who's keeping it going. And there is a lot of excess baggage being toted around on both sides. As a result, this is a very intricate and powerful process. It's rapid, it's persistent, it's largely unconscious, and it's two-way. That makes for a pretty tight vicious cycle.

So why did we take the time to explore the role of the subordinate in the set-up-to-fail dynamic? On the one hand, it helps subordinates realize that they have the exact same biases as their bosses—and understand how they also set themselves up for failure. It also enables bosses to make more enlightened interpretations of their subordinates' actions and to keep a more open mind about attributions. It could even help bosses detect the existence of a set-up-to-fail syndrome in their midst. What until now appeared to be totally irrational behavior, may now make more sense. For example, subordinates who often oppose their boss in public may not be "dumb" or "insolent," but may be desperately trying to have an impact.

Ultimately, though, this chapter is intended to help bosses and subordinates break the dynamic. To do so, they need to be conscious of the psychological baggage in their own minds, but also in each other's mind.

Before turning to how to get things back on track, to which we dedicate many pages, let's examine the cost of the dynamics as they ripple out beyond the two directly involved and seep into the rest of the organization.

# 6

## The Cost Iceberg

Facts do not cease to exist because they are ignored.

—Aldous Huxley

BOSSES HAVE SEVERAL WAYS to protect themselves from the pain of difficult relationships with their perceived weaker performers. One obvious alternative is to disconnect emotionally from these subordinates. Once disconnected from them, bosses tend to underestimate the costs of the situation for the subordinate, in terms of pain and stress, and in terms of missed opportunities and rewards. Bosses also underestimate how much subordinates feeling alienated costs the company in terms of energy lost to reading between the lines, overreacting to perceived slights, or pursuing reassurance—not to mention the talent, efforts, and ideas these subordinates could be investing in the company, but instead elect to invest in personal pursuits outside of work.

Clearly, the firm suboptimizes what it gets from perceived weaker performers. As a result of corporate efforts, their performance goes down instead of up! And as we have described in previous chapters, this doesn't just happen to mediocre people—it can happen to very talented ones as well. For example, Andy Pearson, former CEO of PepsiCo, recently recalled: "I remember bringing one of our market-research women to tears because I told her that the information she was gathering wasn't producing anything. I could just see the breath come out of her. . . . That kind of treatment demoralizes people. I don't think that woman was ever the same. If you're not careful, you might discard a very good person."[1]

How much do bosses forfeit in terms of performance when a subordinate disconnects? Clearly it depends on the activity, but when a subordinate's critical and creative faculties are turned off, the company loses a lot of potential for value added. Consider the testimony of Jane Harper, who as head of IBM's Speed Team was charged with catalyzing internal change.[2] Asked about her most important discovery, she said it involved people's contributions:

> We found many people working at less than 50 percent of their potential. We saw a lot of action, and we saw things moving really fast, but we didn't see people conceiving great ideas. . . . We found that people were failing to live up to their potential because they were afraid of making a mistake, of looking foolish, of taking an idea all the way. As leaders, we must blow up those speed bumps and ignite the passion of our people. Because great people are not just two or three times better than average people—they're one hundred times better.[3]

Subordinate underperformance is but the most visible cost of the set-up-to-fail syndrome. There are a host of other costs to consider, some of them indirect and long-term in nature—with implications for the unit and the wider organization, as well as the boss and the team. This chapter is about those submerged costs.

## The Toll on the Boss

The boss pays for the syndrome in several ways. First, there is the use of the boss's time and the opportunity costs involved. His increased monitoring and involvement produce decreasing returns. He may even have to devote more and more effort simply to *maintaining* the subordinate's performance level. That expenditure of time and energy is unending—and an uphill battle. Uneasy relationships with perceived weaker performers are also emotionally wearing. It can be quite a strain to keep up a facade of courtesy, pretending that everything is fine when both parties know it is not. The unease and the pretense deplete what we call the boss's *energy pot.* Imagine that the boss has one hundred units of energy available. If fifty of these units are devoted to self-monitoring, covering up impatience, displeasure, or embarrassment, and controlling body language, only fifty units are still available for value-adding work.

Next at stake is the boss's reputation within the organization. In the "war for talent," managers are increasingly judged on their ability to develop and bring the best out of people and to pull together a great team. Their failure to do so is quickly exposed by skip-level meetings or the availability of 360-degree feedback. If a boss has one disgruntled subordinate or a recruit who derails, she's considered unfortunate, but if she has several, her own bosses can start to have doubts about her performance. And if her treatment of a subordinate is deemed unfair or unsupportive, observers will be quick to draw conclusions. After witnessing his boss's controlling and hypercritical behavior toward another subordinate, one outstanding performer told us, "It made us all feel like we're expendable." With organizations increasingly espousing the values of learning and empowerment, bosses not only have to cultivate their reputations as coaches but also must secure results. They tend to underestimate the extent to which the mismanagement of weaker performers can damage team spirit and functioning.

## Who Cleans Up? Enter HR

When bosses have difficulty handling certain people, where do they go for help? Enter the human resources specialists. Line managers who have grown tired of dealing with these subordinates typically run out of ideas or patience. Thus, they often need advice, training, support, assistance in moving the employee to another unit (which often involves lying to this other unit!), or—in extreme cases—help in building a strong case to justify dismissal. The situation has often lasted too long, absorbed too much of their attention, and they simply want to be rid of this problem.

Many HR professionals we have spoken with confirm that the set-up-to-fail syndrome is indeed widespread and that dealing with its consequences can be very time-consuming for them. On the one hand, they spend a lot of time helping managers deal with perceived weaker performers or trying to mend those relationships. To that end, they may get involved in facilitation, counseling, or arbitration of differences. HR staff also must deal with the consequences of failed relationships or unfair treatment—which may involve administrating grievance or appeals procedures; handling transfer requests; supervising termination procedures; and conducting exit interviews. To ensure that the company is legally covered in case of a termination, HR staff must be sure to document inefficient performance and to show due diligence.

In one way or another, frustrated bosses and unhappy employees create a lot of work for HR, but it is not real value-adding work. Leading-edge human resource management is supposed to focus on attracting, motivating, developing, assessing, rewarding, and retaining talent, but in practice much of HR managers' time and energy is spent in damage limitation exercises. And while thus engaged, HR specialists cannot participate in (much less drive) strategy formulation and change management. In many companies, the vision of HR as a strategic business partner remains distant.[4]

## The Imploding Team

Lack of faith in lower performers leads bosses to overload their perceived better performers. It is an understandable reaction; bosses want to entrust critical assignments to those they can count on to deliver quickly and predictably—those willing to go beyond the call of duty because of their strong sense of shared fate with their boss. As one boss half-jokingly observed, "It's like avoiding the empty restaurant: If you want something done, give it to someone who's busy—there's a reason why that person's busy." It can be argued that this increased workload may help the "stars" learn to manage their time better, partly by more effectively delegating to their own subordinates. In many cases, however, overburdened strong performers simply absorb the greater load and higher stress. Over time, this takes a personal toll and decreases the amount of time and energy available for other dimensions of their job, particularly those yielding longer-term benefits, such as the coaching of their own subordinates. In some cases, the additional pressure may even lead strong performers to leave for other jobs or—in the worst scenario—to burn out.

The team will also experience performance problems, especially if the work requires collaboration between team members. If some team members have lost enthusiasm or become passive contributors, the team's overall ability to deliver will suffer. Even in the absence of high task interdependence, team members can ask each other for assistance, share insights, or simply listen to each other's preoccupations. The "team" may be little more than the sum of the individual bests, but members still influence each other's performance. A striking example, in sport, was the Australian swimmer who broke the world 100-meter freestyle record on the first leg of the Olympic 4 × 100–meter relay in Sydney. In the most individual of sports, Michael Klim swam faster for his team than for he did for himself. That's the power of a strong team. When people experience trust and friendship on a team, their energy curve rises significantly.

The same principle applies in companies. High-performing teams share a sense of engagement and common aspirations. They fire on all cylinders. Strong teams start with healthy individuals—and the progressive alienation of one or more perceived lower performers has a corrosive effect on team spirit. When one person's attachment to the team is weakened, the cohesion of the whole team suffers. A sense of malaise creeps in because there is now something that separates them and about which they don't talk, like a family secret. Before they had a shared objective but now some of them have a private one: to find a way out.

It becomes difficult for the team to engage in stimulating debate, resolve emotional conflicts, coalesce around a decision, or make the leaps of faith necessary for change and innovation. Those feeling abandoned become more nervous about what others are thinking, saying, and meaning with their words, looks, sighs, and silences. They also make others feel more nervous. They are less likely to make team-specific investments or sacrifices, and they may try to ride on others' coattails. Their colleagues are not sure how much longer they will stick around. Trust is eroded.

Even when members of the boss's out-group try to keep their pain to themselves, other members of the team feel the strain. One manager recalled the discomfort the whole team experienced from watching their boss grilling one of their peers every week, and explained, "A team is like a functioning organism. If one member is suffering, the whole team feels that pain." In such circumstances, when bosses evoke teamwork or being "in this together," employees react cynically. As one disillusioned manager remarked, "Sure, we're a team—but I'm the fuse."

In addition, subordinates who feel hard done by often do *not* suffer in silence or keep their pain to themselves. They lament their situation. They seek out sympathetic ears to vent their recriminations, regrets, and complaints. Typically, they will rehash their stories to anyone who will listen. They gather around coffee machines or in hallways in hushed but animated conversations, trading stories and encouraging negative feedback from others.

Novell's Chairman and CEO, Eric Schmidt, described such an atmosphere:

> In a culture of fear . . . people are worried about getting laid off, and so they suppress their feelings. Instead of complaining to their bosses, whom they fear might fire them, they complain vociferously to their peers. That's what was going on here. This situation created a kind of pervasive bellyaching, a corporate cynicism.[5]

In more extreme cases, complaining becomes a way of life. To observers, the complainers appear to wallow in it. So why do they do it? Partly to verify the injustice through social confirmation and support from others. For a while, close colleagues will listen and show sympathy, but over time, they will grow tired and may start to suspect that the poor performers are bringing this on themselves.

After a while, colleagues may start to avoid them when they see them heading their way. They radiate negative energy. They are dispiriting to be around. Their gloom and cynicism poison the atmosphere, their self-absorption blinds them to the needs or problems of others, and they distract colleagues from productive work and engage them in futile discussions about internal dynamics. Progressively they drive away the very people they need most. Pretty soon they are frozen out of key information loops, which may further impede their understanding of what's going on around them and their ability to make meaningful inferences.

In extreme cases, they become "invisible." They pass unnoticed in corridors. When they enter a discussion, they are heard in silence, as if a pause button has been pressed; on finishing, the conversation resumes as though nothing had been added. For the employee in question, the sense of exclusion and unfairness is only confirmed. For the team, the individual becomes an inhibiting presence. If the boss does not take action, the team may feel impelled to force out their colleague by scapegoating the person for all the dysfunctions of the team.

## When Your Boss Is in the Out-Group

Let's look now at how the set-up-to-fail syndrome affects the welfare of a weaker performer's own subordinates. Subordinates suffer in various ways from their boss's out-group status. Put yourself for a minute in the shoes of a subordinate reporting to a perceived underperformer. First, you are likely to face a set of task-related constraints. For example, if your boss is short on resources, so will you be; if your boss is not privy to the big picture, attempts to keep you informed can be based only on rumor and conjecture; and if your boss receives fairly specific tasks, short deadlines, and close monitoring, the effects of this limited autonomy will necessarily cascade downward to you. Not only that, you'll feel the pressure your boss is under as it will also be put upon you. If your boss must account for even minor variances, you will be sucked into those efforts. When we interviewed subordinates of perceived lower performers, several reported spending more time on explaining away poor results—by identifying plenty of plausible external contributory factors—than trying to identify root causes or addressing them! Inevitably, their bosses' preoccupation with covering up problems or explaining them, rather than fixing them, had repercussions on their work and their freedom to take initiatives. Their own learning and growth were stunted.

Beyond these task-related aspects are emotional repercussions. Working for a boss who is out of favor is no picnic! An insecure boss may not be inclined to give you much visibility upward and may feel more tempted to take credit for your ideas or possibly block them altogether. He will probably set tighter deadlines and try to make sure that all contacts with other units pass through him, in order to maintain his position in the system. He may also feel bad about himself, with a helpless or despondent attitude: "Don't ask me, what the hell do I know? I just do what I'm told."

Paradoxically, many disenchanted managers inflict downward the very behavior they complain about from above. They are like the weakling in the schoolyard who gets pummeled by a bully, then goes home and pummels younger siblings. When members of the boss's out-group have to manage their own employees, they fail to recognize good results and supervise their reports excessively. That is the power of behavioral modeling—it takes a lot more effort to work out the lessons from a negative model than to copy an effective and supportive model. The effect amplifies down the organization.

Employees with ambition will try to extract themselves from such an environment—and some may be lost to the company altogether. Others will remain trapped and underdeveloped.

We are obviously not suggesting that all perceived weaker performers exhibit the same behavior their bosses exhibit toward them. We have indeed seen several managers attempting to resist this temptation, some of them successfully. Note, however, the triple hurdle that weaker-performing managers face when they try *not* to transmit their misery: First they must absorb all the monitoring and pressure applied to them, and they must give their own subordinates a margin of maneuver that they technically do not have. Second, they must fight the temptation to become discouraged and self-protective, instead remaining upbeat and giving their subordinates visibility and credit. Last, they must refrain from mimicking the modeled behavior and instead invent, or call upon memories of, a more empowering and supportive leadership style.

This challenge is not impossible, and we have seen a few managers tackle it successfully. But it is certainly formidable, which explains why so many managers we have observed could not help but pass some of their difficulties on to their subordinates.

## The Ripple Effect

Beyond causing local damage to the boss's team and the subordinate's team, the set-up-to-fail syndrome can have wider consequences. The disenfranchised talk not just to the people in their immediate environment but also to people in other units. They drag their misery around with them and engage in commiseration sessions among the disgruntled, which cut across internal boundaries, possibly gathering momentum. Can the organization tolerate the collective stress and individual pain that these negative spirals generate? When the company makes glib claims that "people are our greatest asset," the hypocrisy of this mixed message is rarely lost on employees. Clearly this failure to live up to espoused values poses an ethical question for the organization in terms of the human cost involved—but it also has implications for the company's image.

Discontent can filter out beyond the organizational boundaries. Customers, for example, may start to notice. The airline industry provides a striking example. When cabin crew staff are angry with their management, customer service suffers almost immediately. When flight attendants feel that the company doesn't take good care of them, they find it difficult to take care of passengers in turn. The situation in the "alleys and the galleys" is an acid test of employee satisfaction within an airline: Are the cabin crew working the gangways (alleys), making themselves available to passengers, or are they at the back of the plane (galleys) bitching about the management?

Beyond the realm of customer service, employees have contacts with suppliers and industry peers. Forgetting those who bad-mouth in the hope of getting back at their employer, dissatisfied staff members rarely make good advertisements for the company. Large-scale mismanagement will pollute not only the internal climate of the company but its reputation and capability to recruit new employees. Disgruntled employees also have new ways of venting their feelings. Purpose-built Web sites, such as Vault.com, allow employees to exchange information about their companies anonymously on online forms. A company may have to pour extra resources into HR marketing to compensate for high turnover and to attenuate the bad impressions that outsiders have of the company. If your company's management has a poor reputation, then the salaries had better be good. These sunk costs all start with bad people management.

## Management Myopia

This discussion of the multiple costs associated with the set-up-to-fail syndrome begs an obvious question: If the costs are so extensive, why don't more managers do something about it? (For a summary of the costs, see table 6-1.) There are two major reasons. The first is

**TABLE 6 - 1**

## Unattended Set-Up-to-Fail Syndromes

A SUMMARY OF THE COSTS

| Who Pays | Costs Incurred by These Employees and Ultimately by the Company |
|---|---|
| Subordinate | • Career damage and heavy emotional toll, including repercussions on personal life |
| Boss | • Lost performance from subordinate(s)<br>• Opportunity cost in terms of time and energy wasted on "lost causes"<br>• Emotional wear and tear<br>• Damage to reputation (for team building, developing people, or fairness) within the firm |
| Team | • Corrosion of team spirit<br>• Strain on cooperation<br>• Burnout or departure of overloaded top performers |
| Other employees | • Downward-cascading pressure and misery, stunting the growth of other employees and creating a defensive "CYA" culture<br>• Damage to the company's public image (if disgruntled employees deal directly with customers or suppliers) |
| Human resources staff | • Time spent on non-value-adding work, such as counseling, advising, and supporting bosses, helping arbitrate differences, handling grievances, appeals, and transfer requests, etc.<br>• Time and resources used to document failure rather than plan for success |

that managers do not realize the full extent of the costs involved. In part they simply cannot observe each and every symptom of the problem. When two subordinates waste an hour or two exchanging horror stories and venting their frustration, or when an unhappy employee alienates a customer, the boss is not always there to see it. And even if the boss happens to observe the scene, management is a complex activity where causes and consequences are often difficult to connect. The subordinates may be frustrated by the boss's behavior, but they could also simply be unhappy at home or angry with a colleague.

The second reason managers tend to underestimate the costs associated with their behavior is that they generally don't feel a strong sense of personal responsibility about the symptoms they observe. These symptoms include the subordinates' performance loss and the impact of the subordinates' negative state of mind on their peers and own direct reports. In part, and as discussed in chapter 3, bosses' role in the dynamic is obscured by the self-fulfilling nature of the process. Successful bosses are also less likely to have been on the receiving end of such a dynamic—or if they were, they understood the need (and found the means) to move on relatively quickly. As a result, they may simply not appreciate how wretched it feels to be trapped in the boss's out-group, with limited development prospects or rewards. Even if they did once experience the discomfort, it did not last very long or grind them down in the same way.

In addition, to acknowledge the subordinate's pain would be to admit a part of the responsibility. Doing so demands a high degree of humility and courage since it may cast doubt on the boss's whole approach to management. If I'm doing it wrong with this person, that must mean that I did it wrong in the past—so how many other subordinates did I set up to fail? When our egos and competence are thus threatened, denial affords instant protection. This is where *unawareness* of our actions and of their impact on others becomes more than a coincidence and becomes a *skill*—in other words, a process we are so good at that we don't even have to be conscious of it. "We didn't know" because part of us actively did *not* want to know! This is the so-called *skilled unawareness* process, which Chris Argyris has described so well.[6]

## Reasons Not to Change

One line of defense is to argue that talent is not evenly distributed and that any group of subordinates is bound to include some duds. As Jack Welch put it: "If I get ten people, one is a star and one won't cut it."[7] Likewise, some executives tell us: "I have twelve people reporting to me. Two of them are not really working out, so I sacrifice a bit of performance. But that's still a good batting average." This view justifies doing nothing. It also fails to take into account all the other costs incurred by letting the situation continue.

Another counterargument is to point to results. "I get great results, therefore I can't be doing this." From our experience, the set-up-to-fail syndrome is not restricted to incompetent bosses. We have seen it happen to people who are perceived within their organizations as excellent bosses. The mismanagement of some subordinates need not prevent bosses from achieving a certain level of success, particularly when the boss and the star performers have high individual output levels. But the likelihood is that they are paying a high personal price—in terms of workload and stress—to achieve that success.

Let's recap the significant costs of the syndrome: emotional and professional toll on the subordinate; job-related and psychological strain on both the boss and on team members who get caught in the cross fire; demoralizing repercussions on other employees farther down the line; and the devaluation of the HR function. So having added up the costs, we clearly have a problem. What do we do to make the costs go away? Is there a solution? Let's start with the obvious one.

## Removing the Thorn

You're a busy manager. You have eight people reporting to you—and one of them is disruptive, demands disproportionate monitoring, and radiates negative energy. What do you do? When we ask the question to groups of executives, they are rarely stuck for an answer: "Fire the person!" they bark. Do they mean it? Well, they have just heard a lengthy denunciation of the behaviors they thought they were "getting away with." So there is probably an element of pent-up frustration and wish-projection in their response. Nevertheless, many see this option as providing rapid resolution and instant relief. It also happens to demonstrate decisiveness, which is no bad thing for impressing the boss; and it serves an example to others, which is no bad thing for "encouraging" would-be slackers.

The managers who favor this option concede that it may be a bit harsh, but they tell us that "life is too short" to straighten out these relationships and that they have to take action "out of fairness to the others who are giving their best." As one executive put it:

> Look, you have to understand, it's a Darwinian world out there. We're under severe pressure. I have fifteen people reporting to me, I'm on seven projects or task forces, two of those in Asia, and the demands are piling up on me all the time. I just don't have time to worry about an individual. Those direct reports are all well paid and they understand the rules of the game. I hired as carefully as I could and I tried to coach as well as I could. It hasn't worked, so I must take them out. End of story.

Some companies actively encourage turnover among less well-evaluated employees, and in fact executives who work for companies with such "up-or-out" systems often are the ones who immediately suggest firing the weaker performer. Following GE's example, a number of companies have started to try to weed out those employees who perform in the bottom 10 percent. That makes it tempting for a manager saddled with one or two underperforming subordinates to look no further. There is the quota!

We are not going to try to argue that this reasoning is wrong as such. Let's instead try to think through the costs of solving the set-up-to-fail syndrome by quickly removing the weaker performer. The first question, of course, is whether we have the *right* 10 percent. Are these really the worst performers or are they just people who got a bad break early on and then went from bad to worse? Perhaps these people could have done well but were poorly managed or underinspired. If you take them out without exploring the issue, you may be firing people who are potentially very good but simply caught in a vicious cycle.

Second, swift termination of the perceived weaker performer(s) may be the fastest "solution," but it is not always the easiest or least costly, especially in countries where labor laws are more rigid. Firing often means rehiring, so the costs of recruitment, induction, and training have to be added to the probability of renewed failure. Why a renewed failure? Because executives who simply fire perceived weaker performers *do not learn from the process*. They just made the symptoms of the particular problem go away. As a result, they are condemned to keep repeating the same mistakes and incurring the same costs.

## The Costs of Perceived Unfairness

Immediate termination of the perceived weaker performer(s) also involves wider costs associated with the repercussions on the rest of the team. Removing people who arguably were set up is bound to create perceptions of unfairness. Does that really matter? Research shows it matters *a lot*.[8] When people perceive that a process is fair, they are more willing to go along with the outcomes, even when those outcomes are unfavorable to them (see "Air France's Brush with Disaster"). Unfair treatment makes people feel expendable. It signals that "people are our number-one asset" applies only if people perform exactly the way they are supposed to. If they falter, they

---

### AIR FRANCE'S BRUSH WITH DISASTER

There's a well-known joke in the United States that turkeys don't vote for Thanksgiving. That is, people never willingly accept outcomes that go against their self-interest. This proposition makes good common sense, but it turns out to be a gross simplification. In truth, people can look beyond short-term outcomes; they can make sacrifices. Take the case of Air France.

Back in 1993, state-owned Air France was a really lousy airline. It was so bad that the previous year, it had lost as much money as all the other major carriers put together. Something clearly had to be done. So the CEO, Bernard Attali, came up with a restructuring plan (energetically called "Return to Break-Even, Part II"). It proposed four thousand staff reductions (mainly through attrition and early retirements) and a two-year salary freeze. The unions didn't even have time to call a strike ballot. The staff, particularly the ground crews, basically went straight out and blocked both Paris airports. With tires burning on the runways, it was more a riot than a strike. After a few days, the French transport minister was essentially forced to withdraw the plan, at which point Attali handed in his resignation.

His successor, Christian Blanc, inherited an unenviable challenge. He was asked to turn around the airline, now in an even more precarious position as a result of the strike, *without any additional industrial unrest*—even though the company's fourteen unions were all fired up, having already tasted blood once. Blanc immediately did a number of things: He met with the strikers and the union leaders on their own ground; he told them that Attali's plan was buried and that no fresh recovery plan would be proposed until all the employees had been

---

become a resource like any other, and we simply kick them out. If that's the deal, then bosses will pay a price in terms of performance, loyalty, and general climate.

## Out-Groups Usually Involve Several Subordinates

When arguing for immediate removal of the perceived weaker performer, executives often change the setting of our discussion by focusing on their single worst, most difficult subordinate. But that

consulted; he set up a massive listening exercise via questionnaire to allow the forty thousand employees to voice their grievances and solutions; and he introduced a weekly newsletter to communicate progress.

After five months as CEO, Blanc came out and said, "Folks, I heard you. What I propose is five thousand departures, a three-year salary freeze, and thirty percent productivity improvement." In other words, he proposed tougher measures than his predecessor. The unions were incredulous and rejected his plan outright. Blanc was unperturbed and told the unions, "We'll ask the staff what they think." So he ordered a referendum. Of the 84 percent who responded, 81 percent of employees gave him their support, forcing the unions to back down. Within the required three years, the company had met all its targets and Air France was again profitable.[9]

So what is the lesson? On the outcome side, Blanc's proposal was in many ways more painful than Attali's. Nobody liked the outcome. But employees believed that the *process* that led to the outcome was fair. So when we think of fairness we need to distinguish the outcome—what happened—and the way it was reached and communicated. Even if the outcome hurts, people will sometimes go along with it, provided the process is acceptable.

We should not expect employees to *propose* measures that are painful for them. But under some circumstances, they *will* ratify those measures—provided the process that led to their identification and communication is acceptable. In short, we should not expect turkeys to *organize* Thanksgiving. Research shows, however, that under some circumstances turkeys *do* vote for Thanksgiving!

is not what we have been talking about. As mentioned earlier, our research focuses on employees whose performance falls short of that of their better-performing colleagues *but still exceeds* the firm's minimum performance threshold. Similarly, studies on bosses' in- and out-groups did not identify the out-group as the bottom 10 percent of the performance distribution; out-groups often include a much larger proportion of the subordinate population. Last but not least, the Pygmalion studies we cited earlier also considered much wider populations than the bottom 10 percent.

In other words, the phenomenon we have been discussing is not restricted to pathological subordinates. While the tension and boss frustration may be most acute for extreme cases, the set-up-to-fail syndrome strikes way beyond the worst-performing subordinate and the bottom 10 percent of the distribution. As a result, the question is not, "Is immediate dismissal the best solution toward the worst performer?" but rather "Is immediate dismissal the best solution for the lower half of the performance distribution?" The latter question is obviously more problematic than the first one.

We will revisit in later chapters the issue of subordinate dismissal as a solution to the set-up-to-fail syndrome. For now, it is clear that immediate dismissal involves nontrivial costs down the line: costs associated with rehiring, training, and so on, of course, but also costs associated with decreased morale if employees think that the process was not fair. Whether they perceive the dismissal as fair naturally depends on many factors, such as whether the boss hired or inherited these employees; how many chances these people have been given in the past; whether they interact effectively with their colleagues or are disliked by everyone; how much performance pressure the unit and the boss are under; how much time the boss has to turn the unit around; and so forth.

We do not argue that dismissal is necessarily a bad option. In fact, we will argue later that it is, *sometimes,* the best solution for all parties. But it is certainly a costly solution, particularly when we remember that the problem involves more than one or two pathological subordinates.

## When Bosses Try to Go It Alone

"So sacking is not optimal. Then I guess I have to do something about it." At this point, bosses can go to the opposite extreme—and propose to tackle the problem unilaterally. They resolve to make immediate changes in the way they handle weaker performers. "OK, I've got the message. It's my fault that some of my people are floundering. So when I go back to work on Monday, they'll see a transformed boss." We ask executives what they'll do. They say they'll treat their weaker performers better, they'll coach them more, and they'll show more patience. They are impressed by the power of the Pygmalion effect and they are determined to make use of it. So from now on, they'll make sure they communicate high expectations. In fact, the first thing they'll do is tell the weaker subordinates just how well they think they can do. And they won't just tell them, they'll show them by giving them stretching assignments: "It's an important project, but I have great confidence in you. Run with it and have a blast!"

The appeal of this unilateral approach is clear. It can be implemented quickly, and it avoids an unpredictable discussion that could trigger recriminations or inflict loss of face. "Some subordinates have a tendency to take things rather personally," bosses tell us, "so this is a way of protecting them." Clearly, bosses are reluctant to risk upsetting the employee and damaging performance further. Instead they sometimes decide to change their behavior and become more encouraging and empowering toward the weaker performers, but without making a formal announcement of it. Essentially, they give the perceived weaker performers a chance to prove them wrong.

While this approach has the advantage of bypassing the discomfort of an open discussion, its chances of producing a satisfactory outcome are low, for several reasons. First, the bosses will find it difficult to wipe the slate clean. In spite of the bosses' best intentions, memories of past subordinate mistakes will linger and may lead bosses to slip from their commitment to become more empowering and supportive and to reflect higher expectations. Second, the last chapter showed how subordinates' cognitive processes and behavior contribute to fueling the set-up-to-fail dynamic. In the absence of a cue that they too should try to wipe the slate clean, subordinates are even less likely than bosses to be successful at doing so.

A single-handed approach is also less likely to lead to lasting improvement because it focuses on only one symptom of the problem—namely, the boss's behavior. It does not address the subordinate's role in the underperformance. Lack of self-confidence or autonomy was one thing, but other elements may have been involved. There is often a performance problem of some kind, irrespective of how it was triggered. Even if the boss's initial label was unfounded, once the dynamic has been running for awhile, some aspects of the subordinate's performance will now be in need of treatment—and trying to fix the problem without the subordinate's active contribution is likely to be self-defeating.

Still, there are two major possible outcomes from such unilateral attempts at behavioral change by the boss. One possible outcome is that the process actually works! The subordinate responds well to increased autonomy and does very well on the important project. The other possibility is that the subordinate is overwhelmed with too much, too soon.

Assuming the attempt is successful, the boss may then decide to change her mind on the subordinate and start treating him more positively. So one subordinate managed to break the cycle and move from the out-group to the in-group, but an underlying problem remains. As a pair, boss and subordinate have not worked on their ability to have a dialogue with or confront each other. Therefore, they will not be equipped to head off future difficulties or deal with a relapse.

For example, a newly appointed manager of an international subsidiary was dismayed by the weak trickle of innovations coming out of his operation. Making inquiries on the front lines, he realized that the flow of new ideas was strangled by the mass of checks and procedures. He set up a task force to investigate and, acting on its recommendations, he significantly decreased the number of procedures. The subsidiary's innovation record shot up. A resounding success? Not entirely. The much deeper question that went unasked was, "So what stopped you from questioning these practices and getting them cut earlier?" Not asking this question was a missed opportunity for learning how something similar can be prevented next time.[10]

Managers have a tendency to rush in and respond to surface behaviors without considering the underlying values or assumptions driving the behaviors. Sustainable progress demands that we consider not just how to cure the problem ("single-loop" learning), but that we explore what has allowed the problem to develop unchallenged in the first place ("double-loop" learning).[11]

A unilateral approach, hence, limits the learning that boss and subordinates could derive from a more up-front handling of the problem. The subordinate and the rest of the team miss out on the chance of observing and learning from how their boss handled the difficulties in the relationship—a problem they may face someday with their own subordinates.

The other possible outcome of this approach, and the other limitation as well, is that the boss may be trying to do too much at once. The subordinate may be overwhelmed by the sudden rush of auton-

**FIGURE 6 - 1**

## How Far Gone Is the Negative Spiral?

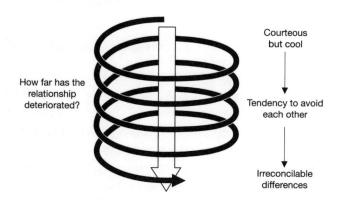

How far has the relationship deteriorated?

Courteous but cool

↓

Tendency to avoid each other

↓

Irreconcilable differences

omy and responsibility. A subordinate who has been carefully encouraged to ask for approval does not instantaneously become entrepreneurial or self-sufficient. The "stretch assignment" may prove to be more than he can handle productively. Unsure why this sudden increase in autonomy is occurring, he may feel stressed or confused. Before starting to run, a stunted employee may need to learn to walk again! In this scenario, the subordinate fails to deliver to the boss's satisfaction, leaving the boss even more frustrated and convinced that the subordinate cannot function without intense supervision. Return to jail.

Overall, unilateral attempts by the boss to interrupt the set-up-to-fail syndrome are risky. At best, if the subordinate manages to live up to the suddenly increased expectations, one member of the out-group manages to move closer to the in-group but the learning for both parties is limited. At worst, if the subordinate cannot improve quickly enough—which would not be surprising—the boss's labeling ends up being supported once more.

This approach is more likely to be successful early in the dynamic, before the relationship really takes a turn for the worse and perceived weaker performer's behavior and output have not yet gone all the way down to boss's low expectations (see figure 6-1).

If the solution cannot be unilateral, then it has to be bilateral. Joint problems require joint solutions. Boss and subordinate must step back and untangle their *complicity* in creating an unhealthy relationship in order to improve their joint performance. And the only way we know to do that is to sit down and talk.

## The Pros and Cons of Trying to Start a Dialogue

Our recommendation that the two parties sit down and talk is not exactly rocket science. Yet we have found that such discussions are rare, mainly because both parties perceive them as presenting a high potential for threat and embarrassment. To reduce this perceived difficulty, we must understand better what bosses and subordinates fear.

We have asked many subordinates caught in such dynamics what, if anything, prevented them from bringing up the issue with their bosses. They gave us two major reasons, to which we will add a third.

First, subordinates are worried about coming across as feeble, thin-skinned, or whiny. One interviewee told us, "It would be very difficult for me to broach the issue—perhaps because I don't want to give my boss an impression of weakness."

The legitimacy of this concern becomes very clear when we ask executives to role-play "setting up the initial meeting" with the subordinate taking the lead. Even in this artificial situation, signs of tension are evident. How do you tell your boss that you sometimes find her unfair, that you feel underappreciated, that you feel she often does not give you a chance to work on your terms, that, basically, you think she does not have much faith in your abilities? In our role plays, one boss's reaction to the subordinate's opening appeal, went something like this: "You came in here wanting to discuss a problem and now you're telling me this is *my* problem? Let's rather start with *your* problems. . . . " And thereby the boss hijacked the discussion and turned it into an opportunity to revisit the subordinate's shortcomings.

Second, many subordinates explain that their boss is aware of the problem and that it would be easy for him to bring up the issue (implying that bosses don't have to be afraid of coming across as feeble and thin-skinned). Since the boss doesn't bring up the issue, his subordinates conclude that he probably *does not want* to discuss it. As one disenchanted subordinate commented, "He must feel the tension as well. He must notice the absence of interchanges. I'm sure he's intelligent enough to say, *'Hey, what's going on here?'* but he chooses not to bring up the topic, so I take it to mean he doesn't want to discuss it." On that basis, many "weaker performers" indicated that they would be delighted to discuss the problem with their boss, but that they would need some sign that the boss was somehow ready for such a discussion.

Beyond these two dimensions that subordinates articulated, another factor may be that subordinates have mixed feelings about the prospect of triggering a serious discussion with their boss. While they would certainly welcome a resolution to their problem, some subordinates are likely to be concerned that the discussion may prove unpleasant for them and, far from leading to a resolution, may make things worse for them.

In light of these concerns and the power imbalance, bosses seem to be in a better position to instigate the process. Unfortunately, most bosses are not very keen to initiate such conversations either. Subordinates are severely misguided when they assume that bringing the problem into the open would be easy for their boss. Most bosses do not relish the prospect of sitting down to give feedback to subordinates, particularly to weaker performers. Countless research studies have documented bosses' tendency to delay giving feedback, but this is one area where we do not need research studies to tell us what we all know: When we look at our agenda and consider when would be best to sit down and have a potentially difficult discussion with a subordinate, especially one with whom we have an uneasy relationship, tomorrow tends to be much more appealing than today!

## Building Up Dissatisfaction

The fallout from an undiagnosed and untreated set-up-to-fail relationship often has a clear ripple effect throughout the organization, and it carries with it a number of hidden costs. It is costly for the firm because perceived weaker performers' output is suboptimized, and because the subordinates' predicament imposes costs on their bosses, HR professionals, and the subordinates' peers and subordinates. This multidimensional set of costs makes the process worth interrupting.

Immediate dismissal of the subordinate will make the symptoms go away for this relationship, but it triggers its own set of costs and does not solve the underlying problem. Nor does the boss who is trying to modify his or her behavior unilaterally and tacitly. As a result, the solution requires some deliberate conversations with bilateral participation. The next chapter explores exactly how these conversations can help and how bosses and subordinates can unlock the full potential of these conversations, to pave the way for a successful turnaround in the relationship.

# 7

---

# Blinders of
# Our Own Making

What [we do] is based not on direct and certain knowledge,
but on pictures made by [us] or given to [us]. . . . The way in
which the world is imagined determines at any particular
moment what [we] will do.

—Walter Lippmann

AS WE SAW IN CHAPTER 6, bosses can be discouraged from taking the initiative to intervene in a failed relationship by a variety of
factors: the low probability that their intervention will be successful, combined with the anxiety and pain that such meetings are
likely to entail, and the significant probability that the situation will
be worsened by the meeting. They have a point. Perceived weaker
performers are indeed unlikely to heed and act on their boss's feedback—but mainly because their boss's behavior toward them fails to
signal a concern for their well-being or for fairness in the way the
feedback was developed and communicated.

In spite of the difficulties we've enumerated, we still maintain
that the boss should try to design and conduct an intervention. To
be successful, this intervention must convince the subordinate that
the boss's feedback is valid, rather than being a sign of an overall
critical disposition and unfair attitude. That means the boss will

have to do a fair amount of preparation and undertake some soul searching, which we will discuss in detail in chapter 8.

Before turning to the intervention as such, however, we must examine why bosses tend to perceive interventions with perceived weaker performers as stressful, and why these interventions often end up being ineffective. The main factor, we believe, is the way bosses approach stressful interactions in general, and feedback-giving in particular.

## The Risks Associated with Giving Feedback

Let's take a moment to examine in some detail what concerns bosses about the *process* and *potential outcomes* of such conversations. For one thing, bosses worry that critical feedback will *hurt* the subordinate's feelings. Most bosses have been trained how to communicate critical feedback as effectively as possible, but their subordinates have often gone to the same training programs and are very skilled at decoding bosses' behavior. They know that after the flowers generally comes the flowerpot. Bosses would prefer not to hurt subordinates' feelings because, like most human beings, they generally don't derive pleasure from inflicting pain on other people, but also because they are concerned about subordinates' reactions.

When their feelings are hurt, some people lash back at the "offender," in an attempt to make their pain go away and/or to share it with the offender. This retaliation can be aggressive: The feedback recipient might accuse the boss of being partial or even biased, question the boss's judgment and integrity, or simply raise the sound volume beyond the threshold that the boss can handle. Subordinates can also retaliate in more submissive ways by expressing their pain clearly enough to make the boss uncomfortable. Just as children's crying can be a defensive mechanism designed to make the parents uncomfortable and hence stop their line of questioning or discussion, adults have ways to communicate to other adults that "you have hurt me and I hope you feel bad about it."

Knowing *ex ante* that the conversation might be hurtful to the subordinate and lead him or her to lash out, bosses often start worrying about the conversation some time ahead. This anxiety has an obvious direct cost for the boss, but it may also have an effect on the

---

## WORKING YOURSELF UP TO A POTENTIALLY ADVERSARIAL MEETING

Some of you may know this joke. A car gets stranded in snow, in a remote area, just before midnight. After circling around the car two or three times, the driver concludes that he needs a shovel to dig the car out of the snow. Seeing a farmhouse in the distance, he sets off to ask for a shovel. It is a long way and as he walks he starts to wonder how the farmer will react. The farmer is bound to be suspicious of this unknown stranger, and probably resentful at being woken up. As he continues to walk he realizes that it is now 1:00 AM and his concern keeps growing. "The farmer surely has to get up early and will probably have additional work with the snow." As he gets closer to the farm, the driver is now downright worried: "And why would he lend a shovel to a perfect stranger in the middle of the night? He is bound to ask for some deposit or some guarantee to get his shovel back. But I have no money!" By the time he reaches the farmhouse, the car driver has convinced himself that the farmer will be unsympathetic to his request. The farmer barely has a chance to open the door before the driver screams out, "You can keep your damned shovel!"

---

way the discussion unfolds later. When we enter a meeting anxious about its outcome and conscious that the atmosphere may become adversarial, we often tend to start off on an aggressive note—just like the driver of the car in the anecdote above (see "Working Yourself Up to a Potentially Adversarial Meeting").

Beyond these costs that bosses pay leading up to and during the meeting, bosses can be concerned about the outcomes of the discussion. If all these discussions led to a productive resolution—that is, if subordinates were to accept the feedback and successfully act on it to improve their performance—the up-front costs would typically be worth it and we would see more such conversations. The problem is, of course, that two other less than optimal outcomes can and do occur.

In both cases, the subordinates push back on the boss, arguing that the feedback is invalid, that the boss does not see the full picture, and so on. At some point the boss will face a choice: to continue the discussion and push back harder, which will lead to an escalation in the tone and content of the discussion, or to end the meeting without a clear agreement but after having made some points. Let's illustrate both outcomes.

In the first case, the boss is often less scared of what he might hear than of what he might say. He is concerned that, if pushed by the subordinate, he may end up saying what he *really* thinks and let loose the frustrations he has accumulated over time. He might start listing all the things that the subordinate does that bug him, all the mistakes he remembers the subordinate made, or even worse, make clear his very limited confidence in the subordinate's ability and potential. Doing so is likely to end up needlessly worsening a poor but tolerable situation.

An executive once gave us a powerful example of a conversation that escalated way beyond his original intention. One of his subordinates produced high-quality work, but the executive thought it was a bit short on quantity. He thought the subordinate's high emphasis on quality was probably responsible for the slower pace of work, and he thought he could tell her that and thus help her rebalance her priorities. This diagnosis was so obvious to him that he didn't question it for a moment. As a result he didn't think of preparing for the meeting, for example by having productivity data available in case the subordinate would disagree with his assessment. The conversation went four rounds, which we summarize below.

> **Boss:** I'd like to discuss your work with you. I think your work is fantastic in quality, but a bit lacking in quantity. My sense is that if you put a little less emphasis on quality you could work more quickly.
>
> **Sub:** I don't understand why you are saying this; I am not slow.
>
> **Boss:** No, look, you *are* slow. There's no doubt about that . . .
>
> **Sub:** But I really don't understand why you are saying this, I meet my deadlines, I do good work . . .
>
> **Boss:** Gee, you're not listening. Look, I'm telling you, *you do work slowly* . . .
>
> **Sub:** But really, I don't see . . .

**Boss:** Look, listen to me: You're so damn slow the whole office makes fun of you behind your back, that's how slow you are!

Such conversations often end on a remark that the speaker would *really* like to take back and erase from the record. Unfortunately, we can correct past statements but we cannot erase them from someone's memory. Once some things have been said, it is impossible to pick up the pieces and continue as if nothing had happened.

Obviously, the boss could have decided somewhere along the line that this conversation was going nowhere and that, in the absence of clear data supporting his point, he should fold for now and come back better prepared. The CEO of a small company provided us with a good example of this approach. One of his direct reports was experiencing difficulty with several of his subordinates. This was reasonably public knowledge within the firm. Lately, however, the problems seemed to have escalated to the point where the CEO was now receiving anonymous mail complaining about his subordinate's leadership style.

Fully determined to tackle this problem, he held several meetings with his subordinate, who initially denied the existence of a morale problem in his department. The CEO patiently stated that he'd heard about the problem from enough different people that there must be some truth to it. He did not divulge the identity of his sources or mention the anonymous letters. The subordinate then changed tactics and acknowledged that, yes, he was riding his troops pretty hard, but he was doing so only because he was asked to produce ambitious results with limited resources. Yes, he was demanding, and maybe his style was better suited to project management than to "steady-state" management, but part of his responsibilities were important projects, and so forth.

The CEO was unsure how to proceed from there. He knew that his subordinate's unit was somewhat under-resourced and he wanted projects to continue to be managed tightly. He also had no direct evidence that his subordinate was really behaving as alleged by the anonymous detractors. In contacts with him, the subordinate was nothing like this. "And, by the way," the CEO asked himself, "why did these people write anonymously? This is a firm where we can speak our minds."

On the basis of these questions, the CEO chose to "fold" and to stop pushing hard on the issues. He continued to mention it periodically to his subordinate, but they reached no specific agreement about the nature, timing, and extent of progress the subordinate was expected to make. Not surprisingly, grumblings and morale problems continue to plague this department.

## An Uphill Battle

Having illustrated the major possible outcomes, we can now go back to the big picture and examine the *probabilities* that should be assigned to the various outcomes. Figure 7-1 illustrates possible outcomes of the boss's intervention.

Let's first walk through the figure with "Yuri," a better-performing subordinate in mind. Given Yuri's overall high level of performance, the feedback his boss ("Zoë") wants to communicate is unlikely to be devastating for him. Some things here and there, nothing major. Even if the feedback is serious, Zoë is bound to start by reminding Yuri of the high esteem she has for him, and that she is offering this feedback to help him optimize what promises to be a successful career. In this context, Zoë is unlikely to experience much anxiety before the meeting. Yuri may feel hurt on the spot but is unlikely to retaliate and will probably instead thank his boss for taking the time and effort. The feedback is likely to be accepted and, given the high capabilities Zoë attributes to Yuri, she is likely to be confident that performance will improve on the dimension discussed. Overall, this is not a very threatening exercise and the prospective cost-benefit analysis is very encouraging for Zoë.

Repeating the exercise with Sara, a perceived weaker-performing subordinate in mind, yields a markedly different picture. As the set-up-to-fail syndrome develops, Zoë and Sara become increasingly uneasy with one another. Sara tries as much as possible to minimize contact with Zoë, who tries increasingly hard to keep a close eye on things, specifies tasks in substantial detail, and intensely monitors Sara's results.

Preparing for the intervention is likely to trigger some anxiety for Zoë, who anticipates a difficult conversation likely to be unpleasant for Sara. Sara may in turn lash out at Zoë and become defensive.

**FIGURE 7 - 1**

## Possible Outcomes of the Boss's Intervention

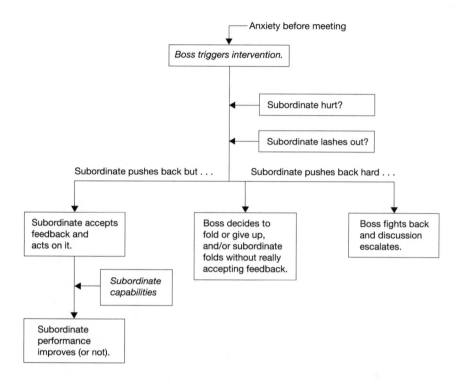

From past experience, Zoë probably doubts that Sara will *genuinely* accept the feedback and suspects that, even if she accepts it, her performance won't improve markedly. Zoë also knows that if she really engages in a performance improvement program with Sara, she will have to follow up regularly on her progress. And, if the outcome does prove to be negative, Zoë will need to take measures to transfer or even terminate Sara's employment, all of which will consume much of her time and energy.

This prospective cost-benefit analysis is much less encouraging for the boss than its equivalent with a perceived high performer, which explains why bosses tend to be reluctant to engage in such processes. As long as the situation remains "bearable," the temptation is hence strong for the boss to leave things as they are and not to intervene. This is exactly what the director of legal services of a very large firm, reputed for its forcefulness with weaker performers, told us. He explained that over the past three years, he had more or less given up on a senior lawyer, caught as he was in a catch-22 situation.

> I realize I can't fire him because I'd have a lawsuit on my hands in a minute. The guy would argue that I abandoned him three years ago and have not given him the chance to develop. Then again, I can't give him any of the interesting assignments because he tends not to perform very well. But if I only give him routine assignments he can't improve either. I guess that with all the work we have to do, I have tended to push this issue aside and unconsciously bide my time; he is supposed to retire in three years.

Note that the director of legal services was not alone in this situation. Although his employer is reputed for its intense performance culture, one of the main criticisms systematically appearing in 360-degree feedback of senior managers of this company is that they do not deal with underperformance promptly and resolutely enough.

A crucial part of this equation is the boss's lack of confidence that the weaker performer will accept and integrate the feedback. Why do bosses feel that way? Is the fear based on fact, or on an assumption that a great many bosses happen to share? We believe that too many bosses have found that weaker performers don't accept feedback, so it can't be pure imagination. So why is feedback so often disregarded?

To understand why, let's turn to research studies aimed at identifying the factors that lead people to accept and integrate feedback.[1] First, these studies tell us that people are more likely to act on feedback when they accept it as valid. That is not surprising and makes intuitive sense.

Studies also find that subordinate acceptance of negative feedback (positive feedback tends to be accepted much more easily!) increases under the following four conditions:

1. The source of the feedback is perceived as reliable

2. The feedback receiver trusts the intentions of the source

3. The feedback receiver perceives as fair the process by which the feedback is *developed*—more specifically, when the boss

- collected all relevant information
- allowed the feedback receiver to provide clarifications and explanations
- considered the feedback receiver's opinion
- applied consistent standards when delivering criticism

4. The feedback receiver perceives as fair the process by which the feedback is *communicated*—specifically, when the boss

- pays careful attention to the feedback receiver's ideas
- shows respect for the feedback receiver
- is supportive of the feedback receiver despite their disagreement.

Looking at this list and comparing it to the differential behavior of bosses toward their perceived better and weaker performers, it is clear that perceived better performers, as members of the boss's in-group, are more likely than their colleagues to trust the boss's motives toward them and to find fair the feedback development and communication processes.

Weaker performers, on the other hand, see a boss who selectively observes and recalls their achievements, attributes their successes to luck but their failures to themselves, gives significantly less attention and weight to their opinions, and is generally much less supportive. In addition, bosses preparing themselves for a tough discussion with a member of their out-group are more likely to try to block out their emotions during the meeting and, as a result, come across as tough and insensitive—as opposed to relaxed and concerned with their subordinates' well-being and career. As a result, many weaker performers are likely to reject the feedback as invalid, believing it's driven not by facts but rather by their boss's critical disposition toward them.

## Approaching Interactions with a Narrow, Frozen Frame

We have discussed in previous chapters how human beings tend to label people and things in order to process information more quickly and make life easier and more manageable for themselves.

Similarly, whenever we face a decision we tend to *frame* it, or to *set a frame* for it. At its simplest, a frame is "the decision maker's image of the situation," the way the decision maker pictures the elements relevant to the decision (including past and current events), and the relationships between these elements.[2] Let's take three examples that shed light on the impact of framing.

A young priest asks his bishop, "May I smoke while praying?" Not surprisingly, the bishop answers an emphatic "No!" Later that day the young priest encounters an older priest puffing away on a cigarette while praying. He scolds the older priest, "You shouldn't be smoking while praying! I asked the bishop this morning and he said I couldn't." "That's strange," the older priest replies. "I asked the bishop if I could pray while I'm smoking, and he said that it was OK to pray at any time." The same request, framed in different ways ("smoking while praying" versus "praying while smoking"), appeared quite different to the bishop and triggered different responses.

For a second example, take a young couple about to welcome a second child. After careful thought, they decide that their house does not offer enough space for the second child and, hence, must be renovated and enlarged. For weeks they examine various proposals from architects and contractors, until their eight-year-old son learns that his neighbor is going to move and asks his parents why people move houses. While trying to answer, the parents realize that they framed their problem as "How should we remodel our current house?" as opposed to "How do we get enough room for our growing family?"—an alternative framing that would have opened up many other solutions than remodeling.[3]

Finally, consider a lesson the Japanese car industry taught to the rest of the world in the early 1980s. For decades, North American car manufacturers developed sophisticated models to calculate the optimum size of production runs, taking into account the cost of changing over production lines, the cost of finished car storage, and so on. Meanwhile, Japanese car companies worked hard at making their entire system more efficient by *reducing* changeover times. They had framed the problem as "what is the most efficient way to produce the requisite variety of models?" while American manufacturers had taken changeover times for granted and hence had excluded their reduction from their problem-solving effort.[4]

By defining the *boundaries* of the decision (which components are in, which are out?) and its *reference point* (how do we define success?), the decision frame also defines a number of important dimensions, such as which issue we are looking at, what information is relevant to the decision, how we are going to weight various bits of information, and, more generally, how we can go about solving the problem.

Having taken a few moments to establish a common vocabulary on the notion of framing, let's examine its relevance to our discussion. In the previous chapters, we have explored the overall relationship between bosses and their subordinates, particularly their perceived weaker performers. We have examined the relationship from a certain altitude in order to identify some of the mechanisms that get triggered. The next step is to move to a greater degree of granularity and look at the way relationships are enacted through interactions (and, in some cases, the lack thereof). It is through interactions with subordinates that bosses have the opportunity to communicate certain messages, including feedback. Bosses will *frame* these interactions, constructing mental pictures of what the issue is about, what the relevant elements are, and how they interrelate.

Chris Argyris's work over nearly five decades has established that human beings, regardless of national cultures, tend to follow predictable behavioral patterns when they face stressful situations. Specifically, Argyris has shown that under difficult conditions (which he calls "situations involving potential threat and embarrassment"), the immense majority of human beings will behave in ways that enable them to be in unilateral control of the situation and to win the "encounter."[5] Our modest observation, consistent with his conclusions, is that when facing stressful situations, bosses tend to frame the issues in rather *narrow, binary* ways and that this framing remains *frozen* during the discussions.

Let's illustrate. An executive faced a concrete and immediate problem. One of her subordinates (Joe) had just resigned, and she could not replace him because the company was in the process of downsizing. To support a class discussion of her situation, she wrote the following caselet (shown in table 7-1), which presents what both parties said (in the right column) as well as the thoughts and feelings that the boss experienced, but chose not to express, during the discussion (shown in the left column).[6]

---

### *The Situation*

Paragraph written by the boss and hence representing the boss's *framing* of the situation:

> Due to a reduction in the number of staff (voluntary resignation), I had to place more work and responsibilities onto one or more of the remaining personnel. I called in the product manager whom I felt was the best suited to take over more responsibilities (based on her former performance and her general background). She refused to take over the product area I was offering, unless of course I wanted to give her a direct order to do so. I chose not to do so and have now placed the extra responsibility with another person. The following is based on the conversation I had with her.

Before getting into the specifics of the dialogue, notice how the boss framed the issue:

- I just lost one employee, hence
- I need to reallocate the work among the remaining managers.
- I am going to select the one I feel is best suited to take the job, then
- I am going to try and convince her to take the additional load on top of her existing work.

From our privileged observer position, examining this case without any time or interpersonal pressure, it is clear that the boss's frame is very *narrow,* in that it *excludes* several interesting avenues, such as:

- Eliminating part or all of Joe's duties (because they are not really value-adding)
- Reallocating Joe's work to several subordinates (not just one)

**TABLE 7 - 1**

## Asking an Employee to Take On More Work

| Thoughts and Feelings | Dialogue |
| --- | --- |
| I hope that [this subordinate] will accept the challenge to take on the vacant job—otherwise we really have a problem. | *Boss:* I have called you to discuss the situation in our department as a result of [Joe] leaving us by 1st October. Due to the uncertainty regarding our future we have not been permitted to hire more staff and thereby fill in the gap that Joe's departure is creating. We have to cover the product area with the remaining staff.<br>   I have thought of who could best take on more responsibilities and I strongly believe that you are the best to do so, as you have performed excellently in the past. I am sure that you have what it takes to generate good results from the turbulent area that Joe has chosen to leave.<br><br>*Sub:* I don't think that it is possible for me to take on more responsibility, as I have already more than enough to take care of. |
| I have always praised her performance so much; she even got a salary increase last year and yet she is unwilling to help out in a difficult situation! | *Boss:* I am of course prepared to give you the necessary backup in the form of support staff and what you may otherwise need.<br><br>*Sub:* Yes, but I don't know anything about the products that you are asking me to be responsible for. |
| Is she stating the real reasons for refusing to accept more responsibilities? | *Boss:* You have the ability to learn fast—you are an intelligent person and, besides, you may attend the courses you find necessary.<br><br>*Sub:* I feel that it should not be our problem alone to cover for staff leaving our function—they should give us help from other functions within the section. |
| Does she not believe me when I am telling her that I have tried everything possible to get more staff? | *Boss:* I have tried everything—believe me. We are simply not going to get personnel from outside.<br><br>*Sub:* Well, you have the right to order me to take over, but I still don't think it is a good idea. |
| She is almost making it sound like a threat. | *Boss:* OK, I regret your attitude. I think we should both give it a second thought and talk about it again tomorrow. |

- Reexamining each manager's workload to identify things we can stop doing, or we can do faster, so that Joe's work replaces, rather than adds to, existing work

- Involving some or all of the team members in analyzing and solving the problem

In addition to being narrow, the boss's frame is *binary*. As demonstrated in her unstated thought at the start of the case, the boss can see only two possible outcomes: the subordinate agrees to the boss's request (success) or refuses to do so (failure).

Finally, the boss's frame is *frozen* to the extent that, in spite of the discussion not going her way at all, she does not revise her framing of the situation. Nor, by the way, did she revise it after the discussion. When we discussed her case, the boss's dominating feeling was still that her subordinate had been disloyal by refusing to help.

The downside of narrow, binary, and frozen frames is that they create situations that are very stressful, *for both parties*. From the boss's point of view, there are only two possible outcomes, a good one (I get my way) and a bad one (I don't get my way). This viewpoint creates anxiety for the boss, who walks into the meeting tense and with a tightly defined game plan. The subordinate feels the boss's tension and quickly realizes there are only two options available: comply or resist. That leaves the two parties very limited room to maneuver.

In addition both boss and subordinate are going to devote valuable energy to monitoring and trying to control their intense emotions during the encounter. They'll both be depleting their "energy pots," using so much energy on their emotions that they'll have little left for more productive pursuits, such as paying real attention to the other party (what he or she is saying, not saying, assuming, or inferring), and trying to imagine a more creative response. For example, if the boss had been able to devote more energy to processing what was going on in real time, she might have been able to ask the subordinate to try to articulate what *really* bothered her in the boss's request. The subordinate mentions lack of time, lack of expertise in this particular area, and a belief that "other departments should help." In the left column, the boss asks herself, "Is she stating the right reason?" Well, why not ask her? See figure 7-2 for a graphical representation of the boss's reduced bandwidth under stressful and threatening conditions.

Compounding the problem is the fact that the boss was *unaware* that she framed the issue in a narrow, binary, and frozen way. In fact, she never thought she was framing anything at all. She just looked at the situation, analyzed it, and came up with a solution.

**FIGURE 7 - 2**

## The Energy Pot

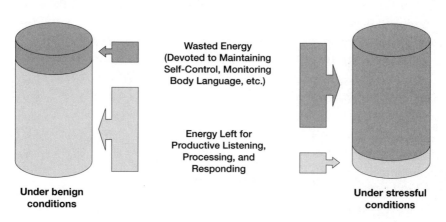

Wasted Energy
(Devoted to Maintaining
Self-Control, Monitoring
Body Language, etc.)

Energy Left for
Productive Listening,
Processing, and
Responding

Under benign
conditions

Under stressful
conditions

This phenomenon is very pervasive. People tend to be unaware of their framing, which prevents them from *articulating* their frame (making it explicit), which then prevents them from *evaluating* whether the framing is appropriate in light of the feedback they receive. In this case, the boss received feedback suggesting that parts of her framing were restrictive, for example, adding Joe's reallocated work to existing duties. She couldn't process this feedback because she was so convinced that it was the only solution.

Note, also, how the boss analyzes the situation in ways that reflect her very partial view of reality, filtered by the biases we examined in the previous chapters. For example, the boss thinks, "I have always praised her performance so much and I even gave her a raise last year," hence, "she owes me." The subordinate might say or think, "I don't owe you anything. Your praising my work and giving me a raise was a reward for all the hard work and dedication I put into my work over the last few years. It settled the past, and we're even." In fact, we might not be even if the subordinate thinks the rewards she received were insufficient to compensate for her input; both parties could be guided by selective memories of who did what, when, and how well.

The boss then seems to overintentionalize the subordinate's behavior by thinking, "Since she owes me, refusing to help shows she is disloyal." This thought presents the disloyalty as a personality trait rather than a response to specific stimuli.

These distortions allow the boss to maintain her "frame blindness," that is, her unawareness of the way she framed the situation and how this framing affected the encounter's process and outcome. In the boss's mind, the problem does not come from the way she approached the issue, but rather from the subordinate's disloyalty (and lack of candor). Case closed.

## How Disagreements Escalate

We have dozens more cases like this one. Bosses can approach easy to moderately easy situations with a reasonably open mind and broad, flexible framing. In difficult and stressful situations, however, their framing tends to be similar to the one presented here: narrow, binary, and frozen.

In addition to creating much tension and anxiety, this situation leaves bosses but two possible generic strategies to "getting their way": to come right out and advocate their point of view, or to ease into it by asking subordinates a series of questions that, if answered "correctly," will lead to the answer the boss wants. The forthright approach was exemplified by the caselet. Note that the boss was very complimentary to the subordinate in the process—she did not do a bad sales job!

The problem with this approach is that if the subordinate—or, more generally, the other party involved—pushes back on the boss, the boss faces a high likelihood that the conversation will escalate. Figure 7-3 provides a visual summary of what often happens in interactions framed this way. In this case the subordinate (Sam) starts the interaction by saying that he did a good job on the project ($S_1$). The boss (Beth) does not vehemently disagree with this assessment and concurs that yes, "It wasn't bad" ($B_1$). Sam could reaffirm his opening bid, but more often than not will try to pull the boss's view closer to his view, by overstating his initial point to "What do you mean, it wasn't bad? It was pretty damn good!" ($S_2$). Beth did not strongly disagree with Sam's initial assessment but does disagree strongly with his inflated statement. She could of course reiterate her first

FIGURE 7 - 3

## Scripted Collisions

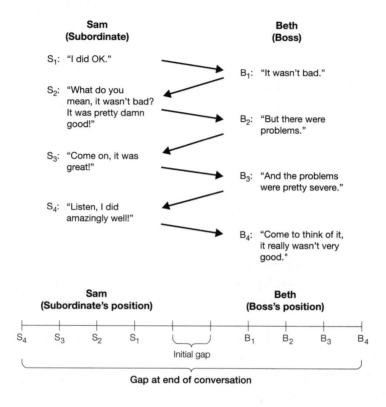

| Sam (Subordinate) | Beth (Boss) |
|---|---|
| S₁: "I did OK." | B₁: "It wasn't bad." |
| S₂: "What do you mean, it wasn't bad? It was pretty damn good!" | B₂: "But there were problems." |
| S₃: "Come on, it was great!" | B₃: "And the problems were pretty severe." |
| S₄: "Listen, I did amazingly well!" | B₄: "Come to think of it, it really wasn't very good." |

statement, but again the temptation is strong to try and pull the subordinate down to her view, "But there were some problems" ($B_2$). The subordinate, in turn, tries to pull the boss's view up, which leads the boss to react in the other direction, and so on. The narrow, binary, and frozen framing of the interaction forced both parties into digging in their heels and led to a corresponding escalation.

As we hinted above, these dynamics do not occur only in boss-subordinate interactions. They are triggered more by the framing of the situation than by the people involved, who can be peers, customers, or suppliers, or even friends or family members. The sidebar below provides a real example of a small disagreement between a husband and wife that degenerates rapidly, because the two parties frame the situation in different ways and, specifically, use different reference points.

## The "Subtle" Approach

In an attempt to avoid the threat associated with such head-on, possibly escalating, confrontations, many bosses choose to approach the interaction less forcefully. Rather than stating up front their choice as dictated by their narrow, binary, and frozen framing, they try to finesse the issue by leading the subordinate to reach the "right" conclusion alone. This tactic, called "easing in," was chosen by an executive who had a difficult piece of news to communicate to one of his subordinates. He wrote the following caselet to describe his approach.

_____

### *Framing by the Boss*

> As chairman of the company's committee for product development, I had to ask one of the members to leave the committee, as she did not contribute satisfactorily to the committee's work. In her daily job this manager reports to me, so we talk often. She performs very well in her daily job as manager of a small group, so the reason for her poor performance on the committee could easily be too much work. I do not think she will like this conversation as the conclusion will be that she must leave the committee and lose status, which is of greater importance to her than to many other people.

_____

Easing in is a risky strategy. The first risk is that the subordinate may either not understand early enough in the conversation that the game is rigged, or understand early enough but refuse to play along with the boss and hence not give the "right answer." In this case, assume for example that the subordinate answers the boss's second question ("Do you feel that you are sometimes wasting time when we have meetings of the product development committee?") by saying, "No, I think these are great meetings and I love to watch you chair them. I learn a lot."

TABLE 7 - 2

## Taking Responsibility Away from an Employee

| Thoughts and Feelings | Dialogue |
| --- | --- |
| I will make her feel that her daily job is important and that she is too busy to participate in the committee. | *Boss:* Are all deadlines met? And how busy are you and your group?<br><br>*Sub:* We have met all deadlines except one, which was caused by a breakdown in our equipment. It is not easy but I think that we are all working very hard, and I must admit that I am very tired in the evening when I go home. |
| I will make her see her role in the product development committee. | *Boss:* Do you feel that you are sometimes wasting time when we have product development committee meetings?<br><br>*Sub:* Yes. Sometimes I cannot see the connection between the points being discussed and my part in it. |
| I must make her understand that she is doing OK in respect to her daily job, but that she does not contribute to the group process in the product development committee. | *Boss:* I also feel that you sometimes are a bit absent-minded and do not get involved in the process. Maybe because your thoughts are with your daily job.<br><br>*Sub:* Yes, that is true. |
| Now is the time to launch the bad news, when she has just acknowledged the small size of her own contribution. | |
| I do not want her to push back on this, so I will not ask for alternative solutions. I will present the one solution that I want. | *Boss:* Could it be of benefit to you and the group if you were no longer a permanent member of the committee, but were invited when your expertise is required?<br><br>*Sub:* Yes, that could be a solution if at the same time I get a copy of the agenda and the minutes from the meeting. |
| She must not lose too much status or enthusiasm in her daily job, so I will let her have the copies. | *Boss:* Of course, you will get the copies. |

There are many ways to role-play this situation, but if you assume that the subordinate has some reason to remain on the committee, you will find that many scenarios lead back to the feedback session outcomes we discussed earlier: (1) an escalation that leads the boss to use increasingly tough vocabulary and probably ends up demotivating the subordinate; (2) a boss who decides to cut his losses and folds somewhere along the line, having failed to get the

## ESCALATION IN EVERYDAY LIFE

Jean-François witnessed the following interaction a few years ago. It occurred between one of his best friends (a dentist who had started his own practice three years before) and his wife (who had been helping with administrative work at the practice). The actual discussion was longer, and each person spoke longer at a time, but we've faithfully reproduced the number of rounds and the basic content of each round.

**Dentist:** I must say that after three years, I'm pretty happy with what we've done. We have grown the business at a rapid pace, the practice is well run . . .

**Spouse:** Yes, the practice is pretty well run . . .

**Dentist:** What do you mean, pretty well run? It is *very well* run. We have well-trained staff, we have procedures, we have . . .

**Spouse:** But a lot of things could be done better. I know, I help with the administration, there's . . . , and . . .

**Dentist:** I can't believe this! Let me tell you, I know more dentists than you do and I dare you to find a three-year-old practice anywhere that functions better and is better run than mine!

**Spouse:** And if it's true that you have the best-run practice, then it really means the others don't know what they're doing because there's really a big margin of improvement. . . .

Witnessing this conversation from the sidelines was very enlightening! At that moment Jean-François proposed a time-out and helped his friends see how an initially small disagreement had escalated into a huge gap. The technical diagnosis is that the two parties are using different *points of reference* in their framing. The dentist focuses on progress made over the last three years, while his spouse focuses on the potential progress that can be made in the future. Beyond the technical aspect, however, this is a striking example of how two people whose starting positions are close (and who obviously enjoy a positive overall relationship) can hang on to their frames and escalate quickly into an apparently irreconcilable difference.

subordinate off the committee and having degraded a once-solid relationship; or (3) a subordinate who realizes at some point that the boss has firmly made up his mind and decides to stop resisting (with a strong possibility of being demotivated as a result).

So the first risk of easing in is that you rely on the subordinate to be willing to provide the "right answers." If he fails to do so, it may be difficult to rescue the conversation before the relationship gets damaged. The second risk is that a boss who eases in and pretends not to do so is essentially lying. The boss is representing herself as open-minded but in fact has already made up her mind. The problem is that we have all sat in front of bosses who tried to ease us into a decision they had already made, and we generally found out somewhere along the way that we were not in a real "discussion." And if we didn't find out on the spot, we found out later. In all cases, we understood that the boss was being disingenuous with us.

If subordinates catch their boss being insincere, they are likely to spend more time asking themselves what else the boss is keeping up her sleeve. At the very least, they will not get a sense of self-determination and relatedness from the interaction. Their boss is treating them like a pawn, leaving them the alternative of playing along or resisting and provoking a confrontation. Our view is that other things being equal, lying is a bad idea for a boss, especially if you know ahead of time that you are almost certain to get caught!

So why did the boss in the caselet think he needed to ease in? Because as in the first case, the boss's framing of the issue was narrow, binary, and frozen. The binary aspect is obvious: The interaction will be a success for the boss if the subordinate agrees to get off the committee without losing her motivation for her "day job"; it will be a failure otherwise. The framing does not evolve as the discussion progresses, as in the first case, though here we understand better why—the subordinate is playing along and not offering much resistance. With respect to the breadth of the frame, the boss enters the meeting with the following reasoning:

- *Implicit belief:* Committee members should talk. If they don't, their performance is deemed to be unsatisfactory.

- My subordinate does not speak much during the meetings of the NPD committee. (I think it's because she is overworked, though I cannot be sure.)

- Hence she must be removed from the committee.
- She pays more attention than most people to external signs of power, hence
- I must be pretty crafty on this one.

This framing is very narrow to the extent that it excludes many valuable solutions the boss might have wanted to examine, such as the following:

- Does the subordinate realize she does not contribute much to the committee?
- If so, why doesn't she talk more? (For example, she might feel that because her boss is the chairman of the committee, he can contribute most of what she can say, and maybe does.)
- Does the subordinate enjoy being on the committee?
- Are there benefits for her to be on the committee? (For example, she may not contribute much but maybe learns a lot; the committee gives her visibility to senior managers; etc.)
- If overwork is indeed an issue, can the subordinate more profitably let go of other duties to free up time and energy?

Overall, the boss framed the issue narrowly: "Let's get her off the committee with minimum breakage." This framing almost dictated the choice of tactic: "This is going to be pretty tricky, so I'd better control the discussion pretty tightly." The boss could instead have framed the interaction fairly loosely: "I have this great subordinate who doesn't say much on the committee. Let's sit down and talk about her work, the committee, her career plans, and how committee membership fits in them." This framing would have been much less threatening for the boss and would not have required a unilateral approach designed to maintain control over the interaction and "win."

## The Way Bosses Frame "Giving Feedback"

Earlier in the chapter we discussed why bosses are often reluctant to engage in performance improvement processes with their perceived weaker performers. Sitting down with members of the out-group to give them solid feedback is simply not very encouraging—the costs seem to outweigh the benefits. In the last section we illustrated bosses' propensity to frame stressful and threatening situations in a restrictive way, and we showed how this framing condemns bosses to use strategies (forthright or easing in) that involve substantial risks of escalation. Let's now join these two discussions and examine how bosses frame interventions where they give feedback to their subordinates.

The very words "giving feedback" give it away: "Feedback" is something that bosses have and subordinates "get." So bosses are going to "give it" to subordinates. The implicit complement is that this feedback is right, of course. On that basis, bosses tend to frame giving feedback as follows:

- Bill's performance is not up to my expectations.
- I know why: Bill has the following shortcomings or skill or character deficiency.
- I want to tell Bill about the problem, but he may not like hearing what I have to say. So he may be hurt (and I don't like hurting people), and he may try to hurt me in return.
- Also, if Bill refuses the feedback and pushes back on me, things may escalate and worsen the current situation.
- So I've got to tell Bill in a way that improves the likelihood he will accept the feedback, even though I have developed significant doubts about Bill's ability to use that feedback to develop.

Once again we see narrow, binary, and frozen framing. In particular, this framing excludes from the boss's mind some potentially interesting issues and questions, such as the following:

- *Bill's performance is not up to my expectations.* Am I right? What exactly am I faulting Bill for? On what evidence am I basing my assessment? Could I be missing part of the picture?
- *I know why: It's Bill.* What about me? Could I be contributing to the situation? If so, how?
- *Bill may not like this and may push back on me.* Then again, Bill is probably very aware of the uneasiness that has

developed between the two of us and may want to discuss it. Bill may also be aware of some of his shortcomings and not know how to go about improving them.

- *I'm not sure Bill can use the feedback to improve.* No, but you cannot be sure either that Bill can't develop. We have established that once caught up in the set-up-to-fail syndrome, Bill did not blossom. But we now understand better how debilitating this syndrome is and how easy it is even for solid performers to get caught in it. So it may well be that if we modify input conditions, Bill has a significant margin of improvement.

Overall, these questions would lead us to modify the framing of giving feedback toward something like this:

> I am not happy with Bill's present performance nor with our relationship. Bill probably feels the malaise as much as, or even more than, I do. He probably wants this job and our relationship to work, at least as much as I do. So we both want the same thing but somehow we're not getting it right now. Let's sit down and discuss why, and how I can help.

This framing is not binary (there's no clear pass-fail criterion), it is broad, and hence it is flexible. It is a good basis for the bilateral intervention that may help bosses interrupt the set-up-to-fail syndrome.

## From Pain to Gain

Managers generally have little difficulty identifying the costs of intervention. First there is the immediate anxiety and threat associated with discussing performance, one's own and the subordinate's. Then there is the time and energy that will be devoted to delivering on the promise—trying to change your own behavior, coaching the subordinate, giving more feedback. There are also concerns that the intervention may only "postpone the inevitable" and may therefore prove a waste of time. Worse still, the discussion may send the wrong performance signals to others. "If I engage in discussion rather than take assertive action, I may be seen as too collaborative, too soft on underperformance. That won't be good for results, and it certainly won't be good for my reputation."

Dealing with the problem through intervention clearly demands time and energy—but, as we have seen in this and the previous chapters, so does *not* dealing with it. The costs are high and the relationship will not spontaneously self-correct. Bosses squander too much time living with "lost causes" of their own making.

As we see it, there *is* a choice. Bosses can continue their tail-chasing efforts to haul subordinates toward acceptable performance, knowing that they will have to pay steadily more—in terms of increased monitoring and control—to offset the subordinate's deteriorating performance. Or else bosses can invest the time helping subordinates become more autonomous, perform better on the job, and demand progressively less attention from above. It is a question of increasing the pull of subordinates—their instinct to learn and develop ownership—in order to lessen the boss's need to push. Our basic assertion is that bosses do *not* need to spend more time with lower performers; they simply need to change the way they use that time to change the dynamics of the relationship.

Imagining a low probability of resolution, bosses figure, "Why put my own back against the wall? Why start a process that engages my own success, not just the subordinate's? If the subordinate doesn't deliver, I will then have to take more drastic action. Who knows where it might end?"

That reasoning is often based on the failure of past interventions. But these previous attempts failed for two predictable reasons: First, weaker performers tend to refuse the boss's feedback, as they perceive it to be developed and communicated unfairly. Second, when bosses finally intervene, they tend to frame the interaction in narrow, binary, and frozen ways—in other words, they approach the discussion with the aim of "fixing the subordinate" or getting the subordinate to own up or understand, at which point the subordinate switches into defensive mode.

Effective interventions are not about the boss giving feedback. They are about the boss and subordinate engaging in a joint dialogue in which their *mutual* behaviors and intentions are up for discussion. Chapter 8 shows what that looks like in practice.

# 8

## Cracking
## the Syndrome

You cannot shake hands with a clenched fist.

—Indira Ghandi

WITH A CLEAR UNDERSTANDING of the common dysfunction found in the dynamic with bosses and subordinates, we are now ready to intervene and try to interrupt the set-up-to-fail syndrome. We'll explore a number of concrete actions bosses can take to be proactive in reversing the syndrome. To illustrate the general principles involved in the process, we present a real-life situation involving two people we met during our research: Steve, a subordinate, and Jeff, his boss. Steve and Jeff's situation is an excellent example of how misperceptions and wrong attributions can create a downward performance spiral that once it is put into motion is difficult to change. We'll walk you through their situation and offer specific tactics and methods for intervention.

## Steve's Story

Steve was a manufacturing supervisor for a Fortune 100 company. When we first met him, he came across as highly motivated, energetic, and proactive. He was on top of his operation, monitoring problems and addressing them quickly. His boss expressed great confidence in him and rated his performance as excellent. Accordingly, Steve was chosen to lead a new production line, considered essential to the future of the plant.

In this new job, Steve reported to Jeff, recently recruited into the company. In the first few weeks of the relationship, Jeff periodically asked Steve to write up short analyses of significant quality-control rejections. Although he didn't really explain it to Steve at the time, Jeff's request had two major objectives: to generate information that would speed their joint learning on this new production process, and to help Steve develop the good habit of systematically performing root-cause analyses of quality problems. Also, being new on the job himself, Jeff wanted to show his *own* boss that he was on top of the operation. After careful consideration, Jeff chose to ask for the analysis in writing instead of verbally because he wanted to give Steve a chance to respond in his own time—and so as not to put Steve on the spot by asking him a question that he might not be able to answer.

Unaware of Jeff's motives, Steve balked; why, he wondered, should he submit reports on information he understood and monitored himself? Partly owing to lack of time, partly to hold off what he regarded as interference by his boss, Steve invested little energy in the reports. Their delay and uneven quality annoyed Jeff, who started to suspect that Steve was not a particularly proactive manager. He asked for the reports again, this time more forcefully. For Steve, this request merely confirmed that Jeff did not trust him. He progressively withdrew from interaction with him, meeting his demands with increased passive resistance. Before long, Jeff became *convinced* that Steve was not proactive enough and couldn't handle his job without help. He increased his supervision of Steve's every move—to Steve's predictable dismay. One year after excitedly taking on the new production line, Steve was so dispirited that he was thinking of quitting.

Like many managers, Jeff and Steve are locked in a negative performance spiral. Before we look at how they might interrupt it, it's worth noting how easily it could have been averted. The development of the spiral rests on a major misunderstanding that occurred within the first few days. It need never have happened if Jeff had been a bit more up-front about what he hoped to achieve and why.

It could also have been averted if Steve had said to his boss, "Look, I feel a bit overmonitored . . . can we talk about this?" But to avoid immediate threat and embarrassment, neither party addressed the issue—and then they started making assumptions about each other's motives, which quickly led the relationship to degenerate. It became a mutual setup. And at that point, it became difficult to fix. So how should they proceed?

## Taking Your Thoughts to Court

It's an old cliché that the first step in solving a problem is to recognize that one exists. But in this case, the cliché is particularly accurate. The set-up-to-fail syndrome is both *self-fulfilling* and *self-reinforcing,* which obscures the boss's responsibility in the process as well as some of the key psychological and social mechanisms involved. Bosses can only develop the openness of mind required to increase the probability of a successful intervention if they accept that they are probably part of the problem.

Once this awareness is achieved, the first step of the intervention must be a serious preparation phase. This phase has two basic objectives: The first is to allow the boss to work on mentally reframing the forthcoming discussions in a broader, more flexible way. At the end of chapter 7 we proposed a reframing of the boss's approach along the following lines:

> I am not happy with Bill's present performance nor with our relationship. Bill probably feels the malaise as much as, or even more than, I do. He probably wants this job and our relationship to work, at least as much as I do. So we both want the same thing but somehow we're not getting it right now. Let's sit down and discuss why, and how I can help.

Each boss must come up with his or her formulation, but the framing must be broad and flexible enough to help the boss avoid the feelings of anxiety and stress that come with narrow, binary framings. This intervention is meant to help interrupt a syndrome that is costly for the subordinate, so the boss should start from the premise that the subordinate will be open to improving the situation. The framing must also explicitly include the boss's contribution to the dysfunctions. If the boss enters the meeting intent on fixing the subordinate, we're back to square one.

Building on this last point, we can look at the second objective of the preparation period: to help bosses gather the data and develop the openness of mind that will allow them to convince the subordinate that, this time, the feedback development and communication process is fair. Notice the two dimensions: the data, on one hand—bosses must be able to support their views—and, on the other, openness of mind, without which the boss will not be able to solicit and take into account subordinates' input on their performance and the conditions they operate in.

More specifically, bosses must separate emotion from reality through self-questioning. They must prepare themselves mentally to be open to the subordinate's views, including the possibility that the subordinate will challenge the "evidence" about performance levels. It will be much easier for bosses to be open to challenge during the discussion if, when preparing for the meeting, they have already challenged their own preconceptions and opened enough of a doubt in their minds.

Reviewing the history of those relationships, bosses need to ask themselves some searching questions: "Were our interactions always so difficult? Has something changed in the relationship? Was Marc [the subordinate] always this bad? In fact, is Marc really as bad as I believe? What hard evidence do I have to support this view? In precisely which areas is Marc really weak?" When thinking through these issues, bosses must try to look at things from the subordinate's point of view. "Given the chance to respond, how might Marc react to these charges? Sure, he would complain about an increased workload, insufficient resources, or disruptive organizational changes. But are those excuses really without merit? Could he have a point? Could it be that, under other circumstances or coming from someone else, I might have viewed them more favorably?"

Turning the question around, "what are the things Marc does well? He must have shown some qualities to be recruited or promoted in the first place. Did these qualities evaporate all of a sudden?"

Then come the awkward questions about the boss's blind spots and prejudices: "Could there be other factors, aside from perfor-

mance, that led me to label 'Sheila' a weaker performer? How did
we reach this point? For example, did she experience a change in
personal circumstances? Could it be that my actions turned a
momentary dip into a long slide? To what extent has my behavior
contributed? In particular, does my behavior reflect a lack of confidence? How can I try to interrupt this process and create a more positive dynamic?"

Taking one's thoughts "to court" in this way is a crucial preliminary step. It allows bosses to question their own defensive
mechanisms and to screen out some of the emotional interference
obscuring their perceptions. This may even involve playing out part
of the conversation beforehand, possibly with a colleague or a partner, who could push back on their preconceptions.[1] If bosses are absolutely *convinced* they know something, their openness to learning
is impaired. The tone of the discussion will quickly become accu-
satory or condescending: They have worked out what the problem
is, and now they have to get the subordinate to own up or understand. Learning means discovering facts that might modify their
causal attributions, not going in with a fixed mind (see "Keeping an
Open Mind").

This introspective phase is critical and often discomforting, but
the real difficulty starts with the next phase. That is when bosses
must discuss their contribution to the subordinate's lackluster performance. Initiating that discussion requires a leap of faith and a
high degree of candor, tolerance, and courage from bosses to invite
commentary on the impact of their behavior. That may not sound
like an attractive proposition, but it is the cost of repairing the damage—or to put it another way, the price of learning.

Before getting to the specifics of the intervention, it is important
to articulate one of its cornerstones. Throughout the meetings and
discussions, the boss must keep in mind the principles of fair
process. The notion of fair process relates not to "was the outcome
favorable or not?" but rather to "was the process that led to the outcome fair?" The distinction between these two dimensions is crucial
because an increasing body of research evidence shows that when
people perceive a process as fair, they are more willing to accept its
outcome, *even when it is unfavorable to them*. We saw that in chapter
6, with the Air France employees who ratified a much tougher

## KEEPING AN OPEN MIND

To enter the discussion with an open mind, the boss needs to prepare carefully. This preparation involves a great deal of introspection, the result of which is captured by three statements:

- **You may be wrong about their performance!** Remember the experiments showing that bosses have selective observation and recall about performance of subordinates. Are you really sure your "observations" are fair? Your interpretation of what you remember observing may be wrong or unrepresentative.
- **You may be right, but there may be reasons!** The performance assessment is accurate, but there are reasons (e.g., the subordinate was never trained to do this task, or you never made it clear that it was a priority for you), not necessarily linked to lack of effort or ability.
- **You may be one of the reasons!** Your own behavior may have been contributing to the subordinate's lack of drive, motivation, initiative, or self-confidence.

More concretely, here are a few summary questions the bosses must consider during their preparation:

1. Reviewing the history of the relationship, were things (e.g., subordinate behavior and performance, the relationship itself) always what they are today? If things have been degrading over time, was there a clear starting point?
2. How bad is the subordinate's performance, *really?* What's the evidence? If confronted with these points, what would the subordinate say? Taking these "excuses" one by one, does she or he have a point on some of these?
3. Let's look at the positive. What qualities can we build on?
4. To what extent am I part of the problem? Which of the behaviors discussed so far do I regularly display with this subordinate? Why do I do these things? Would there be any other way for me to accomplish my objectives?

restructuring plan because they believed it had been developed and communicated in a way they deemed fair.

Based on the research conducted to date, people seem to take into account the following five dimensions when assessing whether a process was fair:[2]

- Were their views heard? Was there some effort to gather and take their views into account?
- Were the decisions and rules applied consistently?
- Did they receive timely feedback?
- Was the decision based on sound facts and reasoning?
- Was communication during and after the process sufficient, sincere, and genuine?

On that basis, let us now turn to the specifics of what we call a "good productive intervention."

## Undoing the Past

As we discussed in chapter 7, there is not much point launching an intervention unless the boss has done some serious preliminary thinking. But even with good preparation, bosses typically still experience some degree of discomfort during these discussions. That is not all bad. The subordinate will probably be somewhat uncomfortable as well, and it is reassuring to see that the boss is human too.

It would be difficult—and indeed, detrimental—to provide a detailed script of what such a conversation should sound like. A boss walking into the intervention's first session with a rigid plan for the conversation would not be able to engage in real dialogue with the subordinate, because real dialogue requires intense listening and real-time processing of, and adaptation to, what the other party says and does.[3] As a guiding framework, however, we offer six components that characterize most effective interventions beyond the initial preparation phase. While a successful intervention will probably involve all six steps, they are not strictly sequential nor do they need to be addressed within the same meeting. The boss and/or the subordinate may feel the need to stop the conversation to take time to process what was said so far and to gain perspective on it. The conversation can resume later.

### First, the boss must create the right context for the discussion.

The first order of business is for the boss to request a meeting with the subordinate. It would be both unfair to the subordinate and probably ineffective to hold the meeting on the spot. If the boss has been preparing the meeting for a few days, she has had a chance to gather her thoughts, examine the evidence, think about the evolution of the relationship, and mentally frame the meeting in broad and flexible terms. The subordinate has gone through none of these steps and hence must be given some time to gather his thoughts and take them to court, to reuse our earlier expression.

This process does not take weeks, however, so the meeting should be scheduled soon after the boss requests it to prevent the subordinate from becoming unnecessarily anxious. An executive commenting on this dimension remarked, "Too often, we tell people a week ahead of time that we really want to meet with them to discuss an important issue. That may be ideal for the boss's schedule, but the subordinate is bound to spend a heck of a bad week!"

The boss should be precise when pitching the meeting so the subordinate doesn't envision a one-sided "blame fest." The session should therefore *not* be billed as feedback, but rather as an exchange. As we have said before, "giving feedback" is a loaded term, evoking a "truth" in need of communication, a one-directional flow, a monologue delivered by the boss to the subordinate. Perceived underperformers are familiar with such sessions and are unlikely to enter into such discussions with a very open mind. They will brace themselves against attack.

Three key ideas may help prevent the subordinate from becoming defensive in anticipation. First, the boss should indicate that he wants to discuss not only the subordinate's performance but also their relationship and their performance as a dyad. He should acknowledge the perceived tension in their relationship and express a desire to use the conversation as a way to decrease it. Second, the boss should confirm his strong desire to improve the situation and state that he is confident that they can do so together. Third, in setting the context, the boss should emphasize the expectation of a genuinely open dialogue. To underline this, he should acknowledge a likely part of responsibility in the situation and clearly signal that his own behavior toward the subordinate will be fair game for commentary.

To help prepare for the forthcoming meeting, the boss could suggest that the subordinate may want to give some thought to a few questions, for example:

- How are we doing as a dyad? How good are our communication and overall relationship?

- Which aspects of your job do you find easiest? Which are you most comfortable with? And which do you find most difficult?

- To what extent do I help you perform? Are there things I do that make life more difficult for you?

- Overall, what can we do to improve your performance, my performance, our joint performance, and our relationship?

The location of the meeting is also important. Logistics matter. The boss should select a time and place for the meeting that reduces the perceived threat for the subordinate. Different surroundings will help both parties break with previous roles, routines, and assumptions—and to see each other in a different light. A meeting outside of both parties' offices, for example, may be more conducive to open dialogue and will also help minimize disruptions.

The boss should also give some thought to requesting help for the meeting. Some bosses have told us that they felt ill equipped for such conversations and, in order to keep them honest and help them be more productive, had requested some help from an internal facilitator or an HR colleague. The downside of this approach is that an outsider's presence, particularly if from the human resources department, can make the discussion seem more formal. A wary subordinate might wonder whether the HR manager is there to help or to document the proceedings for potential future administrative or legal action. Nevertheless, some bosses have told us they benefited from being supported through the process. It is hence an alternative to consider.

*Second, boss and subordinate must come to an
agreement on the symptoms of the problem.*

No employee is ineffective on all aspects of the job. And few—if
any—employees want to do their jobs poorly. Mentioning a few
dimensions where the subordinate's performance is solid or high-
lighting the evolution of the subordinate's performance over time
lends credibility to the boss's comments on dimensions where performance is weaker. They must come to a mutual understanding of
the specific dimensions of the job on which the subordinate is weak.

For instance, with the case of Steve and Jeff, an exhaustive sorting of the *evidence* might have led to an agreement that Steve's
underperformance was not general but largely confined to the quality of the reports he submitted (or failed to submit!). In other situations, it might be agreed that a purchasing manager was weak when
it came to finding offshore suppliers and to contributing in meetings. Or a new investment professional and her boss might come to
agree that her performance was subpar when it came to timing the
sales and purchase of stocks, but they might also agree that her
financial analysis of stocks was quite strong. The idea here is that
before working to improve performance or reduce tension in a relationship, agreement must be reached about what areas of performance are under contention.

We used the word *evidence* to refer to the case of Steve and Jeff.
That is because if the intervention is to be useful, the boss's identification of weak performance should be backed up by facts and data.
It cannot be based on "feelings"—as when Jeff told Steve, "I just
have the feeling you're not putting energy into the reports." Instead,
Jeff needs to describe what a good report would look like and the
ways Steve's reports fall short. Likewise, the subordinate must be
allowed—indeed encouraged—to defend his performance and point
out areas of strength. After all, just because the boss has an opinion
about performance does not make it a fact. In sum, the goal of this
aspect of the intervention is to drive toward a mutual understanding of where performance problems truly exist, based on the best
facts available to both parties.

The boss must keep in mind that her past behavior has probably led the subordinate to regard her as "biased and unfair," and

hence to dismiss a good part of the feedback she has provided in the past. To help the subordinate accept this feedback as valid, the boss must convince the subordinate that, this time, she has developed her feedback carefully and is communicating it fairly. As we discussed in chapter 7, subordinates are more likely to attribute fairness to the feedback *development* process when the boss has collected all relevant information, allows the subordinate to provide clarifications and explanations, genuinely considers them, and applies consistent standards when delivering criticism. As for feedback *communication,* the subordinate is more likely to perceive it as fair if the boss demonstrates during the discussion that she pays careful attention to the subordinate's ideas, shows respect, and is supportive despite their disagreement.

*Third, boss and subordinate should arrive at a common understanding of what might be causing the weak performance in certain areas.*

Once the areas of weak performance have been identified, it is time to unearth the reasons for those weaknesses. Focusing on the subordinate, does he have limited skills in organizing work, managing his time, or working with others? Does he lack experience, knowledge, or capabilities? Do boss and subordinate agree on the order of priorities? Maybe the subordinate has neglected a particular dimension of the work because the boss did not indicate its importance— or else did not specify that timeliness was more important than perfection. Or again, does the subordinate become less effective under pressure? Does he have lower performance standards than the boss? One, some, or all of these reasons may underlie the performance problem(s) at hand, and it is critical to isolate them so that they may, if needed, be addressed or corrected in the future.

These reasons can, and most likely do, include the boss's behavior toward the subordinate. So the boss should bring her behavior up again and invite the subordinate to offer direct feedback on it. The key in this part of the intervention is to uncover and analyze the *reasons* why the employee is not meeting the boss's performance expectations. If the boss acknowledges that she deplores the tension in their relationship, the subordinate will find it easier to bring up his own feelings during the discussion. The boss might even try to describe the dynamics of the set-up-to-fail syndrome. "Does my behavior toward you make things worse?" she might prompt. Or: "What am I doing that leads you to feel so much pressure?" The boss may also level with the subordinate: "By the way, there are certain things you do that really push my buttons and contribute to this."

This component of the discussion also needs to make explicit the assumptions that the boss and the subordinate have thus far been making. Many misunderstandings start with untested assumptions about the other party's intentions. Boss and subordinate must each state their observations and explain the tentative conclusions they drew from them—"Here is what I observed, and it leads me to think that . . . "—and then allow the other party to react. For example, Jeff might have said, "When you did not supply me with the reports I asked, I guess I concluded you were not very proactive." That would have allowed Steve to bring his buried assumptions into the open. "No," he might have answered, "I just reacted negatively because you asked for the reports in writing, which I took as a sign of excessive control." "I meant to help you by giving you more time to work on them, rather than catching you by surprise and on the spot," Jeff could have responded. Mutual irritation blinded them to the possibility of benign explanations.

Similarly, bosses should express to the subordinate the quandary in which they often feel stuck, such as "I realize I typically do not give you assignments that would help you develop your skills, but when I have tried to do so your response has not always been positive, such as in the case of . . . " Or "I realize I monitor you a lot and that you may as a result feel I don't trust you, but my problem is that you often don't volunteer information on problems until it's very late, such as [in this and that case], so I kind of feel I've got to be looking for information myself." As we mentioned before, subordinates often do not understand fully the constraints under which their boss operates, so the boss must help subordinates see that, even with the best of intentions on the boss's part, their behavior sometimes creates difficult dilemmas for the boss.

It is possible that, around this stage of the discussion, subordinates will bring up past injustices they feel were committed toward them. This is not the most pleasant part of the conversation for the boss, whose strong desire is to cast the past aside and set the bases for a brighter future. It is, however, an important moment for subordinates. Bosses should devote some time to listening to the subordinates' gripes, bearing in mind three things. First, it is important to allow subordinates to vent and start "getting the past off their chest." Most of us have people we can call on to listen to our frustrations and allow us some time to vent. Venting does not make the problem go away, but it does, sometimes, help release some of the internal pressure.

Second, listening can help the boss better understand subordinates' sensitivities; we don't always realize how much simple things can hurt others and subordinates can provide bosses valuable information on that front. And third, the boss should be aware that the subordinate's complaints about the past may allow the boss to try to redress an injustice, if appropriate, or at least explain to the subordinate the intentions and reasoning that were guiding his behavior at the time. Bosses often too easily think that because they cannot change the past, they don't need to talk about it. Yes, we can generally not undo what was done, but we can certainly explain why we did it and, when appropriate, apologize for the harm done even if it was not our intention to do harm.

As in medicine, the right diagnosis must take account of all the major symptoms. The difference here is that boss and subordinate identify the root problems *together*. Only then can they discuss how to cure these weaknesses. Of course, a barrier to that discussion is raised if the subordinate categorically denies having a problem.

**When Subordinates Are Unaware of Their Own Weaknesses.** We have so far assumed that subordinates can and will engage in a genuine discussion of their strengths and weaknesses. In our research with subordinates caught in set-up-to-fail syndromes, we have met very few who saw themselves as perfect and in no need of improvement. It is a fact, however, that some subordinates do overestimate the quality of their work performance: they are simply unaware of their weaknesses. A major cause of this phenomenon is that past bosses have been reluctant to confront the subordinates on their shortcomings. In the absence of past negative feedback on key aspects of their behavior and/or performance, subordinates could be genuinely shocked by the boss's feedback and be tempted to reject it as biased and personal. "You're my fifth boss, and no one ever mentioned any of this to me—on the contrary, I was complimented for [this and that aspect]—you must be wrong or biased."

We have no magic wand to make the discomfort of such moments go away, nor any magic pill the boss can give the subordinate to see things in an objective way instantaneously. We do have three pieces of advice. The first one goes back to our discussion of data and evidence. It is always important for bosses to be well prepared for such meetings and be able to provide examples to subordinates—and especially in this kind of case, as these subordinates are much more likely to reject the diagnostic outright than are their counterparts who have received development feedback before.

Our second suggestion is to communicate empathy with the subordinate's predicament. The boss may even want to communicate this empathy first. By not being challenged on important sources of underperformance, the subordinate was failed by his previous bosses, and maybe by his current boss as well. This collective failure, as well as the difficulty that it now creates for the current boss and for the subordinate, has to be acknowledged. In a recent article discussing "difficult conversations," communication expert Holly Weeks considers the case of a boss confronted with a subordinate gifted with such a mean sense of humor that it affected coworkers' performance and, increasingly, their willingness to work with him. No one had ever challenged the subordinate on this issue. Weeks proposed the following introduction to the conversation:

> Jeremy, the quality of your work has been undercut—in part by the reluctance of your colleagues to risk the edge of your humor by talking through problems with you. I share responsibility for this because I have been reluctant to speak openly about these difficulties with you, whom I like and respect and with whom I have worked a long time.[4]

Each boss must choose the words she feels comfortable with and means genuinely. The objective, however, should be to communicate empathy for the difficult situation the subordinate faces, and to acknowledge that past bosses—and maybe yourself, the current one—share some responsibility in this process.

Last suggestion: We mentioned earlier that the intervention could evolve during more than one conversation. It may be particularly appropriate to plan *not* to do everything in one go when the subordinate is likely to be heavily surprised by the diagnostic and evidence. He may benefit from having some time to digest the information before being able to discuss intelligently "where do we go from here?" and "how can we improve things?"

### Fourth, boss and subordinate should arrive at a joint contract on their performance objectives and their relationship going forward.

To pursue the medical analogy, the diagnosing of an illness leads to a prescription. Things are a bit more complex when repairing organizational dysfunctions, since modifying behavior and developing complex skills are more difficult than taking a few pills! Another key distinction is that the object of the exercise is not to "fix" the subordinate but rather to find a joint cure: Boss and subordinate must use the intervention to plot a course of treatment to address their mutual failings.

The cure should include action items for *both parties*. It should identify the ways they can improve on their skills, knowledge, experience, or personal relationship. The time frame of action and expected results should be specified. If the symptoms show no signs of abating, they may have the wrong diagnostic, or the subordinate (and/or the boss) might be experiencing difficulties implementing the agreed-upon changes. Either way, there is a need for progress reviews along the way. The aim is not to wait until the end of the "trial period" only to say to the subordinate, "Sorry, you didn't quite make it. Jolly close, though!"

These review mechanisms also need to be negotiated. This requires an explicit discussion of *how much* and *what type* of future supervision the boss will perform. The proposed solution needs to cater to both sets of needs. Clearly, the boss's excessive involvement can be inhibiting; but she also has ideas, contacts, and resources to contribute, and she knows things that the subordinate does not. Furthermore, the boss is accountable upward and therefore needs to be kept informed of what's going on—but in a way that does not eliminate all autonomy for the subordinate. The subordinate has a right to empowerment, but equally the boss has a right to sleep at night.

Greater latitude, delegation, and trust do not imply abdication. It is legitimate for bosses to monitor and have some involvement in their subordinates' work, particularly when a subordinate has shown limitations on some facets of the job. From the subordinate's point of view, however, such involvement by the boss is acceptable, possibly even welcome, if the goal is to help the subordinate develop and improve over time. Most subordinates can accept *temporary* involvement that relents as their performance improves. The problem is intense monitoring and control that never seem to go away.

### *Fifth, boss and subordinate should build on the conversation they just had, to agree on more open communication for the future.*

While boss and subordinate may have charted a way out of the current mess, they also have to take measures to make sure that they don't slip back into their old ways. The aim is not to engage in periodic "summit meetings" as a pair, but rather to avoid the need for such realignments.

Having set the new trajectory, how can they be sure that they each hold up their side of the bargain? They must convert their intentions into actions. The subordinate has to start delivering, but the boss also has to make an effort to drop the selective observation and recall, and also the biased attributions. As we noted in chapter 4, bosses have an incredible ability to interpret behavior and outcomes to suit their expectations. For the relationship to improve, the boss needs to give the subordinate credit for improvements.

How bosses make this behavioral transition and learn to live by the new rules is discussed in chapter 10. A good starting point, however, is to monitor each other. As part of the closure, the boss could say, "Next time I do something that communicates low expectations, can you let me know right away?" And the subordinate might say, or be encouraged to say, "Next time I do something that aggravates you or that you do not understand, can you let me know quicker, too?" These simple requests can open the door to a more honest relationship almost instantly.

*Sixth, the boss must follow through on the contract that was agreed upon—not as part of the initial intervention but very much as part of the process.*

A manager's preoccupation with fair process must in no way be confused with low performance standards, weakness, or permissiveness. Boss and subordinate agreed to make some changes, perform certain actions, and/or reach certain performance targets by a given date. Remember, the boss must make sure that much communication occurs during the "contract period." She must also reach some closure by the end of that period by reviewing with the subordinate how well they are doing against the contract.

Ideally the contract objectives should be specific enough, and the communication process during the contract period effective enough, that both parties will agree on the assessment of the outcomes. A fair process should also increase the likelihood that the subordinate will be honest in his self-appraisal. Ultimately, however, the boss is responsible for assessing the outcome and deciding on appropriate actions. Possible actions should include removal from the job. Whether that implies removal from the company then depends on a number of criteria, including the needs of the firm (influenced in part by its economic situation) and the skill profile of the employee (e.g., does the employee have major strengths that could be better used elsewhere within the firm, or strengths that could be better used in another company, or a "bland profile" with no major strengths).

## Who Dares, Wins

How high a payback the boss gets and what form it takes obviously depend on the outcome of the intervention. That, in turn, depends on the quality of the intervention, as well as key contextual factors, such as the resolve of the two parties and how long the relationship has been in a tailspin. There are two main dimensions along which an improvement can occur: the subordinate's performance and the quality of the relationship.

We cannot predict the probability of achieving any particular outcome, as it depends on too many factors. We can, however, say that whatever the outcome, there is always some return on the boss's investment. In the best-case scenario, the intervention leads to a mixture of coaching, training, job redesign, and a clearing of the air; as a result, the subordinate's performance improves, the relationship improves, and the costs associated with the syndrome go away—or at least decrease measurably.

A rarer outcome is the scenario in which performance improves but the relationship does not. Of course, this depends on what we mean by *relationship*. It is quite plausible that the boss-subordinate relationship would not change much in terms of warmth, social exchange, and consideration. Their respective personalities, outlooks, and demographic characteristics may mean they are not cut out for that kind of rapport. But a *working* relationship has many other facets, including respect, openness, and trust. It is difficult to imagine an intervention that produces better performance but does not also ease the working relationship *in some way*. The mere fact that the boss sat down, clarified expectations, listened, and offered help must earn some respect from the subordinate. Probably the case where the relationship would improve the least is where the intervention is really an exercise in behavioral control. The subordinate either misunderstood or disagreed with the boss's priorities. Once these are spelled out, the subordinate chooses to comply, in the interests of self-preservation. Thus performance improves in the boss's eyes, but the relationship is not really more trusting or bilateral. Nevertheless, the fact that the subordinate now gets less grief from the boss, and less monitoring or disdain, makes the relationship less stressful. At the very least the relationship is no longer a drag on performance: It has gone from bad to bearable.

The other scenario sees the subordinate's performance improve only marginally, but because the subordinate received an honest and open hearing from the boss, the relationship between the two becomes more productive. Boss and subordinate develop a better understanding of those job dimensions on which the subordinate struggles or does well. This improved understanding provides leverage to try to improve the situation further. For example, it would allow boss and subordinate to explore *together* how they can develop a better fit between the job and the subordinate's strengths and weaknesses. That improved fit can be achieved by significantly modifying the subordinate's existing job or by transferring the subordinate to another job within the company. It may even result in the subordinate choosing to leave the company.

While that outcome is not as successful as the first one, it is still productive; a more honest relationship eases the strain on both boss and subordinate, on the team, and in turn on the people the subordinate manages. And if a transfer results in a better fit with the new job, the subordinate will become a stronger performer. Relocation will also free up a slot for a potentially better performer in the subordinate's old job.

In fact, we do not believe that the nature of the outcome necessarily reflects on the quality of the intervention. The boss can achieve a highly productive intervention with a negative outcome. Even in the worst of cases, bosses have rehearsed and projected fair process, have developed their communication and leadership skills, and have modeled the behavior for other members of the team.

The set-up-to-fail syndrome is not an organizational fatality. It can be cured. The first step is for the boss to become aware of its existence and acknowledge a possible role in the dynamic. The second step requires the boss to prepare carefully, then initiate a clear and focused intervention. Such an intervention demands an open *exchange* between boss and subordinate based on the evidence of poor performance, its underlying causes, and their joint responsibility—culminating in a joint decision on how to proceed, both on the "problem" itself and in their future relationship. (For a recap, see "Starting Over.")

Curing the syndrome requires managers to challenge their own assumptions. It also demands that they have the courage to look inside themselves for causes and solutions rather than placing the burden of responsibility where it does not fully belong. We don't pretend to have a silver bullet that makes such a discussion easy or a sure-fire success, but we can use the case of Steve and Jeff to offer some additional insights on what a good productive intervention looks like and how to undertake a root-cause analysis.

---

## STARTING OVER: A RECAP

A good, productive intervention must be *thought through,* must be *explicit,* and must *culminate in a joint decision.* First, bosses should gather their thoughts and their evidence, then take them "to court" to create the openness of mind required by the meeting and enhance the perceived fairness of their feedback. The intervention process itself involves the following six steps:

1. **Setting the stage.** The boss should acknowledge the tension and admit some responsibility for problems in the employee's performance. The subordinate should feel free to discuss the boss's behavior. Choosing an appropriate context and positioning the meeting well will help.
2. **Agreeing on the symptoms.** Resting on solid evidence, the two parties must come to an agreement on the symptoms they are going to address. In particular, they must identify the specific areas where they concur the subordinate has struggled.
3. **Diagnosing the causes.** The boss and the subordinate must jointly explore the causes of weak performance, including how the boss's behavior has affected that performance. The boss may give the subordinate some space to vent past grievances.
4. **Finding the cure.** The two parties should agree on performance objectives and on specific actions on both sides that will help reach these objectives and improve the relationship.
5. **Preventing relapse.** Both sides should pledge to address future problems earlier and open the door to more open communication.
6. **Monitoring the effectiveness of the treatment.** Beyond the initial discussions, the two parties must hold periodic progress reviews to assess how well the treatment is working and discuss its evolution over time.

---

## Steve and Jeff Unwind

Let's consider how Jeff, Steve's boss, might have tried to interrupt the negative spiral. Jeff would approach the discussion with three objectives in mind:

1. *Acknowledge* and discuss the issue of uneasiness in the relationship

2. *Address* the specific performance issue (the quality of Steve's follow-up on quality-control rejections)

3. *Ensure* that such a problem does not develop again between Jeff and Steve in the future—which requires a discussion of "how did we get to this?"

The first thing for Jeff to do is to decide where to hold the discussion. As mentioned earlier, it is probably best to opt for a reasonably neutral and informal setting, rather than an office, which might be charged with the memories of previous difficult or unpleasant conversations.

Then Jeff could say to Steve something like the following:

> There is something I would like to discuss with you. We have been working together for almost a year now, and I think we both know things have not been working out as well as you and I would have liked. On one hand, I do have a problem with some aspects of your performance, but this problem has also been increasingly affecting our relationship and I don't think we communicate as well as we could and should.

At this point, Steve is probably thinking, "Here we go again. . . . " But Jeff continues:

> However, I'm increasingly realizing that I may have been part of the problem. So could we sit down and try to work out how we get out of this—because I believe in you, I believe in us, and I believe strongly that if we work together we can improve both our working relationship and our joint performance. So could we talk this over, maybe at the cafeteria later today or tomorrow?

When they meet, Jeff could then open up the conversation by expanding on his earlier comments:

> Over the past year I've given you some feedback and suggestions here and there, but we have never really sat down to discuss the way

we work together. I'd like to talk about it today. I don't know how you feel about our relationship, and maybe you can tell me in a minute, but I think I should start the process and tell you how I feel.

Basically, I am starting to feel a fair amount of uneasiness developing between the two of us. There are things I ask you to do, you don't always do them, then I get annoyed, and the more I get annoyed the more I realize I become impatient with you. Sometimes I guess I can even be unpleasant with you, and I don't like this. I don't want to be impatient or unpleasant with you. I would much prefer us to get along well and to have easy and pleasant communications. I wonder whether I'm the only one feeling this tension or if you feel it, too?

Now there are a few things that you do that kind of irritate me. I'm sure that there maybe things that I do that irritate you as well, so I'd like to discuss that, including my own behavior, OK?

Having included himself in the issues that can be debated, Jeff needs to validate the starting point on the performance issue:

Maybe I can start with the main thing I have in mind, but again I would like this to be a discussion, so it would really be helpful if you bring in things that I do that may be contributing to the problem, OK?

What I have in mind is the issue of quality-control rejections in the area, and how and when we follow up on these rejections. I asked you to send me regular reports on the causes of these rejections, and from where I sit the reports are not very helpful; they don't reach me until quite some time after the event, and the analysis of the causes is often fairly superficial, at least in my eyes. If you want I can illustrate what I mean, but I thought I would ask, at a global level first, is my assessment unfair? Are you happy with your reports? Or are you perhaps following up in a way that I can't see?

Jeff should have a few examples in mind and may have some documents at hand. Jeff should also be prepared to let Steve go away and think about the issue and perhaps marshal up some arguments and evidence of his own—so that the discussion can be fair.

When they resume the discussion, there are two possible paths: Steve agrees that the reports are not very helpful, or he disagrees. (Figure 8-1 is a root-cause analysis of Steve and Jeff's situation.) A disagreement on the quality of the reports could highlight an important cause of Steve's behavior. Jeff has assumed so far that the report quality problem is a sign that Steve is not very proactive, which might have to do with a lack of effort on Steve's part and/or a time management problem. There are other possibilities, for example: (a) Jeff is wrong, and the reports are as good as can be; (b) Steve does not know how to write good reports (so the follow-up is performed well but not communicated well); or (c) Steve does not know how to go about analyzing the causes of rejections.

Note that most of these explanations are not related to Steve's level of effort or quality of time management. They relate more to cognitive factors and to Jeff's or Steve's respective understanding of how to perform a certain task. Jeff can then either change his opinion (if he realizes he was wrong) or try to help Steve develop his report-writing skills or his ability to perform root-cause analysis.

Assuming that Steve agrees that the reports are not very good, Jeff can go on as follows:

> Now I can see two possible causes for your writing up reports that you know are not very good. There may be others, but here are the two I see. One is that you don't think that investigating the root cause of quality-control rejections is a good use of your time or a good idea. The other possibility is that you think it is a good idea, but you don't like having to report to me on it. I am quite open to discuss both, but I think we need to be clear about what the issue is.

Here again, there are at least three possibilities. Depending on the nature of the problem, the conversation would veer in three very different directions. First possibility: Steve is less convinced than Jeff of the benefits of systematically investigating quality-control rejections. Jeff would then focus the discussion on this issue, using a combination of *advocating* his own view, explaining to Steve (maybe with the help of some data) why he has come to believe in

FIGURE 8 - 1

## Root-Cause Analysis

STEVE'S CASE

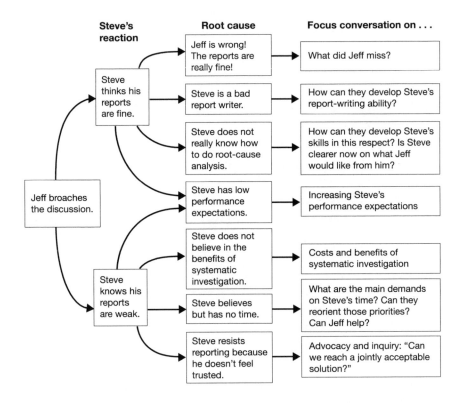

the usefulness of systematic investigation; and *inquiring* into Steve's views by asking Steve what leads him to conclude that systematic investigation is not a good idea.

Second possibility: Steve agrees that systematic investigation is a good idea, but he finds it difficult to set aside the time required to perform the follow-up. This response can trigger a discussion of Steve's time allocation, including what the major demands are on Steve's time, which responsibilities might be delegated, and what Jeff could do to help Steve. The discussion might even cover Steve's work habits and/or work hours.

Third possibility: Steve performs the systematic investigation but is not happy with having to report to Jeff on it. He registers his discontent through "passive resistance," that is, by responding slowly and with lightweight reports. As above, Jeff could use a combination of advocacy and inquiry:

- *Advocating* his views: "I have two fundamental reasons for asking you to report back to me. One is that I need to have an idea of what's going on because my own boss sometimes asks me quite detailed questions. The other is that I know you are busy and I kind of thought that you would be more likely to perform the follow-up systematically if you had to report back to me on it, so I was trying to help you set priorities."

- *Inquiring* into Steve's views: "What is it that bothers you about reporting back to me? Is it the time it takes or does it perhaps make you feel I don't trust you?"

This combination of advocacy and inquiry is important for Jeff. The objective is not to tell Steve that "I trust you completely" if this is not the case. Sooner or later, Steve would see through this lie. If Jeff has good reasons, including past instances of Steve not delivering on promises, Jeff should bring them up to support his difficulties with "fully trusting" Steve. That is the advocacy part. Jeff should also inquire into Steve's views, including what Jeff does that makes Steve not feel trusted. The objective of the discussion is to arrive at a jointly acceptable solution, where Steve feels he has enough leeway and Jeff gets the information he needs and develops sufficient confidence that the rejections are appropriately investigated.

Some of you might be tempted to take a more direct route to resolution. You might advise Jeff to be much more unilateral about requiring Steve to investigate rejections. Jeff could lay down his expectations in no uncertain terms and associate clear and important rewards or punishments to Steve's compliance. This approach might work in the short run, but it would not help meet Jeff's objective of reducing the uneasiness in the relationship; nor would it advance his objective of using the conversation to enhance their joint ability to solve problems in the future. Jeff could spell out this learning objective toward the end of the conversation. The formulation would depend on the precise cause of Steve's behavior. Assuming, for example, that Steve was feeling pressured by having to report something he did anyway, Jeff might say something like this:

> I'm glad we discussed this issue because I now have a better understanding of what happened and how we can improve the situation. I would also like us to make a deal for the future because I would hope that next time something like this happens, we would identify it and address it more quickly! My understanding of what happened is that I asked you to investigate the rejections and report back to me, and you didn't do it to my satisfaction, so I assumed you didn't want to do it. I felt it was important, so I started putting more pressure on you, which I now understand was the very thing that annoyed you in the first place! So I'd like to make the following deal with you. Next time you seem to do something I don't like, I will try not to jump to conclusions and rather ask you what's happening. In turn, next time I ask you to do something that disturbs you, it would be great if you told me that you disagree! This way we could discuss things in real time, rather than both of us becoming increasingly annoyed with one another.

To summarize Steve's case: Jeff develops a perception that Steve is not very proactive. He asks Steve to perform a task and report back to him regularly. Steve does not do so to Jeff's satisfaction. As many bosses frequently do with subordinates they perceive to be weaker performers, Jeff makes a negative attribution about Steve's motives, leading to a negative evaluation of Steve: Steve does not understand why systematic follow-up is important, and/or is not putting in enough effort, and/or is not managing his time well. The inevitable conclusion follows: Steve is simply not "a proactive guy." But our discussion, summarized in figure 8-1, shows that there are many possible reasons for Steve's behavior. Unless Jeff and Steve identify the right cause, or causes, and agree on an action plan, they are doomed to continue in a spiral of mutual misunderstanding and growing exasperation.

As mentioned previously, Jeff will have to follow up on the evolution of the relationship, of his behavior, and of Steve's performance, as agreed with Steve during their discussion. In the ideal situation, Steve's performance will improve markedly. This would indeed have been the case in the real situation. The fundamental problem Jeff and Steve were facing was very largely based on their initial misunderstanding. Clearing this misunderstanding would have had a major impact on Steve's performance.

With a subordinate less skilled and less motivated than Steve, the problem could have been rooted in the subordinate's perform-ance, skill, or effort shortcomings. In these cases the boss should fol-low up on the actions agreed upon and later assess with the subor-dinate the result of their joint effort.

## What about the Slackers?

The real Steve was no slacker. He was a very energetic, ambitious, and driven manager. But Jeff could not tell what lay behind Steve's underperformance. That is why, among the alternatives featured in the decision tree (figure 8-1), there is the possibility that the subor-dinate simply has low performance expectations. Such a problem may be "curable": The subordinate might be demotivated or ex-hausted, he may be going through domestic problems, and so on. In other words, he may be going through a passing phase. But not always. Among the underperformers, there will be some who refuse to raise their performance standards and/or are unable to acknowl-edge and address their own weaknesses.

This may come up during the initial intervention when the boss and subordinate explore their past and discuss the present. It may be, however, that the subordinate chooses to conceal his unwilling-ness to change and credibly attributes his difficulties to other causes. Or perhaps the subordinate only realizes along the way that he is not prepared to put in the effort required by the "joint contract." So we can't exclude the possibility that in some cases the employees will try to fool you, only pretending to go along with what you agreed. Nor can we exclude the possibility that some people, includ-ing very smart ones, are simply unwilling or unable to learn.[5]

A good, productive intervention can succeed only if both par-ties really want to make an effort to deliver on the "contract terms." So what do we do about subordinates who refuse to play ball and with whom there is no improvement either in the performance or in the quality of the relationship? There are two possible answers to this question. One view is that as long as the employee meets cur-rent performance standards, it is his right to refuse to develop fur-ther. It is actually fortunate that some of our employees do not aspire to become CEOs; they are happy doing an adequate job at their level and we should let them be.

The second possible answer—which is the one we ascribe to—is that we live in a world where performance requirements for corporations are constantly being raised.[6] Performance levels (e.g., service levels) we considered outstanding a few years ago are now but a basic condition to stay in business. The same is probably true for individuals. Larry Bossidy, then CEO of AlliedSignal, gave an excellent illustration of this view:

> Recently one guy said, "Well, I don't care if I'm going to limit my potential; I've gone as far as I want to anyway." I said, "No, no, you've got it wrong. You have to keep growing just to stay where you are. And you've demonstrated that you can't do it yourself, so you have to get some help." Then I offered him some suggestions and said, "We're not going to sit here and have the same discussion every year."[7]

Furthermore, we do not live and work in a vacuum. As we discussed in chapter 6, the individual's attitude is bound to have an impact on her boss, peers, subordinates, and all the teams she is a part of. Today's corporations face intense competition that requires very high individual employee performance, very high collective performance of employees supporting one another in the pursuit of common goals, and continuous learning on everyone's part. For corporations to learn, their members must learn and develop. Being happy and content with the skills you have today is simply no longer a viable option. Hence leaders should work hard at helping employees develop their skills, competencies, and self-confidence. These efforts should involve as much fair process as possible, and bosses should modify their behavior to help, rather than hinder, perceived weaker performers. A boss may also need to redesign a job to fit better with a subordinate's skills and abilities.

When, however, in spite of all these efforts, subordinates are not willing or able to elevate their game sufficiently—and the boss must remain the judge of what "sufficiently" involves—the boss must then take decisive action and take the individual out of the unit, or out of the company altogether if the person's skills cannot be used profitably in other parts of the organization. The decision to let someone go is never easy, but the boss *did* give the subordinate a chance and a fair process was respected, which should make the boss's decision more acceptable to others around, if not to the employee in question.

We believe that there are relatively few real "slackers" out there. In our experience, most people, when treated well, want to do a good job. If you try to sit down and talk, if you give people a chance, and if you include your own responsibility in the discussion, the outcome is rarely disappointing. We therefore consider this alternative in the decision tree to be a residual category. It is a fact, however, that some employees have low performance expectations and keep them in spite of the boss's best efforts. In most cases, keeping them around, often in an unhappy state, helps neither the corporation nor, long term, the individuals involved.

## When It's Too Late

We have devoted nearly a chapter to discussing what a good, productive intervention involves and illustrating what it could look and feel like. But an intervention is not always advisable.

In some cases, the relationship between boss and subordinate has gone so far down the negative spiral that the boss simply does not feel up to an intervention; she just cannot imagine mustering up the time and energy required by the process we have described.

Having realized that she is part of the problem, the boss may prefer to acknowledge the situation rather than explore it:

> You and I got into a bad dynamic. I now realize how I contributed to the dynamic and I'm really sorry. It really wasn't my intention. But I've tried to imagine you and me sitting down and working on this and frankly, I don't have it in me. I have nine other regional managers throughout the world. I'm stretched really thin and I don't have time for this.

The relationship clearly has no future, but in recognition of the joint responsibility for the failure, the boss can help the subordinate effect a dignified exit, with compensation and outplacement help, or she can give the person a reasonable amount of time to look around for another opportunity. You may see this as incurring unnecessary expenses, but the rest of the team will take close note of how you discharge your responsibility. Bosses should take advantage of the opportunities they are offered to signal their commitment to fair process. As Eric Nicoli, then CEO of the United Kingdom's United Biscuits, put it:

> You can fire people in a caring way, or you can just fire people. . . .
> I think one of the attractive characteristics of our company is genuine concern. There is a price for that, of course. It's cheaper not to care—in the short term. But that is one of the reasons, I suspect, that we don't lose good people.[8]

## When the Subordinate Wants to Take the Initiative

We examined in chapter 6 why subordinates often find it impossible to approach their boss to discuss their situation. They are afraid of coming across as feeble or thin-skinned, and they tend to overintentionalize their boss's reluctance to trigger the discussion himself. In some cases, however, we have seen subordinates take the lead and approach their boss. The managers reading this book are probably both boss and subordinate. So far we have spoken to you mainly in your boss's role. Let's examine briefly what you can do as a subordinate if you find yourself caught in a dynamic resembling the set-up-to-fail syndrome.

First, you might be able to get some help from a third party—like a mentor or respected senior colleague—someone who can make suggestions in a way that will be heard. Or again, if you have worked successfully at other divisions within the same company, try talking to your former boss. She may be able to give you advice; may be willing to talk to your current boss behind the scenes to help alter her perception of you; or may help you both set up the discussion.

If that kind of option is not available, then you're on your own. But before confronting your boss, you need to do some preparation: *failing to plan is planning to fail.* The following elements will help you prepare your intervention:

- *Get your job in order:* Focus on the things you *can* control, starting with your own work. Being able to show some measure of recent effort and goodwill, or something that is going well, will enhance your credibility.

- *Get your head in order:* Just like you had to do in your boss's role before triggering a meeting, you as a subordinate need to prepare for the discussion. This includes putting yourself in your boss's shoes and trying to understand the multiple pressures and constraints under which she must operate. When you review the many "injustices" you have suffered, which ones really suggest intentional bias? Try a reality check with colleagues who hold a different view of the boss, for instance, among the in-group. As you enrich the diagnostic, you potentially open up other avenues for the solution.

- *Make it easy for the boss:* Broach the issue when your boss is not under time pressure or in a bad mood. Don't make it seem like an ambush, and don't go in assuming your boss will resist. The chances are that these issues have also been fairly high in the boss's mind—but she may not have known how to bring them up. You may be doing both yourself and your boss a service.

- *Don't rush it:* Even if the boss is very receptive to your approach, even relieved, don't accept an on-the-spot meeting. She still needs a chance to get on same page as you—to sort through some psychological garbage of her own—and to think back over the relationship. Let the boss know what you want to discuss ahead of time.

### Inviting Your Boss to a Meeting

We have tried to role-play the invitation encounter with numerous executives. It becomes a very tricky discussion as soon as the subordinate brings up the desire to discuss the boss's contribution to the situation. Remember that your boss may not know what you know today and, as a result, may not yet have identified his role in the spiral of underperformance in which you may be trapped. Our suggestion is hence to request a meeting focusing on your performance and shared relationship. The following formulation might help:

> Look, I sense a certain uneasiness developing between the two of us. I think you feel it too. It's also clear in your eyes as well as in mine that my current performance does not live up to your expectations. Frankly, it doesn't live up to mine either. I certainly don't

come to work in the morning determined to aggravate you or do a
bad job. So the reason I'd like to have this discussion is to see what
I can do to improve my performance, and also maybe to improve
our relationship so that we get rid of this uneasiness and work better together. Can we meet to talk about this, maybe in a day or two
so that you have time to think about it?

The objectives of the meeting are the same as those discussed earlier
in this chapter, and they remain, regardless of who initiates the
process. In this case, however, the boss is probably not yet aware
that he has been a part of the problem and hence must be part of
the solution, so this can only come up later in the discussion. To
adapt to this new situation, you may want to consider the following to guide the meeting.

- *Concentrate first on what you can do for the boss.* Since this discussion is not his idea, a full and immediate exploration of
  the boss's contribution is likely to be unhelpful. Start with
  what you can do for your boss, for example: "I feel you're
  not very happy with my performance/behavior. I think I
  know some of the sources of your dissatisfaction, but it
  would help me to hear in your words how you see things
  and which aspects of my behavior or my work you think I
  need to improve most."

- *Don't get stuck.* Monitor your emotions. If you reach an
  impasse, check your own impatience and suggest breaking
  up the meeting to let you both think the issues through
  before coming back together. The opportunity to digest
  your mutual differences should allow you to resume more
  productively.

- *Allaying the fears.* Make sure you come away with a better
  understanding of the boss's key concerns—and indeed of the
  concerns of the boss's boss—so that you are more capable of
  acting appropriately.

- *Bringing up the boss's contribution to the process.* Having listened to and discussed the boss's point of view, you must at
  some point engage the boss on the way his behavior contributes to your underperformance. One way to do so is to

take one of the boss's pieces of advice and try to show him how it is impossible for you to implement without some change in his behavior. For example, you might say, "I hear you saying that you would like me to delegate more authority to my staff, but that's very difficult for me to do given the very limited autonomy you're giving me. I can't delegate what I don't have!" Or "I hear you telling me that I shouldn't supervise my staff so closely, but I kind of have to do it in order to answer the questions you routinely ask me when we meet by chance in the corridor." The downside of this approach is that your boss may think you're transferring the guilt to him and, as a result, become defensive.

The other alternative, which we prefer, is to summarize the three key items on which your boss wants you to work and say:

> OK, I will work on these three dimensions. Now, let me ask *you* a few things that, if you could do them, would really help me do what you'd like me to do. For example, on the issue of delegating more authority to my subordinates, would it be possible for you to give me slightly less detailed instructions when you entrust me with a task? Maybe a bit more on the "what is needed, why and by when?" and a bit less on the "how it must be done." This would be really helpful because it would allow me to have broader discussions with my staff and involve them more in the choice of "how they should go about it."

Or, assuming you feel a lack of confidence from your boss, you might say something like this:

> One of the things I struggle with is that I sometimes feel you don't trust me as much as I'd like you to do. And on one hand I understand that you do need to have some reassurance that things are going the way they should, but it's also a bit discouraging, sometimes, when I feel this lack of trust. Like for example, when you . . . or when you. . . .

As we have discussed throughout this book, very few bosses actively try to drive their subordinates' motivation into the ground. The vast majority of the time, they are trying to help, and they think their behavior helps! Having owned up to your side of the needed improvement, it will be easier to help your boss see how what he does, sometimes, may hinder your performance. And it may be less threatening for your boss if, instead of crafting it negatively and with respect to the past ("here is how you screw me up"), you frame it positively and referring to the future ("here is how you can help me").

- *Hammer out and jointly agree on a workable plan.* This should be the scaffolding to rebuild your credibility and your relationship.

The next step will be to deliver on your plan. Hopefully, the boss will be willing and able to work on the changes in his behavior that you've discussed. This should help you, but you may also want to consider the following:

- *Prioritize.* Structure your goals so that you can meet the boss's expectations.

- *Communicate.* As you achieve the goals, let your boss know. Schedule meetings with your boss to make certain that you improve her opinion of your work. This is part of rebuilding your credibility.

- *Adjust.* Stop treating your boss as the enemy or hanging out with people who do. If you have to or want to hang out with them, ban discussions about the boss.

- *Persevere.* Work hard at maintaining your self-confidence, without overreaching and overcommitting. As the well-known saying puts it, to build credibility, it's "better to underpromise and overdeliver" than the opposite. This is even more true when you are trying to *rebuild* credibility.

## Catching Problems Earlier

Interrupting the syndrome is good but, of course, it means that things have already got out of hand. Interventions of the kind we've described are not exercises that bosses are eager to repeat too often.

Bosses therefore need to be more alert to the development of vicious cycles in order to take action more quickly. The good news is that holding an intervention discussion will make it easier for boss and subordinate to catch future problems earlier. The intervention process opens up new communication channels; it extends learning and leadership skills. It forces bosses, in particular, to think about their management style. Self-inquiry, together with feedback from the subordinate, yields insights into the effectiveness of the boss's behavior, even in cases where a happy outcome cannot be reached.

Over the long-term, *preventing* the syndrome is clearly the goal. Interruption seems tougher than prevention in that it involves breaking a dynamic that has accumulated momentum and changing patterns of behavior that have become ingrained. It also requires explicit discussions where both parties may feel embarrassed, whereas prevention does not require confrontation. If the boss decides to enroll the subordinate in a joint prevention effort, the discussion is proactive and therefore less threatening.

To avoid triggering vicious cycles, managers do not need to behave identically with all subordinates. They must, however, behave differently in a way that subordinates interpret as supportive and helpful. This is possible, even with more monitoring and direction. Let's explore how leaders can do that in chapter 9.

# 9

## Preventing the
## Set-Up-to-Fail Syndrome

*Lessons from the "Syndrome Busters"*

> I never criticize a player until they are first convinced of my
> unconditional confidence in their abilities.
>
> —John Robinson, football coach

WHEN EXECUTIVES we have worked with begin to realize the
impact of their differentiated behavior on perceived weaker performers, they invariably ask us with great anxiety in their voices:
"Does that mean we should behave the same way with all our subordinates?" The answer of course is no, for two reasons: First, even
if bosses *wanted* to behave the same way, they would not be able to.
It is simply impossible to do! Second and fortunately, they do not
have to. It is quite possible to behave differently with various subordinates without triggering the set-up-to-fail syndrome. The difficulty is in making sure that the difference in behavior does not lead
subordinates to feel they are neither trusted nor valued.

We have studied a number of bosses who succeed in getting
the best from their perceived weaker performers. We call them
"syndrome busters." None of them try to pretend that all their subordinates have similar capabilities. They *do* provide perceived weaker
performers with more guidance up front, and they monitor their
actions and results more closely than they do for their better-
performing colleagues. But this differentiated behavior occurs within

197

an interpersonal context that makes it easier for subordinates to seek help and guidance, as well as to accept feedback from their boss. The boss and perceived weaker performers are not adversaries; they are partners in a relationship aimed at improving subordinate performance and at producing a satisfying personal boss-subordinate relationship. In this chapter we provide a few actionable suggestions to help managers establish and maintain such an interpersonal context.

Our research has shown us that syndrome-busting bosses do six key things that keep the boss-subordinate relationship on the right foot. It is particularly important to establish these ways of working during the formative period in the relationship, starting with the "first hundred days." But there are additional steps bosses can take that help sustain a healthy interpersonal context over the long haul—and we round out the chapter with a broader look at what we call the *twin pillars*.

## Good Foundations: The First Hundred Days

### Framing the Relationship

The preceding chapters have highlighted how subordinates, just as much as bosses, perceive reality through the prism of their impressions of the other party. A subordinate might interpret an action positively if it comes from a trusted boss but negatively from a boss that he perceives to be meddling and controlling. Incoming leaders can choose to be more or less involved in the creation of their subordinates' first impressions. They can choose to let things develop naturally, or they can choose to be more up front and explicit. The sidebar, "Off to a Bad Start," lists a few errors bosses often make early in new relationships.

We think it is important for leaders to *frame* the boss-subordinate relationship up front. Frequent contact in the developmental stages of the relationship gives the boss ample opportunity to communicate with subordinates about key priorities, performance measures, time allocation, and even expectations for the type and frequency of communication. Also, to prevent misunderstandings from polluting a relationship, bosses can be more explicit about their own style, how they work, and what they like and don't like. This kind of clarity goes a long way toward preventing the dynamic of the set-up-to-fail syndrome, which is so often fueled by unstated expectations or misunderstandings about priorities.[1]

For example, take the case of Steve and Jeff in chapter 8. Jeff could have made explicit very early that he wanted Steve to set up a system that would systematically analyze the root causes of quality-control rejections. He could have explained the benefits of establishing such a system with the launch of the new production line, and he might have expressed his intention to be actively involved in the design and the early operation of the system. Jeff's failure to spell out the intention behind his request left Steve to interpret it simply as a lack of faith in his ability.

This point was also emphasized in a recent study of leaders taking charge of a new position. When discussing the need to establish early credibility with employees, the authors state that "setting expectations and shaping the behavior of subordinates and employees are among the new leader's most important tasks." In the words of one executive, "You have to make clear [what are] the behavioral limits. . . . Sit down with each of [your direct reports] and say, 'Here's the way I do things and how I understand things and how we'll get on well as we work together. Here are the things that will drive me crazy and I'll be very angry at.'"[2]

Such communication can take place during a meeting specifically dedicated to this purpose, but it can also occur through more active boss involvement in the early days of the relationship. Some leaders are afraid of coming across early on as micromanagers and hence tend to delegate heavily, observe how things work, and then adjust their degree of involvement as they gather more information. We think this approach is a mistake. Early involvement and guidance by the new boss are not intrinsically threatening for subordinates because they are not triggered by performance shortcomings. The involvement is systematic and meant to help set the conditions for future success. It is part of the normal adaptation process and can be reduced as newcomers settle in. Taking the reverse approach to see how it goes, with low involvement at the start, means that any subsequent increase in boss involvement will clearly signal that something is not working out, which is much more likely to be threatening for the subordinate.

---

### OFF TO A BAD START: COMMON WELL-INTENTIONED ERRORS EARLY IN BOSS-SUBORDINATE RELATIONSHIPS

- **The sink or swim principle:** The boss expects the new hire to hit the job running, to be instantly operational, especially if he has years of work experience. The boss believes that saying something once should suffice.
- **The laundry list approach:** The boss outlines a multitude of managerial responsibilities, without making clear the "critical few objectives," the two or three dimensions on which the subordinate *must* excel.
- **Respecting the honeymoon period:** The boss tries to withhold directions and negative feedback at the outset, assuming that overt criticism may spoil the development of a working relationship.
- **The "not-so-jointly" agreed plan:** The boss overestimates the new hire's willingness to challenge objectives or time frames the boss sets out. The new hire, trying hard to make a good impression, lacks the confidence and the experience to contradict the boss's unrealistic projections. The new hire signs on for "mission impossible."
- **The open-door fallacy:** The boss assumes that the new hire will come to her for advice if he runs into trouble. The opposite is more often the case. The situation may be compounded by vague initial instructions, such that the new hire does not even realize he needs help.

---

## Investing in the Development of Relationships

The formative period of the relationship allows bosses to present themselves, which is important in order to allay doubts or misapprehensions subordinates may have about the new boss. Take the example of Carly Fiorina, the first outsider to be named CEO of Hewlett-Packard. On the weekend before the announcement, she met with Ann Livermore for four hours. Livermore had been the leading internal candidate for the job. Left unattended, her disappointment at being passed over could prompt her to leave, could thwart their working relationship, or could create factions within the management team. To retain her, Fiorina needed to explain what *she* was about and to reassure Livermore about her future role in the new HP. Livermore not only stayed but took responsibility for HP Services, the company's biggest division.

Early contacts also give bosses an opportunity to get to know their subordinates personally, develop mutual respect, and thus start establishing a difference between the *person* and the *performance*. An outstanding boss we interviewed explained:

> The first thing I do when I get a new group is to spend a lot of one-on-one time with the people over the first two or three months. My philosophy there is you want a lot of listening, *a lot of listening,* much more so than talking. And that develops a relationship which is not just work-related; it becomes a personal relationship. Some better than others, but there are personal relationships between people, a real understanding of who they are, and they understand who I am. And that brings acceptance of [our respective] strengths and weaknesses, and the ways we can complement each other.
>
> My previous boss modeled this very well. She took a lot of time with each person. She got to know you as a person and there was mutual respect. She knew your weaknesses and you weren't afraid of that. And I think that's the key thing: There's some respect, some mutual trust here, and an understanding that we need each other.

Carlos Ghosn, who recently led a spectacular turnaround at Nissan Motor Co., also emphasizes the importance of developing mutual respect:

> Mutual respect is also very important. It is very easy not to respect one another. You just have to focus on what is different. Now mutual respect means we don't focus on the weaknesses, we focus on the strengths of the other party. . . . This is basic but it allows a token change in atmosphere in what we want to undertake.[3]

Think about how the work environment differs from home in this respect. At home, your relationship with your child, for example, is generally distinct from your assessment of your child's "performance." Of course, serious performance problems on the part of a child can sometimes jeopardize the overall relationship with the parents, but small ones generally do not. Kids can generally break minor rules without parents ceasing to love them. This distinction is implicit for the two parties, and it is sometimes reinforced by parents saying to their child, "I don't like what you have done. I still love you—that does not change, of course—but I still don't like what you have done." Parents say such things to mark the difference between the person/relationship and performance. This distinction is important because if the relationship is secure, the performance-related feedback becomes less threatening.

There is no such natural distinction in the work context. The raison d'être of an employment relationship is for the subordinate to perform up to certain standards. As a result, performance-related negative feedback threatens subordinates' need for competence and for relatedness (i.e., a safe connection to others), two of the three fundamental human needs identified by *Self-Determination Theory*.[4] Hence it tends to be associated with much evaluation anxiety and defensiveness.

Working to establish a distinction between person and performance in the work context contributes to decreasing subordinate anxiety and defensiveness associated with feedback from the boss. One important way bosses can establish this distinction is to develop personal relationships with their subordinates. As the quote above points out, these relationships will not all be equally strong and positive, but they will at least exist. They thus represent a productive first step toward the subordinate's thinking, "I will still be respected as a person even if my performance is not as high as my boss and I would like it to be."

This is exactly what another manager explained to us when he described how spending time on the road with his boss had improved their working relationship: "Because it's a lot more real. I mean . . . he cares about me as a person. I am valued. Not what I do is valued, *I* am valued. I think that's very important. People need to know they're valued for who they are, not only for what they do."

### Resisting Crude Labeling of People

The human urge to label is deep-seated. Labeling helps us make sense quickly of the world around us. But there are two aspects of the labeling process that bosses can work hard to resist. The first is the temptation to categorize employees in simplistic ways—"he's useless," "she's weak." The trouble is that the boss usually bases those characterizations on the subordinate's performance of certain tasks—or worse yet, as discussed in chapter 4—on behaviors that are not necessarily related to performance. In performance appraisals, this spillover between performance dimensions is known as the "halo effect" if it is positive and as the "horn effect" if it is negative. Labeling *can* be helpful, provided it is specific. It is useful for the boss to bear in mind that the subordinate tends to struggle with particular types of work. That knowledge can be used to tailor assignments more toward the subordinate's strengths and to provide incremental learning opportunities in the areas of weakness.

The second aspect of labeling that gets managers into trouble is premature closure. The fact that a subordinate struggles in a particular area does not mean that he will always do so. Underperformance can have many root causes, such as a lack of confidence, of skills, of understanding, or of effort. The problem is that by the time the subordinate improves, the boss's mind is already made up and the improvement goes unregistered. Bosses therefore need to suspend judgment on subordinates and be willing to revise their labels as they receive new information.

The need to suspend judgment is particularly important for incoming bosses who may be tempted to over-rely on the performance labels handed out by their predecessors. Determined not to fall into that trap when he landed at IBM, Lou Gerstner told his new management team, "I don't care whether you're the next star or on your way out. You start clean with me."[5]

Information recorded in personnel files has been characterized as notoriously mistaken, ambiguous, and irrelevant.[6] Should bosses deliberately avoid looking at subordinates' records for several weeks or months? Or indeed should companies make it a policy to withhold these records for a similar period? The presence and use of such records certainly contributes significantly to the speed at which negative performance spirals are activated in real life—as quickly as one week, as we've seen.

Conversely, bosses can also use such records to try to interrupt past dynamics, by identifying the employees who were in the previous boss's doghouse and approaching them individually to assure them that they will get a fresh start. One of Aesop's fables tells us that the tongue is both the best and the worst tool, and that lesson certainly applies here. The problem is not the existence of employee records and files, but rather the way bosses use them.[7]

## Monitoring Your Evaluations

Labels are preserved and reinforced by mental processes that influence which events we notice and remember, and how we explain them. Recall Jeff and Steve again. Jeff, the boss, takes Steve's slowness to comply as evidence of incompetence, when in fact it is motivated more by resentment at not being trusted. Conversely, Steve takes Jeff's request as interference when, in fact, it is based largely on Jeff's inexperience in a new area and his desire to make a good impression on his own boss.

Becoming aware of the tricks their minds play on them is an important first step for bosses who want to avoid jumping to the wrong conclusions. In particular, bosses must be mindful of their tendency to seek, notice, and remember facts that confirm their initial conclusion—the *confirming evidence bias*. To fight this bias, they must develop new mental habits that include actively searching for *disconfirming evidence* and *alternative explanations*.

Questioning your existing data is a good first step ("How do I know this? What's my evidence? What are the facts?"). Looking for disconfirming evidence goes a step farther. It involves looking for instances where, for example, the subordinate *did* show the quality you'd like to see more of, be it initiative, drive, or good judgment. Reviewing your last interactions systematically, can you think of any times the subordinate exhibited "positive behavior"? If you don't have examples yourself, others (e.g., other subordinates or peers of yours) may—you will find out only if you ask.

Similarly, taking your evaluations and reasoning to court is a good idea. Ask yourself, "How do I know this to be true? What is the reasoning that leads me to this conclusion?" You can go farther by actively trying to create alternative explanations. "Is there another way to explain these events? What could be going through her mind? If I put myself in her shoes for a second, what might she argue?" We know that, especially under stress, we tend to frame events and situations in narrow and binary terms. Once aware of this tendency, we can fight it—for example, by actively searching for broader ways of framing the event(s). One way to do so is to identify first the implicit assumptions and constraints embedded in our reasoning. "What am I assuming about these people (or about the situation)? Is it necessarily true? Is there any way to avoid this reaction?" Having identified questionable implicit assumptions or constraints, we are better able to try to reframe the situation in broader, less biased ways.

### Intervening Early; Asking Rather Than Telling

As illustrated several times before, large problems typically start small and would go away if one of the parties initiated a discussion. That's why we advise intervening earlier rather than later. The longer the boss waits to intervene, the more often subordinates will have repeated the mistakes and hence the more aggravated (and the less productive) the boss will be, and the more threatening the intervention will be for the subordinate.

If you are a boss who has sat on feedback for a while before finally getting down to communicating it to subordinates, you know about the disadvantages of waiting to communicate your thoughts—though, of course, feedback can also be given *too* quickly (see "Fast Feedback").

At the same time, probably all of us have been on the receiving end of delayed feedback—at work or at home—and many of us probably thought at that time, "But why didn't he say something back then? Why did he have to bottle up and carry this frustration for so long?"

So as subordinates, we would typically prefer to be told earlier rather than later. Yet as bosses, we tend to procrastinate on giving feedback to subordinates.[8] As we discussed in chapter 7, managers are reluctant to give feedback because they tend to view it as a threatening event—both embarrassing and a potential source of conflict. They tend to frame feedback as an adversarial situation. It's like a tennis match, instead of two people trying to knock down the same skittles; it's a truth in need of delivery ("giving" feedback), rather than an assumption in need of testing ("exploring" feedback). Feedback evokes a painful monologue rather than an occasion for joint learning (see "The Pain of Giving Feedback"). Bosses

---

**FAST FEEDBACK**

When we recommend that bosses not delay feedback, we are not talking about delays counted in minutes or hours, which are sometimes
quite valuable to allow bosses to control their emotions, gather their
thoughts, and think through how they will broach the subject. As Rick
Mayrer explains in *Feedback Toolkit,* there is a difference between *timely*
feedback and *rushed* feedback. If the feedback concerns an emotionally
charged event, it may be best to wait a day or two. "Sometimes you're
so emotional that it makes sense to wait. . . . Schedule an appointment
and have a meeting. Don't give important feedback in the hallway."[9]

The advice echoes advice handed out over four hundred years ago
by French philosopher Michel de Montaigne: "While our pulse beats
and we feel emotion, let us put off the business. Things will truly seem
different to us when we have quieted and cooled down. It is passion
that is in command at first, it is passion that speaks, it is not ourselves."[10]

---

also tend to assume that, unlike themselves, others will probably try
to deflect the feedback rather than embrace the information as a
means to improve.

We argued in chapter 7 that feedback-giving sessions can be
reframed as performance-related discussions, where boss and subordinate probably both want the same thing: a successful professional
relationship and, if possible, a pleasant personal interaction. We have
also discussed the need to separate person and performance, which
should make the reframing easier. This conversation is not going to
be about how and why Joe is an awful person, Joe is a fine person. It
will be about the "thing" that Joe does that I don't like, that aggravates me, or simply that I would prefer him to do differently.

Another way to help reframe the session in less threatening
terms is to construe it as a discussion where, rather than presenting
their thoughts as uncontroversial evidence, bosses will test their
understanding of the facts and validate their inferences. In other
words, bosses can *ask rather than tell.* "Say, Joe, I was wondering:
Why are you doing this thing this way? What's your reasoning?"
rather than "Joe, I'd rather you would do this thing differently."
Returning again to Jeff and Steve's example, it would have been relatively painless for Jeff to ask Steve, early on, about the weak reports

---

### THE PAIN OF GIVING FEEDBACK

The words *giving feedback* are not especially constructive and mislead many managers. *I will give you feedback* implies that:

1. The purpose is corrective—don't expect any positive feedback.
2. Feedback is something *I have.* (I have all the necessary information, and I have correctly interpreted it when distinguishing your contribution from the impact of contextual factors).
3. And feedback is something *you don't* have; so I am going to give it to you, or rather *administer it to you.* This is unilateral communication, so I just hope you take it constructively and don't try to find excuses. This is painful enough for me as it is. Don't make it worse.

---

Steve was writing. It was, of course, easy *not* to ask him as well—too easy. Why ask if you think you know?

The earlier the boss intervenes, the less often the subordinate will have repeated the same mistake (assuming it is indeed a mistake!) and hence the less emotional baggage the boss will take to the meeting. As subordinates, we would rather be given a chance to validate our boss's perceptions of facts and inferences early. If we must learn something, we would prefer to learn it sooner rather than later. Maybe we should not systematically attribute to our subordinates a significantly greater defensiveness than we would demonstrate. Some subordinates are indeed very defensive, but many of them probably feel the same way we do.

In addition, we can ask rather than tell if we are unsure about our facts or inferences. The answer may give the boss an opportunity to correct the subordinate's approach to the issue. It may also help the boss learn something, if the subordinate's answer turns out to open the boss's eyes to an excellent, though different, way of looking at the issue.

### Getting Subordinates to Jointly Own the Boss-Subordinate Relationship

As discussed in chapter 5, subordinates can play an important role in fueling the development of the set-up-to-fail syndrome. As a result, they are also in a good position to try to prevent it. Much of the advice we've given to bosses in the last few pages can also apply to subordinates. Subordinates should resist crudely labeling their boss prematurely. They should also monitor and challenge their evaluations and, more generally, their tendency to seek, notice, and remember evidence confirming their initial belief about their boss. Ideally, they should also intervene early if they feel their boss is setting them up for failure.

For example, Paula Sims recalls being put right by a subordinate in her first few days as the head of GE's self-managed jet engine plant:

> Not long after I started here, an employee came to me and said, "Paula, you realize that you don't need to follow up with us to make sure we're doing what we agreed to do. If we say we'll do something, we'll do it. You don't need to micromanage us." I sat back and thought, "Wow. That's so simple. I'm sending the message that I don't trust people, because I always follow up." I took that to heart. This was a technician, and I had been at the plant less than thirty days. I appreciated that he felt comfortable enough to tell me this.[11]

As mentioned previously, the fact that this feedback was delivered early in the new relationship, and in the context of self-management, meant that the comments were not particularly threatening or embarrassing for either party. More generally, however, communicating upward feedback is at least as threatening as—in fact, even more threatening than—communicating downward assessments. Subordinates are much more likely to bring up their uneasiness if their boss specifically invites them to do so. Bosses must invite subordinates to feel and *act as joint custodians* of the boss-subordinate relationship. If they experience their boss as being unhelpful or even inhibiting, they should flag the problem and ask for a discussion.

The first step in this process is simple: A boss must, *early on,* explicitly signal her interest in investing in the subordinate and the relationship, indicating that she will be doing her best to contribute to both but that she needs the subordinate's help because she cannot do it alone. The boss should invite the subordinate(s) to keep her honest and bring up problems quickly before they take root. As time passes, she should *periodically* reconfirm this interest by asking the subordinate how things are going.

While some bosses may think that saying these things explicitly is not necessary, we think it is. Subordinates face the same doubts bosses do regarding the other party's potential reactions to feedback. Moreover, they are on the lower end of the power scale and therefore face the additional concerns of coming across as feeble and thin-skinned, and of bringing up an issue that the boss may not want to talk about. In some national and organizational cultures, the power distance between bosses and subordinates may be low enough for subordinates to feel naturally empowered to raise their concerns with their boss. In most of the organizations we work with, however, we think subordinates are more likely to behave as active partners if they are explicitly and repeatedly invited to do so.

Beyond *inviting* subordinate input, the second step for the boss eager to get such input is to create an environment where the subordinate will feel comfortable airing his concerns—and therefore feel able and willing to act as a joint custodian of the boss-subordinate relationship. That is part of the wider issue we tackle next.

## The Twin Pillars of a Learning Environment

So far, we have discussed various ways of avoiding early slippage in the boss-subordinate relationship. But beyond those initial exchanges, the relationship has got to live. So what kind of environment will help keep it productive and nip set-up-to-fail syndromes in the bud? Put simply, an environment where communication can flow freely in both directions. That means, on the one hand, that subordinates, especially the weaker-performing ones, feel comfortable reporting problems to the boss and asking for help. And it means, on the other hand, that feedback from the boss is accepted by subordinates and perceived as supportive, encouraging, and competence-enhancing. Let's examine these two dimensions in turn.

*Upward Pillar: Subordinates Feel Confident*
*Reporting Problems and Asking for Help*

We discussed in chapters 2 and 3 how perceived weaker performers tend to shy away from reporting problems and asking for their boss's help. As a result of these subordinates' propensity to try to maintain their autonomy, the boss often discovers problems late, leaving him little choice but to call a drastic intervention and give forceful directions. This only reinforces the subordinates' conviction that they are better off when their boss is not fully informed. To avoid coming to such extremes, bosses are tempted to be very directive up-front with the subordinates (to try to minimize errors) and to monitor subordinates' performance very closely (to try to detect problems earlier). All these actions reinforce subordinates' feelings that the boss underappreciates them, doesn't trust them, and is overly controlling.

Accordingly, one of the ways to prevent triggering and fueling the set-up-to-fail syndrome is for subordinates to feel comfortable enough approaching the boss with problems or to ask for help. Subordinates are more likely to report problems if they feel that doing so will lead to positive outcomes, or at least won't produce negative ones. The main positive outcome they expect is help from the boss; the main negative outcomes they hope to avoid are unpleasant reactions from the boss and the tightening of their already limited autonomy.

Bosses who manage to prevent the syndrome deliver on both fronts: they respond constructively to bad news, and they don't systematically try to reduce subordinates' autonomy in cases of problems.

**Responding to Bad News.** Syndrome busters do not react in a punitive way when confronted with bad news. There are various ways to be punitive. The most obvious and feared is ranting and raving in public. A softer one is giving a subordinate the cold shoulder for a while. Leaders who work on encouraging early communication of problems have learned to maintain their reaction within a "reasonably calm" zone. One executive explained why it is extremely important for communication purposes not to shoot, or otherwise punish, the messenger:

People told me things that were shocking at times. It wasn't easy to control the anger. But you've got to try to be calm, and ask, "Thanks for telling me. How did that happen?" "Well, there was a problem with the. . . . " "OK, so how are you going to prevent it from happening again?" So that's what promotes trust. And that's when I knew I had it. Instead of trying to cover up, they were telling me.

This testimony shows the manager's determination to control his anger as well as his receptiveness to the causes of the problem and willingness to learn (see "Nobody's Perfect").

Beyond this first dimension of self-control, our research suggests that syndrome busters encourage subordinates by doing three things when they discuss bad news:

- They emphasize the responsibility of, and focus the discussion on, the *process* that caused the problem, or allowed it to happen. More than reaching a slightly better decision in a specific case, these leaders want to improve (a) subordinates' understanding of the process they work with, that is, the cause-and-effect chains that connect actions to results, and (b) subordinates' decision-making processes, that is, the ways they analyze issues and weigh costs and benefits when reaching decisions.

- They emphasize the future. For example, "OK, it happened this time, can it happen again? If so, what can we do to prevent it from happening again, or at least to decrease the magnitude of the problem?"

- They summarize at the end of the discussion the learning points generated during the conversation.

One executive we interviewed summarized why it was so easy to discuss bad news with his boss:

I now know that it's OK to go to her and say, "We screwed up." She will sit down with you and discuss: "How can we fix this? What do you think about that? How about if we approach it this way?" And it's never personal, it's never a personal attack against me. It's never: "You did something wrong, how do we fix you?" It's always: "What's wrong with the process, how do we fix the process?

---

**NOBODY'S PERFECT**

We talk about bosses learning to "control" their anger rather than "eliminate" it. Subordinates do not expect their bosses to look happy when they hear bad news, particularly if they care about what they do. On the other hand, there is a big difference between expressing dissatisfaction with the outcome (which conveys passion) and an intensely emotional outburst, which—even if not specifically directed at the subordinate—is likely to be experienced as pretty unpleasant. An example of the former would be, "Damn, this is not good news!" An emotional monologue along the lines of "How could [you let] this happen!" would be closer to the latter. Subordinates also do not expect their boss to be perfect. They are quite capable of forgiving an occasional outburst from a boss who generally handles well disappointing news.

---

**Supporting Autonomy.** When faced with bad news or a request for help, syndrome busters do not attempt to repossess the decision rights from subordinates and make all the decisions themselves. This is not to say that they allow all their subordinates the same degree of autonomy; they do not. They *do* get more involved with perceived weaker performers. But they do try to preserve some measure of autonomy for all their subordinates. After all, subordinate empowerment is not a zero-one switch. Nor is boss involvement; bosses can be involved without actually *making* the decision. For example, they can be informed at specific junctures, consulted at every stage of a critical process, or even ratify the ultimate decision. Furthermore, when bosses do get involved in subordinates' activities, syndrome busters make sure they highlight the temporary nature of the coaching they are providing. Perceived weaker performers are not hostile to coaching; what is painful for them is *constant* monitoring and supervision, across the *whole range* of their activities, that *never* seems to go away.

*Downward Pillar: Subordinates Do Not Feel*
*Threatened by, and Hence Are More Willing to Accept*
*and Act on, Their Boss's Feedback*

Bosses who manage to get the best from their weaker performers do so because they manage not to discourage and alienate these subordinates, but also because they succeed at helping them improve. We have already discussed why subordinates caught in a set-up-to-fail syndrome are unlikely to accept their bosses' feedback as valid and helpful. Syndrome busters do not trigger their subordinates' defensiveness because they display five important dimensions for subordinates.

**Syndrome Busters Establish a Clear Distinction between the Subordinate's Performance and the Subordinate as a Person.** This distinction is important because it allows subordinates to feel that they can still be respected as human beings even if their performance falls short of their own and their boss's expectations. As a result, critical feedback becomes less threatening; it is a negative comment on the subordinate's performance at a given time and place and under given conditions, but not a sweeping blanket condemnation of the subordinate as a human being.

This is achieved in large part through informal and regular contact. Take the example of Lina Echeverrìa, director of one of the research labs at Corning, in charge of an unruly group of forty-five researchers: "I believe in being in close touch with people as human beings. . . . I can tell you about the family situation of every one of the people who work for me. I know what kind of work environment suits them. I can see when someone is not motivated." How does she do it? By inviting them to talk: "I am always walking into someone's office and saying to that person, 'How does it feel?' How does it feel—in this project? In life? I have this conversation often with people, and *not just people whose performance concerns me.*"[12]

**Syndrome Busters Do Not Jump to Hasty Conclusions about Subordinate Performance.** Even where perceived weaker performers are concerned, they make the effort to remain open-minded about their evaluations of the outcome ("Is this really bad performance?") and their beliefs about the outcome's possible causes. In addition, and consistent with the requirements of fairness in the development and communication of feedback, they give subordinates an opportunity to validate their data and inferences before making up their minds. A manager working for such a leader explained as follows:

Some people say my boss is subjective, but that depends on how you define subjectivity. To me, saying that "being 5 percent under the profit target is bad" is subjective, because the person does not take the time to analyze why profitability is at that level. My boss does not make up her mind on how good or bad a result is before she talks it over with you. She believes that any data is subjective until it is run by you.

Another manager illustrated this dimension by contrasting the behavior of his boss with that of his boss's boss:

My boss's boss tends to jump to a conclusion the minute he sees the data or hears something about your area. At one point, for example, my area's quality level remained at 70 percent for about three months. He called me in and said something like: "Your quality has stayed stagnant for the past three months; it looks to me that your area is either not working the right issues, or not working them right." He doesn't give you the benefit of the doubt; he doesn't leave you room to show that you have identified the issue and you are working it effectively. *One of the problems with this approach is that you cannot be sure he will change his initial bad impression, so that makes you more defensive.*

My boss would have approached it differently. He would have said something like: "The quality went up to 70 percent very quickly but it has not improved over the last three months. Why is that? What are we doing about it?" That would have invited me to explain why quality was not improving—because we are now working on more complex issues, requiring coordination with engineering and with vendors, which takes more time—and what we are doing about it.

When a perceived weaker performer believes that her boss makes an effort to remain open-minded about the causes of poor performance—for example, by giving her an honest chance to validate the boss's evaluations—she is bound to be less anxious and defensive about the boss's evaluation process. As a result, she feels less of a need to systematically and proactively distance herself from likely failures for which she could be held responsible. She is also more open to feedback she perceives to be based on validated facts and an unbiased appraisal of events and outcomes.

**Syndrome Busters Spend Time Discussing Favorable Outcomes.** Several bosses we studied indeed explained that while they agreed in principle with the idea that they could learn from studying favorable variances, time is short and is best spent focusing on measures or issues that need improvement. In the words of one of these managers:

> If the business is real good, you might look at the profit and loss report, thank everyone for their effort, and have a real quick meeting. You don't want to waste a lot of time looking at something that you're doing right when you can spend that time doing more right.

While this traditional management-by-exception approach has intuitive appeal, syndrome busters take the time to try to learn from success by asking subordinates how they solved a particular problem or what factors contributed to a nontrivial favorable variance. This interest in the *causes* of "favorable variances" has four important benefits:

- It contributes to the creation and/or the transmission of knowledge about the process and the cause-effect mechanisms underlying performance. Knowledge is "created" if the boss or the subordinate learns something from the exercise. Knowledge can also be "transmitted" to other subordinates, for example, if the discussion occurs in a team meeting.

- It provides the boss with an opportunity to provide positive reinforcement to the subordinates.

- It reinforces the credibility of the boss's commitment to learning and to understanding and improving the process. Not only is the boss looking for positive results; he also wants to understand how these results were achieved, including the possible impact of exogenous factors on the measure.

- Last, but most important, bosses' attention to favorable variances and interest in the causes of favorable variances increases the legitimacy of their interest in the causes of unfavorable variances. This balance contributes to a lower degree of defensiveness about unfavorable variances on the part of subordinates.

One of our interviewees illustrated her boss's approach and explained its benefits:

> My boss is interested in your results, but also in how you approach the problem and get to its root causes. So it's not like: "Dave, I fixed this problem." "Oh, good. Thank you very much." This provides him with a learning opportunity, so he might say: "How did you fix that? How did you solve this problem?" "Well, I did [this and that]." "That's a great idea; I want to use it myself." Or he might suggest some other way you might have considered and we might discuss them. . . . Like when we reached 100 percent customer satisfaction one month, he said, "I'm going to give you an A, but I would also like to hear how you did that. Can you tell us how so that we can share it with the others?" That made us feel great! It took a lot of effort to reach that result. And now, if we get down to 90 percent satisfaction one month and he asks, "Hmm! What happened here?" I won't feel so bad about having to explain. So it's all in how you approach the positive result and the negative result.

**Syndrome Busters Show: "I'm on Your Side."** Research shows that subordinates are more likely to accept feedback if they trust the feedback provider's intentions. Syndrome busters confirm their good intentions toward their subordinates by showing that they care about them, their performance, and their development. Several of the actions we have discussed also help demonstrate the syndrome busters' personal concern for their subordinates, including the time they take to establish a professional and personal relationship with each subordinate, the distinction they make between person and performance, and the openness and attention they demonstrate when discussing bad news and analyzing causes.

There are of course many other ways for bosses to reflect a personal concern for their subordinates' welfare, development, and career. For example, one of the syndrome busters we studied clearly demonstrated his concern by acting as his subordinates' shield and absorbing a lot of the pressure that was coming down from above, and by supporting his subordinates' career aspirations, even when it was not convenient for him. Thinking back to the bosses you have worked for over the years, you will have no difficulty identifying those who cared personally and the signals that conveyed their intentions.

The net result is that syndrome busters are more likely to be listened to by their subordinates. This is exactly what Rajat Gupta, who has been overseeing McKinsey & Co.'s global expansion since taking over in 1994, explained recently:

> Sometimes, somebody wants to become head of an office and I have to have a discussion with two or three potential candidates and appoint one of them. So I'm going to disappoint the other two in some fashion. But fundamentally, if I convince them that I care about their long-term professional success, then I can give them messages that are not always pleasant. . . . If they really believe that you are always trying to make them successful, they will take a lot tougher messages from you.[13]

**Syndrome Busters Face Up to Their Shortcomings.** Some companies—such as GE, Shell, and Ford—require their senior executives to act as teachers in leadership development programs. One of the main benefits of this approach is the example that senior executives give when discussing the leadership lessons they have learned over the years. It is very difficult for junior executives to excuse their leadership shortcomings by referring to their "inner nature" when some of their senior leaders are very explicit about the difficulties they faced and the personal development efforts they made over the years.

Similarly, syndrome busters model for their subordinates a learning orientation regarding their own shortcomings, which makes it easier for subordinates to accept help and advice. More specifically, these leaders display two types of behaviors: They acknowledge when they make mistakes and are not reluctant to apologize for them. They also invite subordinates to help keep them honest and to alert them on the (hopefully) rare occasions where their behavior is unhelpful. These requests for help can be made early in the relationship, as discussed at the start of this chapter. But it does no harm to repeat them once in a while, like the manager who recalled his boss sending him a report back with two questions and a handwritten comment specifying "and by the way, please keep me honest and let me know if I'm becoming a burden."

When bosses acknowledge personal failure or invite subordinates to confront them when their behavior seems inconsistent with the intentions they announced, they signal that they know they are not perfect and hence probably do not expect others to be perfect. This makes it easier for subordinates to acknowledge that they are themselves not perfect.

Bosses who acknowledge failure in their interpersonal behavior (e.g., "Upon further thought, I did not react very well to what you told me earlier.") also signal that they are monitoring themselves, that they think about the way they behave, and that they are probably interested in improving. They also signal that they can be influenced, that is, that they are flexible enough to change their mind.

Last but not least, acknowledging failure and/or inviting subordinates to help monitor themselves signals respect for others in general, and for the subordinates in particular. It conveys clear messages: "You are important to me and I care about the way we communicate," and "I believe that you can help me improve."

## Weighing Up the Investment

Syndrome busters encourage subordinates to seek help and guidance by reacting productively to bad news, focusing on the process that led to the outcome and on what can be learned from the experience. They also make sure they do not take problems away from subordinates and, when they enter "coaching mode," make sure subordinates understand that the objective of the coaching is to help them outgrow the need for it. Beyond encouraging calls for help, these bosses provide feedback that is more acceptable for a variety of reasons: First, because it is not a reflection on the value of subordinates as individuals (person and performance are clearly differentiated); second, because subordinates have a genuine opportunity to validate the boss's data and inferences on the causes of performance; third, because the leader's attention to bad news is legitimated by a corresponding attention to positive outcomes; and fourth, because they trust their boss's intentions toward them. In addition, these leaders also model a strong personal desire to develop themselves and, with the help of subordinates, contribute to a positive boss-subordinate relationship.

Before they get to create this learning environment with subordinates, syndrome busters invest a lot of time and energy in the early stages of the relationship to frame "the contract." They also try to specify some of their key objectives as well as their professional likes, and dislikes, to build and develop personal relationships, and to monitor their tendency to label subordinates hastily and incorrectly. They make sure problems do not set in too deeply by intervening earlier rather than later and inviting subordinates to do the same should they find the boss's behavior unhelpful.

The up-front investment takes time and energy from the boss. There is not much we can say or do about this. Leaders must decide how they allocate their precious first days and weeks, and all we can do is make a pitch for investing a bit more time on the framing and development of relationships. The key word, however, is *investment*. The time and energy are invested to produce returns later by saving the boss, the perceived weaker performers, and their peers and subordinates the multiple costs we identified and discussed in chapter 6.

Bosses *will* spend time dealing with perceived weaker performers. The question is *how* they want this time to be used: squandering time and energy trying to limit the damage done by these subordinates, or else *investing* the effort into trying to get the best from these employees by developing relationships and subordinates' capabilities. Once bosses understand the nature of the dynamics involved in the set-up-to-fail syndrome, it becomes largely a matter of choice. It is also, however, an issue of skills. The syndrome busters we met were not born this way—they worked at becoming what they are. Chapter 10 examines some of the hurdles they encountered along the way, and some of the measures they took to overcome them.

# 10

# Getting There

I do not try to dance better than anyone else. I only try to dance better than myself.

—Mikhail Baryshnikov

WHEN DISCUSSING the boss's role in interrupting and preventing the set-up-to-fail syndrome, we have tried to provide actionable advice grounded in the research we and others have conducted on this subject. For managers to be able to implement these recommendations in real life, the advice must be concrete enough for them to visualize what it might look like in practice. But the fact that a piece of advice is concrete does not make it easy to implement, particularly under stressful or difficult conditions. We have tried to show how bosses can try to decrease the perceived stress associated with dealing with perceived weaker performers by reframing the interactions in broader and more flexible terms. We have also given examples of bosses—"syndrome busters"—who have been successful at being more directive and involved with their subordinates without discouraging or inhibiting them.

Still, there is a gap between knowing and doing. The methods of interrupting and preventing the set-up-to-fail syndrome we described in chapters 8 and 9 represent a change from many managers' usual practices. Any change requires a transition period, during which managers can experiment with the new ways and learn from their successes and failures. This final chapter intends to help with this transition period by providing a few tools and techniques and high-lighting some impediments managers may encounter along the way. Until now, we have tended to talk about bosses in the third person. In this chapter we would like to engage *you,* the reader, more directly, and as a result we often use the second person.

## Nature or Nurture?

Through our research we have identified several bosses who seem to be able to support and empower all their subordinates. Some give the impression of having always been this way; their ability seems to be a natural part of their personality. For others, it seems to be a skill they acquired along the way. For example, a boss whom we'll call "Maurice" seemed to be able to absorb a lot of the pressure coming from his bosses and yet treat all his subordinates, including the weaker-performing ones, in an empowering and supportive way. One of his subordinates emphasized that this was not some kind of act but rather a true expression of who he was:

> The thing is also that it's natural, it's not forced. You can see it all the time. . . . It's not something he puts on for presentation. It seems to be present in everyday life; he really cares for people. I've known him for quite a few years and I haven't seen him change.

Maurice confirmed that he was indeed "being himself":

> I think I'm trapped in my style . . . with the exception of when I determine that the situation is a crisis. I'm stuck in this style with my kids, too, so it's not something that I bring to work and I don't take home.

When we asked the obvious question—"Were you born or raised this way, or did you have to work at it?"—Maurice's answer was unambiguous: Yes, he did work on his behaviors significantly over the years. People used to find him cold; they didn't know what he thought or felt. He had worked so hard at controlling his emotions over the years that he was coming across as aloof and insensitive. So he worked on becoming more accessible to others—and becoming more comfortable expressing his thoughts and emotions in a productive way. In his words:

> I grew up trying to do everything perfectly. Somewhere along the line, someone taught me "never say you're sorry." That was a bad thing to teach me, but I learned it very, very well. For years I didn't feel a whole range of emotions. Over the last few years, I have tried to stop filtering my visible emotions. Today I think that the people working with me know when I'm up and when I'm down. I used to be a real weird guy, not easy to get inside of and not willing to be vulnerable. Now I'm not a mystery for them anymore.

Other bosses we studied had the opposite problem: They couldn't control their emotions, particularly their anger. One executive explained his evolution on that front:

> When I started on this job, I was the most aggressive person you could find. I was one tough SOB. I could really intimidate people. I have personally evolved into a totally different human being than I was three years ago. I learned, I evolved, as well as my staff, we all evolved, to today, where I take a very humanistic approach toward things. And that's the antithesis of who I was three years ago. Today, I'm much calmer.

Over the years we have noted similar declarations from several high-profile leaders (see "Personal Transformations: Top Executives Tell Their Stories"). In each of these cases, and others we studied, the starting point was different and the path traveled differed. Some had to deal with a performance drive so intense that they overwhelmed subordinates. At the other extreme, others were too reserved and secretive. Yet still others were so skilled at making decisions that they kept doing their subordinates' job even after having been promoted. But whether they struggled with aggression, impatience, timidity, micromanagement, or inexpressiveness, these leaders each had their own cross to bear, specific patterns of behavior that they worked on over time.

---

### PERSONAL TRANSFORMATIONS:
### TOP EXECUTIVES TELL THEIR STORIES

The more effective leaders we studied clearly worked hard over the years at developing certain features of their leadership style. So did a number of high-profile leaders, who reflected on their personal challenges.

Elizabeth Acton, then executive VP and CFO of Ford Credit, credits what she learned to her boss, Don Winkler:

> Don has made me a lot more sensitive to my role as a leader, more aware of the shadow that I cast. Lots of people watch us, so my behavior is elevated out of the day-to-day. I think more strategically about it. What signals am I sending? What's my body language saying? Where am I on the mood elevator, and how does that affect people around me? Don has sensitized me to that.[1]

Raymond Smith, then CEO of Bell Atlantic:

> My biggest personal setback was self-inflicted. In my first year as CEO, I was intensely frustrated because people didn't immediately understand my notions of empowerment, accountability, and teamwork. I finally learned to be less impatient. . . . A lot of impatience was coached out of me.[2]

Arnold Hiatt, former CEO of Stride Rite:

> My personal struggle has always been how far to let someone else go. I'll see someone in the company doing something

---

Executives have a tendency to underestimate how much exemplars have actually worked on themselves. There may indeed be a few "natural leaders," people whose disposition or upbringing makes them naturally good at it. But the majority of effective bosses we observed or studied over the years have worked on themselves substantially.

## Making Change a Priority

There are many models of individual and organizational change. These models differ in many substantial ways, but they all agree on

I know isn't right, because I've been there myself too many times before. But then I grit my teeth and remind myself that I never learned anything by listening to someone else preach."[3]

Percy Barnevik, former head of ABB:

My biggest weakness is that with everything I know about this firm, I tend to think too fast and decide too quickly. This intimidates others, and you don't get the confrontation of views that is vital for good decision making. I find that when somebody says something stupid, I have to force myself to smile and say nothing, letting bad ideas die their natural death. If I act too quickly, that person will never again tell me what he believes to be the truth.[4]

Andy Pearson, former head of PepsiCo then chairman and CEO of Tricon (spun off from Pepsi in 1997), who realized late in his career:

There are a lot of ways to ask tough questions without killing somebody. . . . I think I've gone from making my way by trying to be the smartest guy in the room to just asking questions and insisting that the answers be reasonable and logical.[5]

This behavior was quite a change in Pearson, who was then in his seventies. Before he changed his behavior, a colleague recalled, Pearson "was brutal. He'd just beat the crap out of us. I remember one time he told us, 'A room full of monkeys could do better than this!' That was only three years ago."[6]

one thing: There can be no change without a strong desire to change, without a heavy dissatisfaction with the status quo.[7] This is all the more true in today's environment, which leaves managers with absolutely zero slack time and energy. They are already swamped and overwhelmed with current activities, so that any new activity must involve decreasing the time and energy given to current endeavors. The new activity must have a high enough priority to merit time and attention.

In all our discussions so far, we've been trying to raise your consciousness, as it were: to make you feel dissatisfied with the status quo. Some readers should now have a better understanding of their unwitting role in the set-up-to-fail dynamic and of how they can go about interrupting the syndrome in existing relationships or preventing it from beginning in future ones. That in itself should stimulate their interest in trying to change. It represents the first necessary condition to improve.

While this point is intuitively clear, it is worth emphasizing again. Top executive coaches have noticed, as have we, that in today's hectic environment it is "easy to postpone human resource development in favor of other pressing concerns," and that "personal development is important, but it can be put off. Before you know it, a year has passed and those development issues never made it to the top of the 'to do' list," and that "there are too many things to focus [executives'] attention on, and [they] don't have the personal bandwidth to keep going in the new direction. In other words, [they] *know* better, but they don't *do* better."[8]

Understanding your responsibility in the development of the set-up-to-fail syndrome is a fundamental first step, especially because the self-fulfilling nature of the dynamic seems to exonerate the boss from responsibility. But understanding without action and effort is bound to be sterile. Leaders must decide to devote time and attention to interrupting and preventing the syndrome. To do so effectively, they must learn to produce the behaviors we have discussed in chapters 8 and 9, which for most leaders will require some personal development.

## The Transition Phase

Modifying the functioning of an electronically controlled device only requires getting into its source code and adjusting a few lines of programming. The device will then respond immediately to the new instructions. If only human beings were so simple! We cannot go into executives' heads and tweak a neuron or two to make them more patient, more empathic, more open-minded, or more caring. *They* have to decide by themselves that they want the change, and then *they* have to invest the time and energy to enact it.

We all know that it takes much longer to modify the *culture* of an organization than it does to observe changes in the *behavior* of its employees.[9] For example, we can make employees more customer-sensitive relatively quickly by using a very forceful combination of rewards and punishments. This will not work equally well with all employees and will not be sufficient to obtain perfect customer satisfaction, but a strong investment in measuring customer service quality, coupled with powerful rewards for good service and heavy penalties for bad service, *will* modify the behavior of some employees to some extent. To become part of the organization's culture, however, this new attitude will need to be repeated (and reinforced by the organization) often enough, by a large enough proportion of employees, over a long enough period of time, for it to become progressively part of "the way we do things around here."

The same is true at the individual level. It is easier to modify your behavior in specific instances than it is to modify your inner programming. For example, you can learn to interrupt your bursts of anger by increasing your attention to cues that anger is building up, and learning to interrupt them (e.g., by taking a few deep breaths). It is much more difficult—that is, it takes much longer—to rewrite your inner programming so that certain conditions no longer make you lose your temper.

In the short run, managers intent on modifying their behavior must first work on controlling this behavior to make it consistent with their new intentions. Modifying your approach so that it becomes "second nature" takes time. As one leading coach put it, "Knowing what to do and doing it automatically are two very different things. . . . Leadership style is not about what we know, but about how we operate when the heat is on."[10] Nevertheless, we can provide some advice that has proved helpful to managers who have bridged that gap between knowing and doing. Our suggestions fall under three headings: ask for help, craft your behavior, and prepare for setbacks.

## Enlisting Help

When asked how they plan to pursue a change effort, executives often tell us: "The key thing was taking the decision to make this a priority. I have made that decision, so now I guess it's up to me to make it happen." Resolve and willpower are important, but there are limits to going it alone. In our experience, managers embarking on a personal change effort need two types of help: First, ongoing feedback on how well they are doing and whether their efforts are having the desired effects. Second, a caring, unbiased, and competent third party (or parties), who will listen to them and stimulate them at a cognitive level, and help sustain their resolve over time.

### Encouraging Internal Feedback

The people best placed to give you feedback are the ones you interact with most, including your boss, peers, and subordinates. We discussed in chapter 9 the advantages of inviting subordinates to act as joint owners of your relationship with them. We also illustrated that if you invite subordinates to "keep you honest" and help you be more productive, you communicate three important messages: I'm not perfect, and I don't expect you to be; I monitor myself because I want to improve and develop myself; I care about you and our relationship, and my asking for your help is a sign of my respect for you.

Now, in this new context of supporting your personal development, you can get two additional benefits from telling subordinates, peers, and/or bosses about your commitment to improving your performance, and asking them to help you do so. First, you will probably get valuable feedback from these people; subordinates can tell you right away when you display undesirable behavior, and you now have a legitimate reason to connect periodically with subordinates to ask whether they are seeing progress. Second, "going public" about your commitment to change increases the stakes involved in this process and gives you a major incentive to follow through and stick with your effort—otherwise, you risk losing face. "Broadcasting Your Desire to Learn" illustrates how one senior executive tackled this issue and went about asking for help.

Some managers will probably find threatening the idea of asking their subordinates for help—particularly those for whom they have less consideration. Won't it be seen as a sign of weakness? This may have been true not so long ago. But that attitude is probably less common today, at least in most organizational cultures. Two leading coaches agree with this assessment and posit that notwithstanding the impact of future progress by the boss, the mere fact of involving subordinates will lead to an improvement in subordinates' perceptions:

## BROADCASTING YOUR DESIRE TO LEARN

LeRoy Pingho, a vice president at Fannie Mae, the mortgage giant, realized that he would have difficulty changing his behavior without help.
"Some things are 'flat spots' for me," he explained. "I can struggle with
them alone or get help." So when he got his 360-degree feedback
assessment, he distributed copies to fifty people—bosses, peers, direct
reports, his wife—telling them, "You work with me, so you should
know my strengths and weaknesses. Also, I'm going to ask four of you
to help me work on the things I'm not good at."

He chose two peers, one boss, and one subordinate, to act as his
"spotters," and he met with each of them to discuss the "flat spots"
he'd identified. Then he told them that he wanted to work on two of
those weaknesses (five at once seemed too much). First there was
active listening: "When I'm in meetings, I'm already through the presentation before the presenter has gotten to the first page." Second was
empowerment: "I want to use the input I get from people instead of
disregarding it." He asked his spotters to let him know if they saw him
falter: "You don't have to do this in a formal way," he told them. "But
if you see something, tell me."

Making them jointly responsible for "keeping him in line" proved
liberating: "It's like being on the high bar. Just knowing that there's
somebody to make sure you don't fall helps you become more self-
confident." Over time he would no longer need the spotters, as they
would effectively be in his head.

This story, including all the quotes, was featured in G. Imperato, "How to Give Good
Feedback," *Fast Company,* September 1998, 144–156.

By informing peers and subordinates, the individual can gain support and assistance. . . . [By letting] people know he or she is working on changing dysfunctional behaviors, others tend to make
allowances and offer their support. . . . The more a manager
involves others in the coaching process, the more that manager is
perceived as having improved."[11]

Notwithstanding bosses' misgivings regarding asking for help,
the subordinates themselves may be somewhat reluctant to speak
up, at least initially. As Steve Kerr, then Vice President and Chief

Learning Officer at GE, pointed out: "Candor won't happen of its own accord. . . . From the time we're taught to talk, we're taught to lie—it's called courtesy."[12] Similarly, Dick Sethi, a former director of AT&T's executive education programs, warns executives,

> Do not expect employees to be candid just because you ask for candor. This is probably a new experience for many subordinates and can be daunting for any number of reasons. . . . [They] may not believe that you truly want honest feedback. Let people test you.[13]

Sethi's warning highlights a point that is intuitively clear but deserves emphasis: Your behavior following subordinates' first attempt(s) at giving you feedback will be crucial to their willingness to provide more feedback. If people feel (a) that you will not penalize them for their candor and (b) that you will act on their input, they are much more likely to keep volunteering reactions. If one of these two dimensions is missing, they will come to regard your commitment to improving as another flavor-of-the-month intervention.

Ultimately, we are responsible for the way we frame events. If you frame your view involving subordinates in development efforts as threatening and embarrassing, you won't be able to hide this feeling from your subordinates and won't get the help you need. But if you frame your request as a sign of openness and strength, you are more likely to put your subordinates at ease and, as a result, not only get feedback but also make your subordinates more receptive to feedback from you.

Rich Teerlink certainly seems to have benefited from his subordinates' help. Reflecting on his tenure as CEO of Harley-Davidson, he said: "Many times during the course of my tenure, I slipped in my commitment to inclusive leadership. Each time, [one] or another colleague pulled me up short and reminded me that I wasn't 'walking the talk.' I was always grateful."[14]

### Getting Outside Help

Leaders who are trying to work on their skills can also greatly benefit from the help of third parties to support their learning, reflection, and commitment. This third party can be a personal coach—a costly but increasingly common choice—and/or a mentor. The support of someone who has been through such a change—someone you trust and respect, someone with real insight into your strengths and weaknesses, can be invaluable. Coaches and mentors can provide three forms of assistance:

1. They can help you develop a meaningful plan of action—not a "to-do list with boxes to check off . . . [but rather] a thoughtful program that encourages learning."[15] Jointly, you can identify one or two high-impact areas that stir your passion and energy, and you can try to focus on directly observable behaviors. The developmental challenges should be structured in a way that moves from easier behavioral changes to progressively more entrenched behaviors. For example, a simple behavioral change might involve deciding to stop cutting off weaker performers; a more complex one would be to allow their perspectives really to influence your own. Structuring your efforts in this way will generate "quick wins" and will avoid premature exposure to failure. It will therefore build up your sense of self-confidence and your motivation to persevere and stretch further.

2. Second, mentors and coaches can help you track progress. To get a lift from small victories, you need to be able to measure progress, but you also need someone to celebrate with—someone whose own journey allows him to understand the full significance of particular improvements. Without this chance to see or share progress, you may find the change effort frustrating and be tempted to abandon. This is a particular danger in the event of a serious setback, which drives home the fact that you still have "so far to go." It is at this juncture that a reminder from your mentor or coach about how far you have come may be enough to keep your effort on the rails. Indeed, research shows that feedback framed as gains (ground covered) supports self-efficacy, whereas the same feedback framed in terms of shortfall (ground that remains to be covered) diminishes it.[16] The mentor's role in times of difficulty is to provide

perspective, above all by encouraging you to focus on progress made rather than on unfavorable comparisons with others' achievements or on some unattainable ideal.

3. The coach or mentor can help ensure that your developmental effort remains a priority. One of the main barriers to implementing and maintaining a change effort is that it tends to get crowded out by more pressing problems for which you are accountable to someone. In order to change, "We need someone to be a stake in the ground . . . a tether that will hold us steady against past conditioning and the present demands on our lives that distract us from learning new behavior."[17] The coach or mentor forces you to block out or make time by scheduling regular meetings—allowing you to break off from the immediate distractions and to reflect on your daily practice. He or she acts both as your conscience and your shield to make sure that the action plan is implemented.

**The Benefits of Mentors: An Example.** Mack Tilling, cofounder and CEO of Instill, a business-to-business technology company for the food-service industry, has monthly breakfasts with his mentor, David Garrison, CEO of Verestar Communications and former head of Netcom. Tilling claims that being able to talk about your work with an experienced executive can help anyone—even a CEO—make better decisions. "Mentors help you see things in a way that you might not have thought about," he says. "They've all been there many times before, often under diverse and challenging circumstances."

He was so thrilled with the experience that he suggested that the company extend the idea to all senior executives. All senior executives were asked to choose a mentor whom they admire, usually an executive at another company but in the same functional area. Mentors had to be approved by the Instill board and had to sign confidentiality and no-conflict agreements. In exchange for their commitment, they were offered a small amount of stock in Instill. By all reports, the innovative leadership development plan has proved a rousing success. The executives who had found mentors described the relationship as having had a "huge impact" on their effectiveness as bosses.[18]

**Developmental Partnerships.** Building on the two ways of getting help we've just discussed, two organizational psychologists at the Center for Creative Leadership go one step farther by suggesting that leaders should actually cultivate a *range of relationships* to buttress their developmental efforts.[19] From working with executives who achieved their change objectives, they developed a taxonomy of essential roles:

- *Feedback provider* to provide ongoing data on how you are doing
- *Sounding board* to help you think through alternatives and consequences
- *Comparison point* to gauge progress against someone facing a similar challenge
- *Feedback interpreter* to help you make sense of complex data
- *Dialogue partner* to challenge your perspective and underlying assumptions
- *Assignment broker* to propose experiences or responsibilities that will stretch you
- *Accountant* to monitor your progress and remind you of your commitment
- *Role model* to observe and try to emulate
- *Counselor* to provide emotional support and act as a confidante as you struggle with the goal
- *Cheerleader* or *reinforcer* with whom you can share small successes
- *Cohort* to empathize with your struggles and provide "good company" along the way

These psychologists point out that different people, with different skills and dispositions, can fulfill these roles and provide different forms of support, feedback, and stimulation. They believe that there are just too many roles for one person to handle, and in fact no one person should be burdened with all those expectations. Certain roles, such as *assignment broker* and *accountant,* fall more naturally to the boss. Others, like *dialogue partner, feedback interpreter,* or *counselor* would tend to be associated with a mentor. And others still—such as *feedback provider, comparison point,* and *cohort*—could be covered by a trusted colleague. But subordinates, spouses, previous bosses, and even people from other companies who attended the same training course may also have roles to play. For example, Lourdes Townsend, international marketing manager for Stride Rite, realized that some of the best development help she could get was actually from peers in other companies: "I never thought about learning from someone on my level. I always looked two to four levels above me and wondered what I had to do to get there. But the people who have the best solutions to the problems I face are often the people [in other companies] facing those problems themselves."[20]

In other words, these alliances can be external as well as internal; they can vary in intensity; and they can be targeted to particular development needs. For example, for someone just passed over for promotion, the counseling role may be particularly important, but if it is more a case of changing an ingrained habit, then role modeling, feedback, and encouragement may be more important.

The idea of constructing something resembling a "supporting cast" around you may mean involving a larger group than you may want to consider initially. Yet this is an important constituency. Your personal development effort will compete with numerous other demands on your time. Most of these demands come with supporting casts of their own, that is, people who make sure that their action items remain high enough on your priority list and give *you* feedback on how well you are meeting their needs. Bosses, peers, and subordinates will make sure that their professional needs are well tended. Your family members have ways of raising their preoccupations higher on your priority list. The people with whom you play a sport or do charity work will remind you that they're "counting on you Saturday."

Amid all these stakeholders fighting for your time and attention, who—besides yourself—are you accountable to regarding your personal development, and who will make it a point to give you feedback along the way? Making public your commitment to development will raise the stakes and encourage you to deliver. But you also need ongoing feedback, help, and support to make sure you keep investing the necessary time and energy.

## Crafting Your Behavior

As we mentioned previously, reacting productively to problems or difficult situations requires less effort when the pressure is less intense and when you are dealing with your perceived stronger performers. The real test comes when the pressure mounts and emotions start running high. That is when it is easy to revert to your dominant behavior, which may involve imposing your solution, not listening, cutting people off, or chewing them out. In these situations, you need to find ways of overriding your automatic response. The following techniques can help you.

### Slowing Down the Process

When we are engaged in a discussion, we rarely stop to reflect on what we should say at each particular point in time. This is particularly true when the discussion becomes heated; the Ping-Pong ball travels faster and faster between one party and the other, each pushing his or her point more and more vigorously. During these discussions we do not consciously examine each utterance, and words tend to fly out of our mouths. Yet these words are not just spoken randomly—*something* is organizing them. Following Chris Argyris and many others, we call this something our "master program." That is the mental software that has developed over the years and which, at a given time, directs our behavior.[21]

We have shown in previous chapters that many aspects of our master program can get us into trouble in our dealings with subordinates, particularly perceived weaker performers. We have argued that this is particularly true under conditions of stress. These conditions often limit our ability to process information effectively by engaging specific cognitive biases. They also trigger well-internalized mechanisms designed to bypass perceived threat and embarrassment. Yet under these stressful conditions, we tend to react so quickly that we don't give ourselves a chance to craft our response and behavior consciously. We react spontaneously, that is, we let our master program dictate our behavior.

If we know that this master program can lead us to react in dysfunctional ways, particularly when under stress, we must *interrupt the normal reaction process* and give ourselves a chance to *craft our behavior consciously* along the lines of the principles we have discussed in chapters 7, 8, and 9. The first step is to slow down the conversation process. We must take the time to listen actively to what the other party said (and did not say), process this information, and construct an appropriate response.

This process requires a conscious effort of self-control, whereby we have to tell ourselves, "Listen, process, do *not* react immediately!" It also requires the introduction of what one of the managers we studied called a "buffer between your head and your mouth." This buffer allows the speaker to consider what he is about to say and to determine whether it is likely to be a functional response under the circumstances and whether it fits with his intentions and guiding principles. Take the following example:

- A perceived weaker performer enters your office and says, "Boss, we have a problem with this client. It looks as though we're going to lose their business."

- First thing that comes to your mind is "My God, I need this like I need a hole in the head! This bum screwed up again! I have been warning him for months about this client and as usual he didn't listen. . . . "

- Submit this initial reaction to your internal buffer for examination.

- Result of the examination: Nonproductive response, punitive for the subordinate and not oriented toward a resolution of the issue. Suppress this response.

- Generation of alternative responses, which has two facets:
  - Guiding principles: Try to get as much information as possible before making an evaluation of the subordinate's performance. Try also not to take the problem away from the subordinate—can we use this event for coaching purposes and/or to fix a process?
  - Possible answers: Tell me more about this. What happened? Please summarize for me the recent events that led to this reaction.

Note that the possible responses tend to look like questions. When your emotional levels are running high, a good option is to ask questions. Starting with questions gives you a chance to calm down, to gather more information, and to avoid compounding the problem unnecessarily. Strong emotions like anger make us jump to conclusions. We are likely to try to solve the problem on the basis of incorrect assumptions and with insufficient data. Also, for reasons explored in chapter 4, we are likely to place disproportionate blame on the individual as opposed to the circumstances. To avoid this, we need to slow down, to get a clearer picture of what has happened and why—and to make sure we take account of the subordinate's viewpoint. That means playing back what you think you have heard in your own words, so that the subordinate can clarify misunderstandings and make further inputs.

It could be that you as the boss cannot, at that point in time, process the information and react productively. This may be the third successive item of bad news you have received, leading to a "system overload." When you feel your emotional intensity rising uncontrollably, one option is simply to break off and give yourself a chance to calm down. We talked in chapters 6 and 7 about your "energy pot." Rather than engaging in a difficult discussion when you already feel stressed or irritated, with a significant proportion of your energy devoted to keeping a lid on your emotions, it may be wiser simply to take yourself out of situations where you may be unnecessarily harsh toward subordinates. While venting may provide instant relief for you, it often generates significant costs downstream in terms of patching up relationships. If you feel unable to handle a productive discussion, you need to acknowledge that feeling and be prepared to withdraw (explaining to the subordinate why) rather than risk undermining your change efforts. A possible response could simply be . . . the truth! "Look, this is the third piece of bad news in a row I've heard, and that's a bit much for me! Please give me a few minutes. I'll get back to you when I can process this effectively."

To be able to take time-outs and ask questions under pressure, you must learn to "catch the cue(s)" that you're about to lose your ability to craft your behavior consciously. This loss of control to your dominant behavior is typically preceded by a growing sense of impatience, frustration, or anger. You need to improve your monitoring of these rising emotions. For example, if you tend to blow up at people, that means learning to recognize the rush of adrenaline that typically precedes anger. More generally, you need to develop a better understanding of your "hot buttons" and what situations trigger problematic behavior. Learning to read those early warning signals will allow you to activate the buffer between your mind and your mouth.

At this point, some of you are probably thinking, "Oh, my God, this sounds like an incredibly contrived and unnatural reaction!" Well, yes and no. On one hand, slowing down the process to craft your behavior consciously is different from what most of us do most of the time. In that sense it does not come "naturally." But we must consider two additional points.

First, what we call our natural reaction feels natural today, but it is the product of a master program that has been constructed over a lifetime. Part of it is probably genetically driven, but a large part of it has been constructed by society and our experiences. We have slowly learned over the years that under condition $X$, response $Y$ tended to be productive for our purposes. Over the years, we have progressively *internalized* this behavioral rule so that today we no longer have to think about it. Like riding a bicycle, it has become a skill, something we just do without conscious processing. That does not make it natural, because it is still the result of a socially constructed process.

Second, we have established that our master program and the natural reactions that it triggers are often dysfunctional. We should not be condemned to use dysfunctional rules forever simply because we have unconsciously internalized them over time. Therefore we must rewrite our existing master program to incorporate other rules that will, we hope, produce more productive outcomes.

Hence while it may feel unnatural to slow down the conversation, the underlying idea is to substitute a consciously constructed, explicit set of rules for a mostly tacit set of rules that our experiences have constructed over a number of years. In essence, we are saying:

> I do not like the responses that my current master program dictates under these and those conditions. I would prefer to react based on

a different set of guiding principles. I have not yet internalized these new guiding principles, so they do not come naturally. As a result, for some time I must consciously force-fit the new guiding principles on to my behavior. In time, I will internalize these new rules so that they come naturally to me.

In terms of process, this is very similar to what you do when you try to improve your golf game. As a learner, you have a natural, instinctive golf swing, usually involving bent arms. You get advice from a pro on how to improve your swing and then try to control each of your movements to replicate precisely what the pro has advised you to do. You will need to hit a few hundred, possibly a few thousand, balls before you start internalizing this new movement. At that point your new swing will have become natural. Until then you will have to monitor your movements very consciously.

Let's continue with this golf analogy, because the process we just described is exactly what Tiger Woods went through between July 1997 and February 1999. Although his swing had allowed him to win the 1997 Masters by a record twelve strokes, Woods felt that his swing was not reliable enough to allow him to win when his timing wasn't perfect. He hence embarked on a swing-improvement program, which required him to deconstruct and then rebuild his swing completely. Woods spent the next eighteen months "pounding hundreds of practice balls, reviewing tapes of the swing, and repeating both of the above." During that period Woods won only one of the tournaments he was registered for, having previously won four tournaments in his first seven months on the pro tour. His new swing started to come together effortlessly in May 1999, and by the close of the year Woods had won an extraordinary ten out of fourteen events.[22]

Woods's swing now looks natural, but he certainly worked extremely hard to make it so!

## Preparing for, and Reflecting on, Interactions

To react more productively *online,* during actual conversations, it is not enough to slow things down; you also need to invest time *offline,* in preparation and reflection. Avoiding mistakes, and learning better from them, depends on thinking ahead and thinking back.

**Thinking Ahead.** As discussed in chapter 7, much of the stress and fear that we project into discussions is driven by the way we frame the underlying situation. When dealing with weaker performers, in particular, we expect problems—so we go in with a negative mind-set and to try to leave as little open to chance as possible. Typically we have a strong sense that "this is going to be difficult," and we think, "I hope I can contain the emotion." In many cases, the subsequent collision or deadlock seems almost scripted in advance. We set out to solve the wrong problem or overlook key objectives or options. We head up a blind alley or into a stalemate. We lurch painfully toward ineffectual solutions that destroy trust, goodwill, or the subordinate's sense of autonomy and participation—in large part because of the mental frame we created for approaching the issue.

Frames play tricks on our minds because we are often unaware of them or else assume they are self-evident. Although we "know" that reality is a personal perspective, we are not continuously, actively thinking that other people could see the world differently. We tend to enter situations thinking *not* "This is how I see it," but rather "This is how it is." Our personal view and the truth are one and the same. And if our personal view *is* the truth, then everybody should be able to see it. This phenomenon is called "frame blindness."[23]

Productive discussions are the result of thoughtful and flexible framing—and that means *taking the time* to think ahead, realizing that others may see the situation entirely differently from you, and not relying on predetermined solutions.

Another way to think ahead is to use spare moments to craft imaginary conversations in your head. You have to talk to "Jane" in two days about this tricky issue. What will you say? What will she say then? How will you react if she says that? You can practice these sessions mentally on your own, or you can ask a trusted third party to role-play Jane's position. The objective is not to try to imagine every conversation path possible and prepare ready-made answers for each; that would be both impossible and dysfunctional, because you would be stuck in a frozen frame. Instead, the objective is for you to realize over time, as you repeat this exercise, that some types of reactions lead to more productive discussions than others. So rather than imagining "if she says this I'll say that," you will progressively identify what *not* to say in certain circumstances. The exercise will also probably lead you to develop more empathy for Jane's point of view, as well as a better understanding of your own mental and emotional maps, both of which may be very helpful during the actual discussion.

An executive we interviewed mentioned another way to think ahead to situations and conversations. When in doubt, he asks himself two questions to stimulate his reflection: "How would those two great bosses I have had over the years approach this situation? And if I were the subordinate involved, how would I want my boss to approach me in this situation?" The objective of these questions is neither to replicate mindlessly past bosses' behavior nor to project his personality and likely reactions onto subordinates, but rather to bring different lights to the issue at hand and thus broaden his framing and reasoning.

**Reflecting on Conversations and Interactions.** The wise words and sayings of philosophers encourage us to learn from our mistakes. For example the Romans used to say, *"Errare humanum est, persevere diabolicum"* (to err is human, to persist is wicked). Luminaries of the business world preach the same lesson. Akio Morita, cofounder of Sony, advised: "Don't be afraid to make a mistake. But make sure you don't make the same mistake twice." Financier George Soros concurs: "Once we realize that imperfect understanding is the human condition, there is no shame in being wrong, only in failing to correct our mistakes."[24] And a very senior Indian executive we work with recently reminded his staff worldwide that the definition of insanity is "doing the same thing again and again and expecting a different outcome."

Experience can be a great platform for learning, but learning does not follow automatically from experience. You need to *make sense* of the experience and infer useful lessons. This is particularly true with respect to modifying your behavioral patterns over time. In order to change your behavior, you must increase your ability to learn from experience. One way to do so is to devote more time to reflecting on human interactions you engage in or witness.

Reflecting on interactions you were part of involves evaluating your conduct after the event, replaying the discussion mentally to assess what can be learned from the exchange. Did you get impatient, did you cut people off, did you listen properly, did you get to the root cause and agree on a joint solution? What about the other person? How were your arguments received? What reactions did they produce? Did you test or inquire to make sure your intentions were not misread? And what about *your* reaction to what you heard? Did you understand what the other person said, and did you check that you had understood? What reactions did you feel obliged to suppress along the way, and why? Did the person do anything that triggered an emotional reaction on your part (e.g., irritation, embarrassment, fear)? Why does this type of behavior lead you to feel this emotion? What is the button that is being pushed?

Reflecting on past events can help you understand the impact your actions (and other people's actions) have on others and why others react the way they do. Better understanding the implications of your actions on subordinates is an essential component of learning to develop more productive responses. Subordinates' reactions are partly guided by their individual personalities, of course, but you may still identify certain trends and tendencies. For example, one executive told us that over the years he had learned to ask, "What can *we* do about this?" rather than "What are *you* going to do about this?"

> There's a significant difference between the two formulations. One is, "I am shedding any association with the problem by saying, "What are *you* doing with it?" I just put the monkey on *their* back. The other is, "What can *we* do about it?" I'm letting them know that I've enlisted myself in the solution to the problem. . . . At this point, I no longer have to think consciously about using "we" rather than "you." I'm now comfortable in that approach. I did have to work at it, though it's not something that's just totally natural. I got it by observing the behavior of several bosses and the results they were getting, and I said, "Ah! Everybody hates this guy, and everybody loves that one." And they're asking the same thing, but the way they're asking it is totally different. And so you sort of observe things and learn from them.

The discipline of personal reflection can be developed with the help of a mentor, a coach, or a sparring partner. This third party can question your assumptions, play devil's advocate, or even role-play your subordinate's perspective. Keeping a diary or a log can also help: Making notes about what goes well and less well, looking more systematically at causes and effects, identifying discrepancies between expectations and how things actually turn out—all these things can help accelerate your learning process. And you can begin to acknowledge where your own behavior has been inadequate: "This is what went wrong; this is why I think it went wrong; this is what I'll do so it doesn't happen again; this is what I've learned."

Another helpful exercise is writing a caselet about an interaction, such as those in chapter 7. On the right side of the page, you record the actual dialogue as you remember it, and on the left side you write your unexpressed thoughts and feelings. Writing such a "split-page" exercise can help you reflect on difficult interactions. This kind of writing can give you a window into your own mind and help you ask yourself why you acted and reacted the way you did. It can also help you become increasingly aware of the untested attributions and evaluations you make about others. Understanding better the impact of your actions on others is an important subject of reflection, but so is understanding better your own existing master program and the impact of others' behavior on you.

Yet another tool that can help you analyze your behavior is taping or videotaping important interactions. John Seely Brown, Xerox's Chief Scientist at Palo Alto, used this approach to assess the extent to which his behavior could be inhibiting his staff:

> As a leader, I could be the team's biggest obstacle in the unlearning process. Each of us can send out signals—by raising our voices, squinting our eyes, stiffening our bodies—that block open conversation and shut people down. To try to curb those signals, I started videotaping important meetings to see exactly how I acted and what subliminal cues I sent out.[25]

Each tool and approach has its advantages and disadvantages. Videotaping meetings provides richer data than your own recollections, but it is also less transparent to others than writing caselets. Whichever support you choose to use, the first step is to develop the discipline of devoting some time to learning from your interactions.[26]

---

**CRAFTING YOUR BEHAVIOR CONSCIOUSLY: SUMMARY**

- Slow down the conversation.
- Listen and think.
- Maintain a buffer between your brain and your mouth. Consider your response carefully in light of your new guiding principles.
- Ask questions to get relevant information.
- Catch the cue(s).
- Ask for time-out (that is, postpone your response) if need be.
- Prepare for, and reflect on, interactions.
- Think ahead to conversations and interactions.
- Reflect back on conversations and interactions.

---

For a summary of all the recommendations of the last few pages, see "Crafting Your Behavior Consciously."

## Preparing for Setbacks

Research into personal change has shown that it hardly ever follows a linear trajectory. Successful change efforts include improvements, plateaus, regressions, and recoveries. Reversals are therefore to be expected. For example, it takes smokers an average of three to four attempts before they can break the habit in a sustainable way. And New Year's resolvers report five or more years of consecutive pledges before maintaining the behavioral goal for at least six months.[27] Numerous leaders have experienced this problem. Here are some testimonies.

A consultant had confronted Ralph Stayer and his top management team at Johnsonville Foods with an uncomfortable truth about the source of their difficulties. "*You* are the problem," he told them. "You state your opinions first. . . . You cut people off. . . . You insist on making every decision. No wonder people don't take responsibility. You won't let them." They were stunned, especially after listening to tape recordings of their meetings. They saw that their leadership behavior *was* counterproductive. So they resolved to change. Stayer recalls, "At the next meeting we tried to remain quiet.

That lasted about three minutes. We tried to stop providing the answers. That lasted about as long. It was tough being different."[28]

Jim Chartrand rose through the ranks to become plant manager at International Paper in his mid-thirties. He was forced to work on his leadership style following the refusal of all the plant's employees to obey a direct order he had given them. He commented on his evolution as follows:

> In the past, when I made a floor visit, I was looking for fires to fight. I'd want to jump in and solve every problem. Now my role on the floor is to help people solve their own problems. I can offer support and resources, but it's mainly their responsibility. More than anything, my job is to listen. . . . I still have problems listening rather than speaking. . . . I have to force myself to listen and comprehend. . . . I still want to jump to conclusions. I have to fight that constantly. I think I know the answer before investing any time into investigating a problem. . . . While the evolution has been rewarding for me both professionally and personally, it wasn't an easy road.[29]

Back in 1992, David Pottruck was told in no uncertain terms by his boss, Larry Stupski, then president of Charles Schwab, that his peers could not stand working with him: "You're overwhelming. Like a freight train." Pottruck was devastated, but he worked hard with a personal coach to overcome the problem and went on to become co-CEO. But even today, it's a daily struggle to restrain himself. At a recent meeting he tried to force an idea on colleagues. They confronted him on it and he acknowledged the error. "I don't want to sound like a recovering alcoholic," observed Pottruck, "but under stress, we revert to old ways."[30]

So you can take for granted that, no matter how hard you try and how good you are, there *will* be breakdowns. There *will* be occasions where you fail to live up to the values you espouse and display the behaviors you are trying to internalize. That's the bad news.

The good news is that an occasional breakdown need not destroy your subordinates' entire faith in your commitment. Remember that subordinates, just like bosses, interpret their boss's behavior through the prism they have developed based on their interactions with the boss, particularly early ones. If your subordinates have decided that you are truly working hard on your behavior and that you really mean well, they are likely to interpret your behavior through that lens and, as a result, forgive and forget the occasional lapse.

A manufacturing supervisor working two levels below Maurice, whom we mentioned at the beginning of the chapter, gave us a sensitive illustration of this process. In anticipation of the likely completion of a number of units during weekend overtime production, he had asked the required quality support staff to come in for the weekend. The units were not completed in time, which meant that the quality staff was paid for nothing. The supervisor remembered Maurice asking him with an acerbic tone, "Why did you have quality staff come in during the weekend if you're not shipping anything?" The supervisor of course explained that he was *hoping* to ship the products, and commented to us on the incident:

> No, I was not angry at him. He is not a vindictive man. I was simply puzzled. I figured he wanted to yell because the product wasn't shipped on time, so I figured he was trying to vent his frustration. But being the polite and thoughtful man that he is, that's all he could muster.

In addition to creating conditions that will increase subordinates' propensity to be understanding, bosses can help themselves by handling such occasional breakdowns productively. Research on customer satisfaction conducted in the early 1990s by British Airways showed very clearly that the happiest customers were not those who had enjoyed a seamless travel experience, but rather customers who had experienced a problem that was resolved to their satisfaction.[31]

Similarly, a breakdown is an opportunity to reaffirm your commitment to the new approach, your confidence in subordinates, the difficulty of what you are trying to do, and the fact that you are doing it for them (too). Now, we're not claiming that breakdowns are desirable, but if you handle them productively, they can provide a means of bouncing back. Bosses who are prepared to acknowledge a failure in their interpersonal behavior ("Look, on reflection I didn't react very well to what you told me earlier. . . . ") signal that they are monitoring themselves, that they think about the way they behave, and

## CAPITALIZING ON BREAKDOWNS

A plant manager, we'll call him George, was becoming frustrated at the lack of progress shown by his managers in terms of workstation organization. So one day he simply went out and put little red "reject" stickers all through the factory floor on objects he felt were misplaced.

That very afternoon, two of the managers came to his office to let him know just how furious everybody was. "Why?" he asked. "It was so demeaning," they explained. "It made us feel like we were little kids being told to clean our rooms." George asked them whether that was the general perception. "Yes," they answered, at which point he realized he'd made a mistake: "Oops. It sounds like I blew it."

The next morning, without telling the managers, George went to every single operator on the floor and apologized personally. "Hey, I guess I offended everybody with these reject stickers yesterday," he admitted. "I'm sorry. I screwed up."

The employees had never seen anything like it before—from George or any of his predecessors. In the words of one manager, "It blew everybody away," not just because George was willing to face up to a mistake but also because he was willing to accept corrective feedback. Looking back, George realized, "I wasn't trying to get any mileage out of it. I was just feeling like I screwed things up. But it was a real turning point. From that day on, the whole plant of over two hundred people and myself were truly one. . . . It was a truly cementing event for all of us."

that they are genuinely interested in improving. They also signal that they are "confrontable," in that they are capable of changing their minds. Consider the example in "Capitalizing on Breakdowns."

Productive reactions to breakdowns can therefore have a dual impact: restoring momentum for the person making the change, but also providing reassurance for those who provide feedback and who see that the person is serious about change. Indeed, an additional benefit is that subordinates get to *see* how the boss actually handles breakdowns—making it more likely that the subordinates themselves will be able to reproduce the behavior with *their* own subordinates.

This kind of modeling is very important in terms of encouraging others to prevent set-up-to-fail syndromes. Indeed, research suggests that observing "masterly models" who perform effortlessly is less helpful than observing "coping models," who begin uncertainly and are seen to overcome difficulties. As behavioral models, those who do not perform with "consummate ease" seem less distant from ourselves, making the behavior seem more accessible.[32] They also demonstrate both the need for perseverance and the means of recovering from setbacks.

This matters because leaders cannot "model" the behavior much beyond their first and, in some cases, second reports. As a leader, your ultimate goal is not simply to prevent set-up-to-fail syndromes with your own direct reports, but to try and eradicate them from the whole chain of relationships below you. Subordinates hence play a key role in diffusing the learning message and reinforcing an environment where everyone learns from everyone else.

Mark Maletz, a change consultant affiliated with McKinsey & Co., reached the same conclusion:

> Leaders and change agents should obviously avoid going public every time they screw up. But . . . occasionally admitting that you're wrong sends an incredibly powerful message that you're serious about engaging in a healthy debate. And it surprises me how few senior executives are willing to do that. They think that acknowledging even one mistake will make them appear as ineffective leaders, when in fact the reverse is true.[33]

## Investing in Yourself

We have met many executives who, after such discussions, conclude with resignation: "This is probably too difficult a path for me. I guess I am who I am and, at this point, it's probably too late for me to change." This is a decision each of us has to make. Our own view has been shaped by our work with executives. In particular by the fact that the most effective leaders we have studied—two of whom we quoted earlier in this chapter—have invariably told us that they were not always so effective and that they had improved over the years by working on their behavior.

On that basis, we no longer buy the "I'd like to change but I am the way I am" argument. It is clear that at any given point in time, some things do come more easily to some people than to others, but the fact that most of us will never become Grand Masters does not mean we cannot become better chess players. Mikhail Baryshnikov is one of the greatest ballet dancers of his generation, yet as indicated in this chapter's opening quote, he tries only to dance better than himself, not better than others.

At the end of the day, however, no researcher, consultant, or teacher can give you *conclusive* evidence that you *can* change, for one simple reason. No one but you can answer the key questions: What price are you willing to pay in order to succeed? How much time and energy are you willing to invest in this process?

In this respect, we are often struck by the fact that some leaders who argue that developing their leadership skills is beyond their capabilities, still devote significant amount of time, energy, and money to improving their tennis or golf game. When it comes to these pursuits, they accept that it will take years to improve their backhand or their swing significantly. In the case of golf, they persevere through setbacks and are willing to spend hours with their elbows strapped to internalize how to hold their arms properly. In some ways, improving their golf or tennis game is easier than modifying significant aspects of their leadership style. Tennis and golf provide instant feedback on the result of their efforts, and no one gets hurt when they encounter failures. At work, these leaders do not get immediate and unambiguous feedback on the impact of each of their actions, and they *can* hurt themselves and others as they experiment with new ways of managing.

But it is still striking that so many managers are willing to invest years to improve their performance in a hobby, yet resist the idea of investing time and energy into becoming more effective at an activity that is much more fundamental for them. Managers' jobs have several facets, but maximizing their subordinates' contribution undoubtedly ranks among the critical ones. Indeed, as mentioned in chapter 1, the failure to establish good relationships with peers and subordinates typically rates as the number-one cause of career derailment among executives.

Quality Guru Edward Deming often reminded participants in his seminars that "Learning is not compulsory, but neither is survival."[34]

We like to use an analogy to make the same point. If you think of yourself as a business, then you must attend to all facets of your value chain. That means spending time on sales and marketing, developing networks and managing impressions. It means spending time on production, striving to reach your business goals and objectives. It also means investing in R&D, spending time on the development of your skills—existing ones as well as new ones. You would not invest in a company operating in a dynamic environment that invests nothing in its R&D, would you?

Improving work performance is an important subject. It has, in fact, become a condition for survival in an increasingly demanding world. We believe it is possible to improve the performance of subordinates, particularly those who appear to be weaker performers, in a way that creates less human pain than the "common-sense" approach most managers have internalized over the years. We have tried to describe what this way looks like. We hope that our efforts will help yours, and we look forward to hearing from some of you about the results of your interventions.

# Notes

## Chapter 1

1. J. P. Kotter, *What Leaders Really Do* (Boston: Harvard Business School Press, 1999), 52–53.
2. W. Bennis and J. Goldsmith, *Learning to Lead* (Reading, MA: Addison-Wesley, 1994), 4. See also *Charismatic Leadership in Organizations,* by J. A. Conger and R. N. Kanungo (Thousand Oaks, CA: Sage, 1998), particularly pages 1–11 for a good discussion of the differences between "leadership and managership."
3. "Three-hundred-and-sixty-degree feedback" involves collecting information on a manager's behavior from a variety of respondents, such as the manager him- or herself, the boss, peers and colleagues, and subordinates.
4. E. L. Axelrod, H. Handfield-Jones, and T. A. Welsh, "The War for Talent, Part Two," *McKinsey Quarterly* 2 (2001): 9–12.
5. Unpublished research by Jodi Taylor and her CCL colleagues, cited by J. M. Kouzes and B. Z. Posner, "When Leaders Are Coaches," in *Coaching for Leadership,* eds. M. Goldsmith, L. Lyons, and A. Freas (San Francisco: Jossey-Bass/Pfeiffer, 2000).
6. For a review of previous studies and additional support, see E. Van Velsor and J. B. Leslie, "Why Executives Derail: Perspectives across Time and Cultures," *Academy of Management Executive* 9 (1995): 62–72.
7. See A. Fisher, "Don't Blow Your New Job," *Fortune,* 22 June 1998, 79–81.
8. A. Howard and D. W. Bray, *Managerial Lives in Transition: Advancing Age and Changing Times* (New York: Guilford Press, 1988).

9. Quoted in S. Milne, "Managers Under Stress," *Guardian*, 1 December 1998, 4.

10. D. Costello, "Stressed Out: Can Workplace Stress Get Worse?" *Wall Street Journal*, 16 January 2001, B1.

11. Specifically, a survey of 930 employees in Michigan (United States) found that 27.2 percent had been "mistreated" in the previous twelve-month period. See L. Keashly and K. Jagatic, "Workplace Abuse and Aggression" (paper presented at the American Public Health Association conference, Chicago, November 1999). For further documentation, see <http://www.bullybusters.org>.

12. More specifically, the British study estimated that victims of workplace bullying took an extra seven days off a year compared with other employees. See C. Cooper and H. Hoel, *Survey of Workplace Bullying* (Manchester, UK: Umist/British Occupational Health Research Foundation, 2000).

13. M. F. Hirigoyen, *Stop au Harcèlement Moral!* (Paris: Editions Syros, 1998).

14. F. Collomp and P. M. Dechamps, "La violence au travail," *L'Expansion*, 27 May 1999, 48–62.

15. D. Chappell and V. Di Martino, *Violence at Work* (Geneva: International Labor Organization, 1998).

16. This 1998 study was conducted by researchers at the University of North Carolina and is cited in S. Vaughn, "Career Challenge," *Los Angeles Times*, 1 July 2001, 1.

17. John Sullivan, head of the HRM program at San Francisco State University, cited in G. Imperato, "How to Hire the Next Michael Jordan," *Fast Company*, December 1998, 212–219.

## Chapter 2

1. For a review of the very extensive research on leadership, see B. M. Bass and R. M. Stogdill, *Bass & Stogdill's Handbook of Leadership* (New York: Free Press, 1990); see also G. Yukl, *Leadership in Organizations* (Englewood Cliffs, NJ: Prentice-Hall, 2001).

2. The following notes provide several references to this stream of research. The first draft of this book contained an Appendix summarizing the key findings in this field. We ultimately had to exclude it due to space constraints, but you can download it easily and free of charge from the knowledge base of our Web site <http://www.set-up-to-fail.net>.

3. F. Dansereau, G. Graen, and W. J. Haga, "A Vertical Dyad Linkage Approach to Leadership within Formal Organizations: A Longitudi-

nal Investigation of the Role Making Process," *Organizational Behavior and Human Performance* 13, (1975): 46–78.

4. A recent review identified close to 150 publications on the subject. See C. A. Schriesheim, L. L. Neider, and T. A. Scandura, "Delegation and Leader-Member Exchange: Main Effects, Moderators, and Measurement Issues," *Academy of Management Journal* 41 (1999): 298–318.

5. See, for example, S. L. Robinson and E. W. Morrison, "Psychological Contracts and OCB: The Effect of Unfulfilled Obligations on Civic Virtue Behavior," *Journal of Organizational Behavior* 16 (1995): 289–299. See also M. A. Konovsky and S. D. Pugh, "Citizenship Behavior and Social Exchange," *Academy of Management Journal* 37 (1994): 656–667.

6. A. Bandura, *Self-Efficacy: The Exercise of Control* (New York: Freeman, 1997).

7. J. Schaubroeck and D. E. Merritt, "Divergent Effects of Job Control on Coping with Work Stressors: The Key Role of Self-Efficacy," *Academy of Management Journal* 40 (1997): 738–754.

8. M. Blittner, J. Goldberg, and M. Merbaum, "Cognitive Self-control Factors in the Reduction of Smoking Behavior," *Behavior Therapy* 9 (1978): 553–561.

9. R. Wood and A. Bandura, "Impact of Conceptions of Ability on Self-Regulatory Mechanisms and Complex Decision Making," *Journal of Personality and Social Psychology* 56 (1989): 407–415.

10. E. J. Langer, *Mindfulness* (Reading, MA: Addison-Wesley, 1989).

11. The concept of "learned helplessness" was introduced by J. B. Overmier and M. E. P. Seligman in "Effects of Inescapable Shock upon Subsequent Escape and Avoidance Learning," *Journal of Comparative and Physiological Psychology* 63 (1967): 28–33.

12. M. E. P. Seligman, *Helplessness* (San Francisco: Freeman, 1975).

13. D. C. Klein, E. Fencil-Morse, and M. E. P. Seligman, "Learned Helplessness, Depression and the Attribution of Failure," *Journal of Personality and Social Psychology* 33 (1976): 508–516.

14. E. L. Deci and R. M. Ryan, *Intrinsic Motivation and Self-Determination in Human Behavior* (New York: Plenum, 1985); see also R. M. Ryan and E. L. Deci, "Self-determination Theory and the Facilitation of Intrinsic Motivation, Social Development, and Well-being," *American Psychologist* 55 (2000): 68–78.

15. G. C. Williams, V. M. Grow, Z. R. Freedman, R. M. Ryan, and E. L. Deci, "Motivational Predictors of Weight Loss and Weight-Loss Maintenance," *Journal of Personality and Social Psychology* 70 (1996): 115–126.

16. A short and easy-to-read summary of research on Self-Determination Theory can be downloaded easily and free of charge from our Web site <http://www.set-up-to-fail.net>.

17. R. M. Ryan and J. P. Connell, "Perceived Locus of Causality and Internalization," *Journal of Personality and Social Psychology* 57 (1989): 749–761.

18. A short and easy-to-read summary of research on the Pygmalion Effect in schools and work organizations can be downloaded easily and free of charge from our Web site <http://www.set-up-to-fail.net>.

19. R. Rosenthal and L. Jacobson, *Pygmalion in the Classroom: Teacher Expectations and Pupils' Intellectual Development* (New York: Holt, Rinehart & Winston, 1968).

20. Some studies, though, have failed to detect this effect. Meta-analyses suggest that failures to detect the Pygmalion effect tend to occur when the teachers' expectations are manipulated after the teacher had an opportunity to develop his or her own independent expectations. When the manipulation occurs within the first two weeks of the teacher meeting the pupils, the effect is robust. See S. W. Raudenbush, "Magnitude of Teacher Expectancy Effects on Pupil IQ as a Function of the Credibility of Expectancy Induction: A Synthesis of Findings from 18 Experiments," *Journal of Educational Psychology* 76 (1984): 85–97; see also R. Rosenthal, "Critiquing Pygmalion: A 25-year Perspective," *Current Directions in Psychological Science* 4 (1995): 171–172.

21. A. E. Smith, L. Jussim, and J. Eccles, "Do Self-fulfilling Prophecies Accumulate, Dissipate, or Remain Stable over Time?" *Journal of Personality and Social Psychology* 77 (1999): 548–565.

22. Most of these experiments have been conducted by Eden and his colleagues in collaboration with the Israeli Defense Forces. These studies stand out by their clever design and powerful results. The military context provides fantastic opportunities for matched comparisons, standardized tests, and measurable outcomes. Beyond that, Eden was careful to manipulate leader expectations as lightly as possible, often changing just one word in a five-minute briefing.

23. D. Eden and A. B. Shani, "Pygmalion Goes to Boot Camp," *Journal of Applied Psychology* 67 (1982): 194–199.

24. D. Eden and G. Ravid, "Pygmalion vs. Self-expectancy: Effects of Instructor- and Self-expectancy on Trainee Performance," *Organizational Behavior and Human Performance* 30 (1982): 351–364.

25. S. Oz and D. Eden, "Restraining the Golem: Boosting Performance by Changing the Interpretation of Low Scores," *Journal of Applied Psychology* 79 (1994): 744–754.

26. E. Y. Babad, J. Inbar, and R. Rosenthal, "Teachers' Judgment of Students' Potential as a Function of Teachers' Susceptibility to Biasing Information," *Journal of Personality and Social Psychology* 42 (1982): 541–547.

## Chapter 3

1. C. O. Word, M. P. Zanna, and J. Cooper, "The Nonverbal Mediation of Self-fulfilling Prophecies in Interracial Interaction," *Journal of Experimental Social Psychology* 10 (1974): 109–120.
2. The problem-solving experiment is discussed in D. Cervone and P. K. Peake, "Anchoring, Efficacy, and Action: The Influence of Judgmental Heuristics on Self-efficacy Judgments and Behavior," *Journal of Personality and Social Psychology* 50 (1986): 492–501. The physical performance experiment is reported in R. S. Weinberg, D. Gould, and A. Jackson, "Expectations and Performance: An Empirical Test of Bandura's Self-efficacy Theory," *Journal of Sports Psychology* 1 (1979): 320–331. For an exhaustive discussion of the relationship between self-efficacy and performance, see A. Bandura, *Self-Efficacy: The Exercise of Control* (New York: Freeman, 1997).
3. This does not mean that higher self-confidence *systematically leads* to leader effectiveness or career advancement. Self-confidence has its drawbacks, particularly at very high levels in an organization. For a discussion of the need for balance between humility and resolve, see J. Collins, "Level 5 Leadership: The Triumph of Humility and Fierce Resolve," *Harvard Business Review,* January 2001, 66–76. For an exhaustive review of decades of research on traits associated with leader effectiveness, see chapters 4 and 5 of B. M. Bass and R. M. Stogdill, *Bass & Stogdill's Handbook of Leadership* (New York: Free Press, 1990); or chapter 10 in G. Yukl, *Leadership in Organizations* (Englewood Cliffs, NJ: Prentice-Hall, 2001).
4. J. W. Hunt, "Four Minutes to Impress," *The Financial Times,* 14 July 1999, 13.
5. L. K. Stroh, H. B. Gregersen, and J. S. Black, "Closing the Gap: Expectations versus Reality among Repatriates," *Journal of World Business* 33 (1998): 111–124.
6. From J. Welch and J. A. Byrne, *Jack: Straight from the Gut* (New York: Warner Books, 2001), 29.
7. D. Eden and G. Ravid, "Pygmalion vs. Self-expectancy: Effects of Instructor- and Self-expectancy on Trainee Performance," *Organizational Behavior and Human Performance* 30 (1982): 351–364.
8. Two studies produced these findings. The first, using men as interviewers and women as interviewees, is reported in M. Snyder, E. D.

Tanke, and E. Berscheid, "Social Perception and Interpersonal Behavior: On the Self-fulfilling Nature of Social Stereotypes," *Journal of Personality and Social Psychology* 9 (1977): 656–666. The second study, conducted by other researchers, switched the roles and is reported in S. M. Andersen and S. L. Bem, "Sex Typing and Androgyny in Dyadic Interaction: Individual Differences in Response to Physical Attractiveness," *Journal of Personality and Social Psychology* 41 (1981): 74–86.

9. C. B. Handy, *The Age of Paradox* (Boston: Harvard Business School Press, 1994).

10. R. J. Bies and T. M. Tripp, "Beyond Distrust: 'Getting Even' and the Need for Revenge," in *Trust in Organizations,* eds. R. M. Kramer and T. R. Tyler (Newbury Park, CA: Sage, 1996), 246–260.

11. M. R. Leary and J. A. Sheppard, "Behavioral Self-handicaps versus Self-reported Handicaps: A Conceptual Note," *Journal of Personality and Social Psychology* 51 (1986): 1265–1268.

## Chapter 4

1. In its old-fashioned original form, the quote went: "The human understanding when it has once adopted an opinion . . . draws all things else to support and agree with it. And though there be a greater number and weight of instances to be found on the other side, yet these it either neglects and despises, or else by some distinction sets aside and rejects, in order that by this great and pernicious predetermination the authority of its former conclusions may remain inviolate." F. Bacon, *The New Organon and Related Writings* (New York: Liberal Arts Press, 1960/1620).

2. N. Nicholson, "How Hardwired Is Human Behavior?" *Harvard Business Review,* July–August 1998, 134–147.

3. R. C. Liden, S. J. Wayne, and D. Stilwell, "A Longitudinal Study on the Early Development of Leader-Member Exchanges," *Journal of Applied Psychology* 78 (1993): 662–674.

4. J. Z. Burns, "Prediction of Leader-Member Exchange Quality by Jungian Personality Type" (unpublished Ph.D. diss., Georgia State University, 1995).

5. See J. E. Russo and P. J. H. Schoemaker, *Decision Traps* (New York: Simon & Schuster, 1990), 88–89.

6. N. T. Duarte, J. R. Goodson, and N. R. Klich, "Effects of Dyadic Quality and Duration on Performance Appraisal," *Academy of Management Journal* 37 (1994): 499–521.

7. H. J. Klein and J. S. Kim, "A Field Study of the Influence of Situational Constraints, Leader-Member Exchange, and Goal Commitment on Performance," *Academy of Management Journal* 41 (1998): 88–95.

8. S. J. Wayne and G. R. Ferris, "Influence Tactics, Affect, and Exchange Quality in Supervisor-Subordinate Interactions: A Laboratory Experiment and Field Study," *Journal of Applied Psychology* 75 (1990): 487–499.

9. See, for example, S. J. Wayne, L. M. Shore, and R. C. Liden, "Perceived Organizational Support and Leader-Member Exchange: A Social Exchange Perspective," *Academy of Management Journal* 40 (1997): 82–111, and E. M. Engle and R. G. Lord, "Implicit Theories, Self-schemas, and Leader-Member Exchange," *Academy of Management Journal* 40 (1997): 988–1010.

10. Liden, Wayne, and Stilwell, "A Longitudinal Study on the Early Development of Leader-Member Exchanges."

11. Notably Dansereau, Graen, and Haga, "A Vertical Dyad Linkage Approach to Leadership within Formal Organizations," G. Graen and J. F. Cashman, "A Role Making Model in Formal Organizations: A Developmental Approach," *Leadership Frontiers,* eds. J. G. Hunt and L. L. Larson (Kent, OH: Kent State Press, 1975): 143–165; R. C. Liden and G. Graen, "Generalizability of the Vertical Dyad Linkage Model of Leadership," *Academy of Management Journal* 23 (1980): 451–465; Liden, Wayne, and Stilwell, "A Longitudinal Study on the Early Development of Leader-Member Exchanges," 662–674.

12. S. Oskamp, "Overconfidence in Case Study Judgments," *Journal of Consulting Psychology* 29 (1965): 261–265.

13. The interpersonal predictions are reported by Lee Ross and his colleagues: see D. Dunning, D. W. Griffin, J. Milojkovic, and L. Ross, "The Overconfidence Effect in Social Interaction," *Journal of Personality and Social Psychology* 58 (1990): 568–581, and also R. P. Vallone, D. W. Griffin, S. Lin, and L. Ross, "The Overconfident Prediction of Future Actions and Outcomes by Self and Others," *Journal of Personality and Social Psychology* 58 (1990): 582–592. The role of anxiety in boosting overconfidence is reported by J. E. Sieber in "Effects of Decision Importance on Ability to Generate Warranted Subjective Uncertainty," *Journal of Personality and Social Psychology* 30 (1974): 688–694.

14. L. Kellaway, "Inside Track," *Financial Times,* 5 February 2001, 15.

15. Quoted in A. Muoio, "The Truth Is, the Truth Hurts," *Fast Company,* April 1998, 93–102.

16. See C. G. Lord, L. Ross, and E. R. Lepper, "Biased Assimilation and Attitude Polarization: The Effects of Prior Series on Subsequently Considered Evidence," *Journal of Personality and Social Psychology* 37 (1979): 2098–2109.

17. H. Kelley, "The Warm-Cold Variable in First Impressions of Persons," *Journal of Personality* 18 (1950): 431–439. This classic study has stood

the test of time and still features prominently in social psychology textbooks—see, for example R. Smith and D. M. Mackie, *Social Psychology* (Philadelphia, PA: Psychology Press, 2000). The findings were replicated in a more recent study by M. Goldman, M. D. Cowles, and C. A. Florez "The Halo Effect of an Initial Impression Upon Speaker and Audience," *Journal of Social Psychology* 120 (1983): 197–201. This study added a new dimension by also manipulating the expectations of the instructor, who was led to expect either a "warm" or "cold" audience. Predictably the strongest effects occurred when the expectations of both parties were manipulated in the same direction.

18. E. E. Jones, L. Rock, K. G. Shaver, G. R. Goethals, and L. M. Ward, "Pattern of Performance and Ability Attribution: An Unexpected Primacy Effect," *Journal of Personality and Social Psychology* 10 (1968): 317–340.

19. The *fundamental attribution error* and the *actor-observer bias* are discussed in most social psychology textbooks. See, for example, D. Gilbert "Ordinary Personology," chapter 20 (pp. 89–150, but particularly pp. 127–134), in *The Handbook of Social Cognition,* 4th ed. vol. 2, eds. D. T. Gilbert, S. T. Fiske, and G. Lindzey (New York: McGraw-Hill, 1998). For a review of studies suggesting that non-Western cultures tend to be less vulnerable to the fundamental attribution error, see chapter 11 of Z. Kunda, *Social Cognition: Making Sense of People* (Cambridge, MA: The MIT Press, 1999).

20. A. Hastorf and H. Cantril, "They Saw a Game: A Case Study," *Journal of Abnormal and Social Psychology* 49 (1954): 129–134. This is another classic study, which actually serves as the opening illustration of "What is social psychology?" in the textbook by R. Smith and D. M. Mackie, *Social Psychology* (Philadelphia, PA: Psychology Press, 2000).

21. R. L. Heneman, D. B. Greenberger, and C. Anonyuo, "Attributions and Exchanges: The Effects of Interpersonal Factors on the Diagnosis of Employee Performance," *Academy of Management Journal* 32 (1989): 466–476.

22. J. S. Uleman, "Consciousness and Control: The Case of Spontaneous Trait Inferences," *Personality and Social Psychology Bulletin* 33 (1987): 337–354.

23. H. E. McDonald and E. R. Hirt, "When Expectancy Meets Desire: Motivational Effects in Reconstructive Memory," *Journal of Personality and Social Psychology* 72 (1997): 5–23.

24. This example is from A. Tversky and D. Kahneman, "Judgment under Uncertainty: Heuristics and Biases," *Science,* 27 September 1974, 1124–1131.

25. C. Cohen, "Person Categories and Social Perception: Testing Some Boundary Conditions of the Processing Effects of Prior Knowledge," *Journal of Personality and Social Psychology* 40 (1981): 441–452.

## Chapter 5

1. R. C. Liden, S. J. Wayne, and D. Stilwell, "A Longitudinal Study on the Early Development of Leader-Member Exchanges," *Journal of Applied Psychology* 78 (1993): 662–674.
2. As B. F. Skinner famously put it, "If we do not know why a person acts as he does, we attribute his behavior to him." In *Beyond Freedom and Dignity* (New York: Alfred Knopf, 1971), 53.
3. This groundbreaking model was first introduced in H. A. Simon, "A Behavioral Model of Rational Choice," *Quarterly Journal of Economics* 69 (1955): 99–118.
4. This perspective is at the heart of the "Group Value Model," which holds that people use experiences with authorities as a source of information about their position within the group. If people are treated insensitively or unfairly, it suggests that they are not valued members of the group. It communicates marginal social status. See E. A. Lind and T. R. Tyler, *The Social Psychology of Procedural Justice* (New York: Plenum, 1988).
5. R. J. Bies, T. M. Tripp, and R. M. Kramer, "At the Breaking Point: Cognitive and Social Dynamics of Revenge in Organizations," in *Antisocial Behavior in Organizations,* eds. R. Giacalone and J. Greenberg (Thousand Oaks, CA: Sage, 1997), 18–36.
6. P. M. Sias, "Constructing Perceptions of Differential Treatment: An Analysis of Coworker Discourse," *Communication Monographs* 63 (1996): 171–187.
7. The tendency to seek out information that supports our existing instinct or point of view while avoiding information that contradicts it is known as the *confirming evidence trap*—as described in J. S. Hammond, R. L. Keeney, and H. Raiffa, *Smart Choices: A Practical Guide to Making Better Decisions* (Boston: Harvard Business School Press, 1999), 198–200.
8. R. M. Kramer, "The Sinister Attribution Error," *Motivation and Emotion* 18 (1994): 199–231.
9. S. L. Hannigan, and M. T. Reinitz, "A Demonstration and Comparison of Two Types of Inference-based Memory Errors," *Journal of Experimental Psychology* 27, no. 4 (2001): 931–940.
10. For a discussion of this psychological trap, see Hammond, Keeney, and Raiffa, *Smart Choices,* 211–212.

11. K. Leung, S. Su, and M. W. Morris, "When Is Criticism *Not* Constructive? The Roles of Fairness Perceptions and Dispositional Attributions in Employee Acceptance of Critical Supervisory Feedback," *Human Relations* 54 (2001): 1155–1187.

12. J. S. Adams pioneered the field of *equity theory* by suggesting that workers adjust their contribution up or down so that the perceived ratio of their contribution to their monetary rewards remains similar to that of their fellow workers. See J. S. Adams, "Inequity in Social Exchange," in *Advances in Experimental Social Psychology* vol. 2, ed. L. Berkowitz (New York: Academic Press, 1965), 267–299. More recent work suggests that employees' concept of equity and justice includes many aspects beyond money, and that their response to perceived inequity does not stop at reducing effort but can go all the way to vengeance. See, for example, R. Hogan and N. P. Helmer, "Retributive Justice," in *The Justice Motive in Social Behavior,* eds. M. J. Lerner and S. C. Lerner (New York: Academic Press, 1981), 125–144. Or more recently, J. A. Colquitt, D. E. Conlon, M. J. Wesson, C. O. Porter, and K. Y. Ng, "Justice at the Millenium: A Meta-Analytic Review of 25 Years of Organizational Justice Research," *Journal of Applied Psychology* 86 (2001): 425–445.

13. See B. J. Bushman, R. F. Baumeister, and C. M. Phillips, "Do People Aggress to Improve Their Mood? Catharsis Beliefs, Affect Regulation Opportunity, and Aggressive Responding," *Journal of Personality and Social Psychology* 81 (2001): 17–32.

14. J. W. Brehm, *Responses to Loss of Freedom: A Theory of Psychological Reactance* (Morristown, NJ: General Learning Press, 1972).

15. Work-Out designates a process developed in the late 1980s at General Electric. The first objective of these sessions is to force the organization to review its processes and procedures to eliminate their non-value-adding components. This is achieved by gathering forty to fifty employees from all levels in a department or business unit, which also has the important benefit of breaking down functional and hierarchical barriers. Concretely, the group has three days to study the issues and come up with recommendations for the department's head, who only has three possible responses: "Yes," "No," and "I'll get back to you within one month." For more information on this process, see, for example, R. Slater's *The GE Way Fieldbook* (New York: McGraw-Hill, 2000).

16. Both of these examples come from H. Lancaster, "Managing Your Career," *Wall Street Journal,* 17 June 2001, B1: 1.

17. This concept, known as the *biased punctuation of conflict,* is presented by Bies, Tripp, and Kramer in "At the Breaking Point."

18. R. J. Bies and T. M. Tripp, "Beyond Distrust: 'Getting Even' and the Need for Revenge," in *Trust in Organizations,* eds. R. M. Kramer and T. R. Tyler (Newbury Park, CA: Sage, 1996), 246–260.

19. Ibid.

## Chapter 6

1. D. Dorsey, "Andy Pearson Finds Love," *Fast Company,* August 2001, 78–86.

2. For details on IBM's Speed Team see, S. Kirsner, "Faster Company," *Fast Company,* May 2000, 162. Also available online at <http://pf.fast company.com/online/34/ibm.html>.

3. A. Layne, "Report from the Past—Jane Harper," *Fast Company,* January 2001, <http://www.fastcompany.com/feature/rftp_harper.html>. This was a "Web-exclusive" interview, following up on a previous feature.

4. For an excellent discussion and illustrations of how HR departments can add more value by becoming strategic partners, see D. Ulrich, *Human Resource Champions* (Boston: Harvard Business School Press, 1997).

5. This quote is extracted from Bronwyn Fryer's interview with Eric Schmidt, published under the title "Leading Through Rough Times," *Harvard Business Review,* May 2001, 116–123.

6. See, for example, *Reasoning, Learning and Action: Individual and Organizational* (San Francisco: Jossey-Bass, 1982). Or, more recently, *Flawed Advice and the Management Trap: How Managers Can Know When They Are Getting Good Advice and When They're Not* (New York: Oxford University Press: 2000).

7. Cited in C. Hymowitz and M. Murray, "Welch's Ideas on Motivating Employees," *Wall Street Journal,* 21 June 1999.

8. A short review of the key findings from studies on fair process can be downloaded from our Web site <http://www.set-up-to-fail.net>. See also the article by W. C. Kim and R. Mauborgne, "Fair Process: Managing in the Knowledge Economy," *Harvard Business Review,* July–August 1997, 65–76; R. Folger and R. Cropanzano, *Organizational Justice and Human Resource Management* (Thousand Oaks, CA: Sage, 1998); or S. Gilliland, D. Steiner, and D. Skarlicki, eds., *Theoretical and Cultural Perspectives on Organizational Justice* (Greenwich, CT: Information Age Publishing, 2001).

9. For more details on the Air France turnaround led by Christian Blanc, see our case "Pulling Out of Its Dive: Air France Under Christian Blanc" and its accompanying Teaching Note, ECCH # 398-079-1 and 398-079-8, respectively (Fontainebleau, France: INSEAD). French-speaking readers can also look at Part IV of F. Autier, G. Corcos, and G. Trépo, *Air France: Des années héroïques à la refondation* (Paris: Vuibert, 2001).

10. Adapted from C. Argyris, "Good Communication That Blocks Learning," *Harvard Business Review,* July–August 1994, 77–85.

11. Ibid.

## Chapter 7

1. Reviews of the scientific literature on the effects of feedback can be found in D. R. Ilgen, C. D. Fisher, and M. S. Taylor, "Consequences of Individual Feedback on Behavior in Organizations," *Journal of Applied Psychology* 64 (1979): 349–371; and more recently in A. N. Kluger and A. DeNisi, "The Effects of Feedback Interventions on Performance: A Historical Review, a Meta-Analysis, and a Preliminary Feedback Intervention Theory," *Psychological Bulletin* 119 (1996): 254–284. The effects of fair process on acceptance of feedback have been identified more recently and are illustrated particularly clearly by two studies discussed in K. Leung, S. Su, and M. W. Morris, "When Is Criticism *Not* Constructive? The Roles of Fairness Perceptions and Dispositional Attributions in Employee Acceptance of Critical Supervisory Feedback," *Human Relations* 54 (2001): 1155–1187.

2. This definition comes from L. R. Beach, *The Psychology of Decision Making: People in Organizations* (Thousand Oaks, CA: Sage, 1997) 22–23. Beach provides a good treatment of framing and related decision-making issues, quite readable but also providing scholarly references. For treatments written more specifically for managers, see J. E. Russo and P. J. H. Shoemaker, *Decision Traps: The Ten Barriers to Brilliant Decision-making and How to Overcome Them* (New York: Fireside, Simon & Schuster, 1989); J. S. Hammond, R. L. Keeney, and H. Raiffa, *Smart Choices: A Practical Guide to Making Better Decisions* (Boston: Harvard Business School Press, 1999); or chapter 10 of P. Senge, *The Fifth Discipline: The Art and Practice of the Learning Organization* (New York: Doubleday/Currency, 1990). For a much more complete discussion of framing and mental schemas, see T. S. Fiske and S. E. Taylor, *Social Cognition,* 2d ed. (New York: McGraw-Hill, 1991).

3. Both illustrations are taken from Hammond, Keeney, and Raiffa, *Smart Choices,* pp. 200 and 26–28, respectively.

4. This example comes from J. E. Russo and P. J. H. Shoemaker, *Decision Traps: The Ten Barriers to Brilliant Decision-making and How to Overcome Them* (New York: Fireside, Simon & Schuster, 1989), 16–17.

5. Argyris has written extensively on how and why people tend to behave unproductively in situations they see as threatening or embarrassing. See, for example, *Reasoning, Learning and Action: Individual and Organizational* (San Francisco: Jossey-Bass, 1982) or *Knowledge for Action: A Guide to Overcoming Barriers to Organizational Change* (San Francisco: Jossey-Bass, 1993). These books build on Argyris's earlier work with Don Schön, including the seminal *Theory in Action: Increasing Professional Effectiveness,* originally published by Jossey-Bass in 1974 and reprinted as a *Jossey-Bass Classic* in 1992.

6. This case format was pioneered by Argyris and Schön in their 1974 classic *Theory in Action.* Peter Senge also refers to such cases in *The Fifth Discipline.*

## Chapter 8

1. Role-playing conversations beforehand with the help of a "neutral friend" is also part of the advice Holly Weeks gives in her article "Taking the Stress Out of Stressful Conversations," *Harvard Business Review,* July–August 2001, 112–119. To prepare for such encounters, she also encourages managers to become more self-aware of their reaction under stress. Under what conditions do I become unproductive, what are some of the "buttons" that make me lose my emotional and/or intellectual balance? Becoming more aware of their vulnerabilities allows managers to develop coping mechanisms (e.g., specific sentences) ahead of time, while they are not under stress, and to identify more quickly the symptoms and causes of their discomfort when it happens in real time.

2. For more on fair process, see C. Kim and R. Mauborgne, "Fair Process: Managing in the Knowledge Economy," *Harvard Business Review,* July–August 1997, 65–75; "Building Trust and Cooperation through Fair Process," *The Antidote* 14 (1998): 33–36; or R. Folger and R. Cropanzano, *Organizational Justice and Human Resource Management* (Thousand Oaks, CA: Sage, 1998).

3. Dialogue is a difficult art, and we cannot do justice to it in these few pages. Readers interested in improving their abilities in this respect can consult William Isaacs's book, *Dialogue and the Art of Thinking*

*Together: A Pioneering Approach to Communicating in Business and in Life* (New York: Doubleday: 1999).

4. H. Weeks, "Taking the Stress Out of Stressful Conversations," *Harvard Business Review,* July–August 2001, 112–119.

5. For an insightful discussion of this paradox, see C. Argyris, "Teaching Smart People How to Learn," *Harvard Business Review,* May–June 1991, 99–110.

6. This is increasingly true all over the world. Even in countries like Japan, India, or France that have historically proposed life-long employment, increasingly global competition for products, services, and manpower is forcing companies to decrease their tolerance for under-performance, and even for "good enough" performance. In Japan and India, the forerunners of this trend are Nissan and Tata Steel, respectively, while in France, Michelin broke dramatically with a long tradition of paternalistic management by announcing layoffs at the same time as posting record profits in 1999.

7. Quoted in N. M. Tichy and R. Charan, "The CEO as Coach: An Interview with AlliedSignal's Lawrence A. Bossidy," *Harvard Business Review,* March–April 1995, 69–78, 76.

8. Quoted in C. Farkas, P. De Backer, and A. Sheppard, *Maximum Leadership 2000* (London: Orion, 2000), 61.

## Chapter 9

1. Executives in some companies are encouraged to develop a personal "leadership point of view," also called "teachable point of view," to support their role in executive training. This point of view should include the leader's thoughts on how the business can become more successful, but also—and more to our point here—the leader's key *beliefs* and *values* regarding leadership. Even if your firm does not require you to participate formally in leadership training activities, developing and articulating your own leadership point of view could be a valuable exercise that will yield multiple benefits. Developing this point of view will lead you to reflect on your beliefs and values, maybe challenge them, and will probably help you learn much about yourself. Once articulated, the resulting output will help you be clearer and more explicit during the formative periods of your relationship with new subordinates. Noel Tichy has written extensively about the teachable point of view in articles such as "How Leaders Develop Leaders" (with Eli Cohen), *Training & Development,* May

1997, 58–71; "The Teachable Point of View," *Journal of Business Strategy,* January–February 1998, 29–33; and "The Teachable Point of View: A Primer" (82–83) in Suzy Wetlaufer's "Driving Change: An Interview with Ford Motor Company's Jacques Nasser," *Harvard Business Review,* March–April 1999, 76–88.

2. In D. Ciampa and M. Watkins, *Right from the Start: Taking Charge in a New Leadership Role* (Boston: Harvard Business School Press, 1999), 97–98.

3. This quote is extracted from E. Nuss, "Why Should We Change? The Nissan Revival Plan," *INSEAD—The Business Link,* no. 3 (2000): 18–22.

4. E. L. Deci and R. M. Ryan, *Intrinsic Motivation and Self-Determination in Human Behavior* (New York: Plenum, 1985).

5. Quoted in B. Morris and J. McGowan, "Big Blue," *Fortune,* 14 April 1997, 68–79.

6. K. C. Laudon, *Dossier Society: Value Choices in the Design of National Information Systems* (New York: Columbia University Press, 1986).

7. Aesop was a slave in ancient Greece. Xanthus, his master, told him to prepare an important banquet but was disappointed to find that the feast consisted only of tongues, cooked in many fashions. When he asked why, Aesop explained that the tongue was responsible for teaching and inspiring, and for all the kind and pleasing words that made people happy. Unimpressed, Xanthus ordered his slave to prepare another feast, but this time "of the worst you have." To his surprise, Aesop again prepared tongues. Why this time? Because the tongue is also responsible for the worst: for lying, slandering, cheating, scolding, and boasting.

8. See, for example, C. F. Bond and E. L. Anderson, "The Reluctance to Transmit Bad News: Private Discomfort or Public Display?" *Journal of Experimental Social Psychology* 23 (1987): 176–187; see also J. F. Veiga, "Face Your Problem Subordinates Now!" *Academy of Management Executive* 2 (1988): 145–152.

9. As explained in R. Mayrer, *Feedback Toolkit* (Portland, OR: Productivity Press, 1994). The quote is from G. Imperato, "How to Give Good Feedback," *Fast Company,* September 1998, 144–156.

10. M. de Montaigne, *Les Essais* (The Essays 3rd edition), tome 2 (Paris: Presses Universitaires de France, 1999).

11. C. Fishman, "Engines of Democracy," *Fast Company,* October 1999, 174–198.

12. C. Fishman, "Creative Tension," *Fast Company,* November 2000, 359–388.

13. J. V. Singh, "McKinsey's Managing Director Rajat Gupta on Leading a Knowledge-based Global Consulting Organization," *Academy of Management Executive* 15 (2001): 34–44.

## Chapter 10

1. K. Hammonds, "How Do We Break out of the Box We're Stuck in?" *Fast Company,* November 2000, 260–272.
2. R. M. Kanter, "Championing Change: An Interview with Bell Atlantic's CEO Raymond Smith," *Harvard Business Review,* January–February 1991, 119–130.
3. N. Stone, "Building Corporate Character: An Interview with Stride Rite Chairman Arnold Hiatt," *Harvard Business Review,* March–April 1992, 104.
4. M. Kets de Vries, "An Interview with Percy Barnevik of ABB," *INSEAD Video,* (Fontainebleau, France, 1994.)
5. D. Dorsey, "Andy Pearson Finds Love," *Fast Company,* August 2001, 78–86.
6. Ibid.
7. See, for example, John Kotter's eight-step change model in "Leading Change: Why Transformation Efforts Fail," *Harvard Business Review,* March–April 1995, 59–67; and *Leading Change* (Boston: Harvard Business School Press, 1996); Todd Jick's perspective in "Implementing Change," *Managing Change: Cases and Concepts* (Chicago: Richard Irwin, 1993) and "Managing Change," in *The Portable MBA in Management,* ed. A. R. Cohen (New York: John Wiley & Sons, 1993). For perspectives from consulting, see Price Waterhouse Change Integration Team, *Better Change: Best Practices for Transforming Your Organization* (Chicago: Richard Irwin, 1995), or J. D. Bruck, *The Change Monster: The Human Forces that Fuel or Foil Corporate Transformation and Change* (New York: Crown Business, 2001).
8. Respectively from B. Kaye, "Career Development—Anytime, Anyplace," 235–246; W. Hawkins and T. Pettey, "Coaching for Organizational Change," 307–315; D. Allen, "Re-grooving Critical Behavior," 231–234. All in *Coaching for Leadership,* eds. M. Goldsmith, L. Lyons, and A. Freas (San Francisco: Jossey-Bass/Pfeiffer, 2000).
9. See, for example, the chapters in Section 1 and 4 of *The International Handbook of Organizational Culture and Climate,* eds. C. L. Cooper, S. Cartwright, and P. C. Early (Chichester, UK: John Wiley & Sons, 2001).

10. Allen, "Re-grooving Critical Behavior," in *Coaching for Leadership*, eds. Goldsmith, Lyons, and Freas, 231–234.

11. These quotes are extracted from pages 127–128 of D. Grayson and K. Larson, "How to Make the Most of the Coaching Relationship for the Person Being Coached," in *Coaching for Leadership*, eds. Goldsmith, Lyons, and Freas, 121–130.

12. C. Hymowitz, "How to Tell Employees All the Things They Don't Want to Hear," *Wall Street Journal*, 22 August 2000, B1.

13. D. Sethi, "Coaching from Below," in *Coaching for Leadership*, Goldsmith, Lyons, and Freas, 143–147, 144.

14. R. Teerlink, "Harley's Leadership U-turn," *Harvard Business Review*, July–August 2000, 43–48.

15. J. Waldroop and T. Butler, "The Executive as Coach," *Harvard Business Review*, November–December 1996, 111–117.

16. F. Jourden, "The Influence of Feedback Framing on the Self-regulatory Mechanisms Governing Complex Decision Making" (Ph.D. diss., Stanford University, 1991).

17. Allen, "Re-grooving Critical Behavior," 231–234.

18. J. Reingold, "Want to Grow as a Leader? Get a Mentor!" *Fast Company*, January 2001, 58–60.

19. C. D. McCauley and C. A. Douglas, "Developmental Relationships," in *Handbook of Leadership Development*, eds. C. D. McCauley, R. S. Moxley, and E. Van Velsor (San Francisco: Jossey-Bass, 1998), 160–193.

20. C. Dahle, "Women's Ways of Mentoring," *Fast Company*, September 1998, 186–197.

21. Chris Argyris and Don Schön first developed the notion that human behavior is guided by "theories of action" in *Theory in Action: Increasing Professional Effectiveness*, mentioned in an earlier note. They distinguished two types of theories of action: the "espoused theory," which comprises the individual's beliefs, attitudes and values and characterizes the way the individual would like to behave, and/or likes to think he behaves; and the "theory-in-use," which really governs the individual's behavior. The term "master program" appeared later, probably reflecting the increasing presence of computers in our lives. For example, Argyris explains [in *Overcoming Organizational Defenses: Facilitating Organizational Learning* (Needham, MA: Allyn and Bacon, 1990), 12–13] that: "We can think of human beings as having been taught, early in life, how to act in ways to be in control. . . . People transform these lessons into theories of action. The theories of action, in turn, contain rules that are used to design and implement the

actions in everyday life." He goes on to describe "theories-in-use (as) the master programs that individuals hold in order to be in control." See also several references to "master programs" in C. Argyris, *On Organizational Learning*, 2d ed. (Oxford: Blackwell Business, 1999).

22. *Time Magazine* put Tiger Woods on its cover page and ran its lead story on Woods's improvement effort. See in Dan Goodgame's article "The Game of Risk: How the Best Golfer in the World Got Even Better," *Time*, 14 August 2000, 34–44.

23. For more on frame blindness, see any of the first three books referenced in chapter 7, note 2

24. Morita's quote is taken from A. Morita, M.E. Reingold, and S. Mitsuko, *Akio Morita and Sony: Made In Japan* (London: Collins, 1990): 150, and Soros's quote from G. Soros, B. Wien, and K. Koenen, *Soros on Soros* (New York: John Wiley, 1995): 11.

25. A. Muoio, "The Art of Smart," *Fast Company,* July–August 1999, 85–97.

26. Don Schön has written extensively about the role of "reflection-in-action" to improve practice, particularly for professionals. See *The Reflective Practitioner: How Professionals Think in Action* (New York: Basic Books, 1983) and *Educating the Reflective Practitioner: Toward a New Design for Teaching and Learning in the Professions* (San Francisco: Jossey-Bass, 1987). Peter Senge's chapters on personal mastery and mental maps in *The Fifth Discipline* are also of interest. For a discussion of reflection focused on interactions, see W. Isaacs, *Dialogue and the Art of Thinking Together: A Pioneering Approach to Communicating in Business and in Life* (New York: Doubleday, 1999).

27. Social psychologists emphasize the idea that relapse is an integral part of successful change. See, for example, A. Bandura, *Self-Efficacy: The Exercise of Control* (New York: Freeman, 1997). It is also stressed by psychotherapists who work more intensely with people trying to break free of addictive behaviors. See, for example, J. O. Prochaska, C. C. DiClemente, and J. C. Norcross, "In Search of How People Change," *American Psychologist,* September 1992, 1102–1114. The evidence of relapse in smokers comes from S. Schnacter, "Recidivism and Self-cure of Smoking and Obesity," *American Psychologist* 37 (1982): 436–444. The fall-out rate in New Year's resolutions comes from J. C. Norcross and D. J. Vangarelli, "The Resolution Solution: Longitudinal Examination of New Year's Change Attempts," *Journal of Substance Abuse* 1 (1989): 127–134.

28. J. A. Belasco and R. C. Stayer, "Why Empowerment Doesn't Empower: The Bankruptcy of Current Paradigms," *Business Horizons,* March–April 1994, 29–41.

29. R. Wellins and J. Worklan, "The Philadelphia Story," *Training* 31 (1994): 93–105.

30. P. Sellers, "Get over Yourself," *Fortune,* 30 April 2001, 62–67.

31. C. Weiser, "Championing the Customer," *Harvard Business Review,* November–December 1995, 113–116.

32. For a review of the evidence, see A. Bandura, *Self-Efficacy: The Exercise of Control* (New York: Freeman, 1997), 99–101.

33. C. Dahle, "Resistance Fighter," *Fast Company,* December 1999, 390–399.

34. This quote is often attributed to Deming. We were unable to trace its provenance and hence contacted the French Deming Association. Its president, Jean-Marie Gogue, did not remember reading this sentence in Deming's writings but confirmed that he indeed heard Deming repeat it on a number of occasions. He also remembers that this phrase once featured on the poster advertising a Deming keynote speech.

# Index

actor-observer bias, 79, 80
Air France, case study of, 126–127
anchoring, 70
    effects of, 74–76
Argyris, Chris, 123, 145, 235
Attali, Bernard, 126, 127
attribution biases, 79–84, 95
autonomy
    fostering of, 212
    importance of, 38
    and motivation, 37

bad news
    differential boss response to,
        23, 26, 29–31, 52, 58–60
    productive handling of,
        210–212, 216, 218, 237
Barnevik, Percy, 225
Bennis, Warren, 3
bias
    actor-observer, 79, 80
    attribution, 79–84, 95
    confirmatory, 76–77, 91, 204
    in observation, 77–78

overconfidence, 74–75
overintentionalizing, 88–89,
    94, 149
in recall, 84–85, 91–92, 94, 96
self-serving, 79
Blanc, Christian, 126–127
bosses. See managers
Bossidy, Larry, 188
bullying, workplace, 12
    incidence of, 12–13
    outside United States, 13
    worker responses to, 13

Camus, Albert, 101
career derailment, 10–11
change, personal
    behavioral, 235–244
    desire for, 225
    importance of, 224–226
    internal feedback for, 228–230
    master program alteration for,
        235–236
    personal investment in,
        248–250

271

change, personal *(continued)*
  preparing for setbacks in,
    244–248
  reflective techniques for,
    239–244
  third-party support of,
    230–234, 242–243
citizenship behavior, 82
coaches, assistance provided by,
    231–232, 242–243
confirmatory bias, 76–77, 91, 204
Cooper, Cary, 12
covert lobbying, 103
  counteracting of, 103–105
  effects of, 105
customer satisfaction
  effects of set-up-to-fail syn-
    drome on, 121
  research on, 246

delayed problem recognition, 58
Deming, Edward, 249
dialogue
  context for, 168–170
  importance of, 132–133
  regarding problem origins,
    171–175
  regarding problem symptoms,
    170–171
directions, disguised, 29–30
disagreements
  escalation of, 150–154
  scripted collisions, 151

easing in, 152
  risks of, 152–156
e factors, 55
energy pot
  depletion of, 115
  preservation of, 237

under normal versus stressful
    situations, 149
equity theory, 99
escalation of disagreements,
    150–154
  everyday manifestations of,
    154
expectations
  impact on subordinate perfor-
    mance of, 42
  importance of, 47–51

fairness
  assessment of, 167
  perceived, 171
  perceived lack of, 98, 125–126
fair process, 125–127, 165, 177,
    188, 190
feedback
  communicating disappoint-
    ment, 212
  costs of giving, 158–159
  dialogue in delivering,
    168–179, 206–207
  discounting of by subordi-
    nates, 97–99, 105
  easing in of, 152–157
  effective delivery of, 142–143
  fairness of, 98
  framing of, 156–158
  importance of timeliness of,
    205, 206
  pain of giving, 207
  positive, 215–216
  risks of giving, 136–140
  self-monitoring by giver,
    204–205
  solicitation of, for change,
    228–230
  subordinate acceptance of,
    140–143

360-degree programs, 17–18, 115

Fiorina, Carly, 200–201

frame blindness, 240

framing, 143
    articulation of, 149
    boundary and reference point definition in, 145
    case study of, 146–150
    examples of, 144–145
    of feedback, 156–158
    frozen, 145–146, 148
    limited view, 148
    points of reference in, 154
    self-evaluation of, 149–150
    of stressful situations, 145

fundamental attribution error, 79

Gerstner, Lou, 203

Ghosn, Carlos, 201

Golem effect, 40

Gupta, Rajat, 217

Hiatt, Arnold, 224

human resources
    dealing with set-up-to-fail syndrome, 115–116
    effects of set-up-to-fail syndrome on, 122

hypervigilance, 92

in-group
    composition versus performance, 72–73
    extension of attribution biases to, 79–84
    preferential treatment of, 24, 30
    relationship with boss, 94
    responses to feedback, 98, 140

interruption of the set-up-to-fail syndrome
    assessing the problem, 170–175, 180
    the case of slackers, 187–189
    case study, 161–163, 180–187
    costs and benefits of intervention, 132–134, 158–159
    importance of fair process, 125–126, 177, 188
    limits of unilateral approach by manager, 128–132
    lost causes, 189–190
    outcomes of intervention, 177–180
    preparation of the intervention, 163–167
    steps, 167–177, 180
    triggered by subordinate, 190–194

justice. See fair process

Kerr, Steve, 229–230

Kotter, John, 2

labeling
    anchoring and, 70
    attitudes and, 71–74
    confirmation of, 91–93
    distorting power of, 93–94
    durability of, 74–76
    faulty information and, 70
    premature closure of, 69–70, 203
    resisting, 202–204, 213–215
    by subordinates, 87–96
    value of, 68–69, 203

leader-member exchange theory,
    23
leaders. *See also* managers
    distinguished from managers,
        2–3
leadership point-of-view, 198–199
learned helplessness, 35
    research on, 36
learning environment
    analyzing positive outcomes
        in, 215–216
    autonomy building in, 212
    importance of, 209
    nonpunitive nature of,
        210–211
    reflection and, 241–244
Livermore, Ann, 200–201
lying, dangers of, 155


managers
    bias in recollections by, 84–85
    career success variables for,
        10–11, 123
    competing demands on atten-
        tion of, 3–4
    conscious crafting of behavior
        by, 235–244
    differential awarding of credit
        by, 78–84
    differential behavior toward
        subordinates by, 21–24,
        28–33
    dilemmas facing, 4–5
    distinguished from leaders, 2
    feedback for development of,
        17–18, 228–230
    incoming, difficulties faced by,
        108–109, 200–201
    interpretation of employee
        behavior, 82–84
    maturation of, 224–227

in out-group, 119–120
overconfidence of, 75–76
personal development of. *See*
    change, personal
pressures on, 11, 75
responses to failure and success
    by, 30–32, 172–173
selective observation by, 77–78
setting expectations of subor-
    dinates, 198–200
stress and, 11, 12, 75, 124, 136,
    145, 148–150, 163, 204,
    235, 237, 240, 245
third-party coaching of,
    230–234
toll of set-up-to-fail syndrome
    on, 114–115
and weaker performers, 9–10,
    22–25, 46–47, 51–55
master program, internal, 235
    overriding of, 235–238
    rewriting of, 238–239
    self-control to combat, 236
memory reconstruction, 84–85
mentors
    assistance provided by,
        231–232, 242–243
    benefits of, 232
mindlessness, 35
Morita, Akio, 241
motivation
    impact of expectations on,
        38–41
    intrinsic, 28
    loss of, 6, 27, 34, 37, 41, 60,
        64, 155
    perceived lack of, 7, 54, 82
    sources of, 34–38


nature or nurture, 222–224
Nicoli, Eric, 190

out-group
    behaviors of, 91–96
    consignment to, 73–74
    effects on team of, 117–118
    manager in, 119–120
    managerial perceptions of,
        80–81
    membership of, 126–128
    signs of assignment to, 29–33
    turnover among, 24
overconfidence
    effects of, 74–75
    universality of, 75
overintentionalizing, 88–89, 94,
        149


Pearson, Andy, 113, 225
peers
    as developmental partners,
        233–234, 242–243
    internal feedback from,
        228–229
personal development. See change,
        personal
personnel records, judicious use
        of, 203–204
Pottruck, David, 245
prevention of set-up-to-fail syn-
        drome, 194–195, 197–198
    building subordinate confi-
        dence and, 210–211
    creation of the right environ-
        ment for, 209–218
    early intervention for, 205–207
    investment in, 217–219
    knowing-doing gap in,
        221–222, 227
    partnership of boss and subor-
        dinate, 207–209, 242
    relationship development for,
        200–202

relationship framing for,
        198–199
    resisting biased evaluations,
        204–205
    resisting premature labeling,
        202–204
    role of trust in, 216–217
    syndrome busters and,
        197–198, 210–218
productivity
    managers and, 4–5, 9–10
    set-up-to-fail syndrome and,
        11–14
psychological abuse, 12. See also
        bullying, workplace
Pygmalion effect, 38
    research on, 38–41
    speed of, 50–51


reactance theory, 101
recall
    memory reconstruction,
        84–85
    phantom recollection, 94, 96
    selective, 91–92
relationship, boss-subordinate
    defined, 178
    deteriorating, 131
    development of, 200–202
    framing of, 198–199
    irreparable, 189–190
    joint ownership of, 131–133,
        176–177, 207–209
resistance to change, perceptions
        of, 80–81
root-cause analysis, 183–184


satisficing, 89–90
    consequence of, 93–94
Schmidt, Eric, 118

Seely Brown, John, 243
selective observation, 77–78
self-confidence
    importance of, 28
    of managers, 48
    research on, 35
    volatility of, 48–49
self-control, importance of, 236
self-determination theory, 36–38
    needs identified by, 202
    research in, 36–37
self-efficacy
    and business performance,
        34–35
    and health, 34
self-fulfilling prophecy, 55–56,
    64–65, 163
self-handicapping, 61, 62
self-reinforcing process, 56–59,
    67–68, 163
self-serving bias, 79
    extension to in-group of,
        79–84
setbacks
    coping with, 245–246
    opportunities provided by,
        246–248
    types of, 244–245
Sethi, Dick, 230
Set-Up-to-Fail Syndrome
    beyond boss-subordinate rela-
        tionships, 8
    costs of, 9–14, 113–122
    interruption of, 158–195. See
        also interruption of set-up-
        to-fail syndrome
    managerial discounting of,
        121–124
    prevention of, 194–219. See
        also prevention of set-up-
        to-fail syndrome

Pygmalion/Golem effect and,
    38–41, 49–51
as self-fulfilling prophecy,
    55–56, 64–65, 163
self-reinforcing nature of,
    56–59, 67–68, 163
as vicious cycle, 46–47, 58–60
Simon, Herbert, 89
sink or swim principle, dangers
    of, 200
skilled unawareness, 123
skip-level meetings, 103–105, 115
slackers, dealing with, 187–189
Smith, Raymond, 224
spontaneous trait inference, 82
Stayer, Ralph, 244–245
stress
    managers and, 11, 12, 75, 124,
        136, 145, 148–150, 163,
        204, 235, 237, 240, 245
    subordinates and, 113, 116,
        131, 148–149
stronger performers. See also
        in-group
    characteristics of, 22
    effects of set-up-to-fail syn-
        drome on, 116–118
    management of, 23
    perceived motivations of, 83
    Pygmalion effect and, 38–41
    reactions to feedback of, 140
    signals sent by managers to,
        28–33
Stupski, Larry, 245
subordinates
    building supportive environ-
        ment for, 210–218
    categorization by bosses of,
        20–22, 71–74
    confirmation biases of, 91–96
    defined, 3

hypervigilance by, 92
interpretation of boss behavior
    by, 95
labeling by, 87–91
mobilization of, 2
motivation of, 6, 27, 28,
    34–41, 54, 60, 64, 82, 155
preemptive strikes by, 107–109
proactive responses to set-up-
    to-fail syndrome, 190–194
provocation of boss by,
    102–103, 104
reactions to feedback, 97–99,
    136–143
rehashing the past, 99–100,
    104, 173
selective recall by, 91–92
social corroboration of assess-
    ment by, 92–93, 94, 96, 118
as source of feedback, 228–230
and stress, 113, 116, 131,
    148–149
syndrome, 7
syndrome buster(s), 197–198
    attention to positive outcomes
        by, 215–216
    born or made, 222–224
    caring for subordinates by,
        216–217
    creation of supportive environ-
        ment by, 209–218
    distinction between person
        and performance by,
        201–202, 213
    early investment in relation-
        ships by, 198–202
    enlisting help becoming,
        227–234
    feedback from, 205–207,
        214–215
    first 100 days of, 198–209

investment by, 218–219
and labeling, 202–205,
    213–215
personal growth of, 222–227
response to bad news,
    210–212, 216, 218, 237

team(s)
    effects of set-up-to-fail syn-
        drome on, 122
    effects of stronger performers
        on, 117
    effects of weaker performers
        on, 117–119
Teerlink, Rich, 230
termination, 124–125
    disadvantages of, 125–126
    ramifications of, 128, 134
threat and embarrassment
    managerial behavior when
        facing, 145, 148–149, 163,
        235
360-degree feedback programs,
    17–18, 115
Tilling, Mack, 232

unawareness
    in framing, 149
    skilled, 123
underperformance
    expectations and, 47–51
    by subordinates, 113–114
unfairness, perceived, 92, 119,
    125–126
unilateral remedies by manager,
    128
    appeal of, 129
    prognosis of, 129–131
    risks of, 132
unsolicited advice, effects of, 29

vicious cycle, 46–47, 58–60
videotaping of interactions, 243
vigilance, 92

weaker performers
    alliance-making by, 103–106
    characteristics of, 5, 21
    differential treatment of,
        21–24, 28–33
    difficulties facing, 51–55, 76–86
    erosion of self-confidence of,
        27–28, 49
    expectations and, 41–43
    feelings of injustice on the part
        of, 93, 99, 100, 108, 173,
        191
    identification of, 20–22, 71–74
    managerial reluctance to give
        feedback to, 136–143

negative energy of, 118–119
overstriding by, 60–61
past grievances of, 99–100,
    104, 173
provocative behavior by,
    102–103, 104
resistance to feedback by,
    140–141
slackers, 187–189
"standing up to the boss" by,
    100–101, 104
termination of, 46, 115–116,
    124–128, 187–189
withdrawal from contact with
    manager, 26–27, 58–60
withdrawal from job, 27
Welch, Jack, 49, 123
Winkler, Don, 224
Woods, Tiger, 239

# About the Authors

JEAN-FRANÇOIS MANZONI is Associate Professor of Management at INSEAD (Fontainebleau, France), where he directs the *INSEAD-PwC Research Initiative on High Performance Organizations.* His research, teaching, and consulting activities are focused on the management of change at the individual and organizational levels. Among his most recent works are *Process Re-engineering, Organizational Change and Performance Improvement* (with Soumitra Dutta), and *Performance Measurement and Management Control: A Compendium of Research* (edited with Marc Epstein). A three-time winner of INSEAD's Outstanding Teacher Award, Jean-François has also received awards for his research and case-writing activities, including two Case of the Year Awards from the European Foundation for Management Development. In addition to being a frequent keynote speaker at various conferences on leadership and change, Jean-François performs training and consulting work for several large international organizations.

JEAN-LOUIS BARSOUX is Senior Research Fellow at INSEAD, where he specializes in organizational behavior, particularly cross-cultural issues and dyadic relations. His doctorate in comparative management provided the foundation for the book *French Management: Elitism in Action* (with Peter Lawrence) and the *Harvard Business Review* article "The Making of French Managers." Jean-Louis is the author or coauthor of nine books. Among his most recent books are *Managing Across Cultures* (with Susan Schneider) and *The Global Challenge* (with Paul Evans and Vlado Pucik). His study of the uses of humor in organizations, *Funny Business,* won the Management Consultancies Association Prize for *Book of the Year.*